The Exile
into Eternity

The Exile
into Eternity

A Study of the Narrative Writings
of Giorgio Bassani

Douglas Radcliff-Umstead

Rutherford • Madison • Teaneck
Fairleigh Dickinson University Press
London and Toronto: Associated University Presses

Associated University Presses
440 Forsgate Drive
Cranbury, NJ 08512

Associated University Presses
25 Sicilian Avenue
London WC1A 2QH, England

Associated University Presses
2133 Royal Windsor Drive
Unit 1
Mississauga, Ontario
Canada L5J 1K5

Library of Congress Cataloging-in-Publication Data

Radcliff-Umstead, Douglas.
The exile into eternity.

Bibliography: p.
Includes index.
1. Bassani, Giorgio—Criticism and interpretation.
2. World War, 1939–1945—Literature and the war.
3. Jews in literature.   I. Title.
PQ4807.A79Z85   1987   853'.914   86-45739
ISBN 0-8386-3296-3 (alk. paper)

Printed in the United States of America

To Lula Louisa Ey with Love

Contents

Preface

With this work, I hope to introduce readers of English to the narrative writings of Giorgio Bassani, who is best known outside of Italy for the motion picture version of his novel *The Garden of the Finzi-Continis*. Because Bassani turned entirely to poetry and essays in 1974, the collection of his tales and novels in *The Romance of Ferrara* constitutes a closed literary world for critics to explore.

Because the last few years in the United States have witnessed an increase of scholarly interest in Holocaust studies, one must include Bassani's fiction, since the nightmare of extermination determines most of his narrative writings. Within the well-defined bounds of Bassani's fictive world there is enacted a drama of optimistic aspirations in Fascist Italy, unfulfilled promises, and cynical political treachery as bewildered Jewish citizens find themselves to be outcasts or prisoners marked for possible destruction. The Italian author transforms a history of internal political exile into an exile in the eternity of literary art.

Once again, I wish to thank Lula Louisa Ey for her inspiring support of my research. I also want to express appreciation to colleagues who furthered my work on this book: Mark Musa and Peter Bondanella of Indiana University, Stelio Cro of McMaster University, Charles Klopp of Ohio State University, Robert Di Pietro of the University of Delaware, and René Girard of Stanford University. To the National Endowment for the Humanities I express gratitude for a summer stipend that permitted me the freedom to pursue my writing.

The Exile
into Eternity

Introduction
The Closed World of Giorgio Bassani

BASSANI'S CLOSED WORLD

Among Italian writers of Jewish experience, Giorgio Bassani in his narrative works expresses conflicting emotions of intense attachment to place and anguished awareness of alienation. The very titles of his collected tales and novels reveal the desire for a space of freedom and security along with a painful realization of a destiny in exile: *The Garden of the Finzi-Continis (Il Giardino dei Finzi-Contini), Behind the Door (Dietro la porta),* and *Within the Walls (Dentro le mura).*

At the center of Bassani's beloved but precarious literary world stand his home city of Ferrara and its surrounding Emilian countryside along the Po River valley. The prominence of Ferrara as the setting for most of the tales and novels led the author in 1974 to entitle the single-volume edition of his narrative works *The Romance of Ferrara (Il Romanzo di Ferrara).* In his novels and stories, Bassani frequently represents the traumatic events of the decade from late 1937 to early 1948, which started when Italian Jews discovered they were "strangers at home" to be victimized by the anti-Semitic policies of the Fascist government that sought to deprive them of civic identity.[1] The image of Ferrara thus becomes an ambiguous one of forcible exclusion and wounded affection as an oppressive reality of persecution closes in on the officially designated "Italian citizens of the Jewish race."

For Bassani, the city of Ferrara and the plains of the Po delta represent "an idea with physical boundaries," as a literary geographer has described William Faulkner's Yoknapatawpha County.[2] The reader's vision of the walled trapezoidal city and marshlands of the Po valley is precisely demarcated. In "Ravenna," which appears in the volume *The Smell of Hay (L'Odore del fieno),* the author clearly establishes the boundaries of his world in northeastern Italy: from the location of Ferrara on the branch channel of the Po known as the Po di Volano, one moves twenty miles southward to the left embankment of the Reno River, where the Romagna plain begins, and continues with straight roads eastward to the ancient town of Ravenna and then southward to the Adriatic Sea, with its beach resorts like Rimini and Riccione frequented during summer vacations by members of Ferrara's middle class. To the southwest of Ferrara, on the Reno River, lies its victorious rival city, Bologna, the regional capital of Emilia-Romagna.

Bassani relates in his tale "The Walk before Supper" ("La Passeggiata prima di cena") that a sordid political intrigue in the late nineteenth century secured the major railroad junction in northern Italy for Bologna rather than Ferrara, so that Bologna became the region's economic and industrial center. That thirty-mile railway line between Ferrara and Bologna figures prominently in the author's short novel *The Gold-Rimmed Eyeglasses* (*Gli Occhiali d'oro*), with its daily trips in third-class compartments by Ferrarese students commuting to the prestigious University of Bologna.

As an urban environment, Ferrara represents a continual battle against the encroaching marshlands of the Po delta, with the threats of flood and malaria. Rising from the plains with its equally protective or imprisoning walls, the city appears to be a fortress opposing capricious nature. Byzantine exarchs, Lombard chieftains, and popes all used the town as a stronghold over the Po valley. But the noble family who succeeded in gaining control of Ferrara for over three and a half centuries and gave the city its physicospiritual character was the Este, who ruled from 1240 to 1597. Under Estense domination, Ferrara developed the contrasts that Bassani repeatedly points out in his tales: the old medieval town of the southern half of the city with narrow, crooked streets and the resplendent northern section with broad Renaissance avenues and luxurious palaces built under the direction of the imperious Duke Ercole I D'Este at the close of the fifteenth century. Cultural historians have called Ferrara the "first truly modern city in Europe," with its urban planning under ducal administration, its large well-built dwellings, and its skillful management of a Renaissance university.[3]

Because of the administrative efficiency of the reigning family, the Ferrarese based their wealth on the surrounding farmlands at the cost of flood control measures and land reclamation throughout the delta region. One particular policy of the Estense designed to ensure their dominance affected the development of the area until present times: By suppressing guilds of merchants and artisans, the Este lords prevented a politically powerful burgher class from arising and concentrated the city's resources in agrarian enterprises.[4] Ferrara consequently never enjoyed the leadership of entrepreneurial wool merchants and financiers like the Medici family in Florence. Even in the twentieth century, any political party seeking to control the city and its countryside would have to turn to the support of large landowners.

As a result of this history of economic restriction dating from the Este family, magnates in Bassani's novels like the Finzi-Continis or Edgardo Limentani in *The Heron* (*L'Airone*) derive their fortunes as anachronistic feudal landholders of estates in the Ferrarese province. Thus, as Bassani's fictitious characters drive along the roads of Emilla-Romagna, they view the hemp, sugar beets, gravevines, wheat, fruit, and livestock on which Ferrara's economy principally depends. The area's somewhat economically backward conditions, resulting from the Estense efforts to retain control, continue to determine the outcome of political power in the region.

Although magnificence, glory, and power characterized the Este lords and their drive toward architectonic grandeur, the increasing taxation required to sustain their patronage of the arts brought about the hostility of the Ferrarese populace, who, with the death of the last legitimate heir to the Este duchy in 1597, welcomed the return of papal rule. Under the papal legates, Ferrara began its rapid economic and cultural decline until it became the dismal, half-empty town where Bassani's characters seek in vain to escape the all-pervading provincial mediocrity. Under ecclesiastic administration, a petty, restrictive atmosphere enveloped the lethargic city and its mutually exclusive districts. The group who most visibly suffered from the physical constrictions of urban life under church rule were the Jews. As early as 1275, it had been a vital part of Este policy to invite Hebrew immigration to Ferrara in the hope of stimulating the city's economy in exactly those areas of banking and finance where the ducal family feared the presence of gentiles who might constitute a political threat. As a minority, Jews could never menace the rulers on whom they, in fact, depended totally for protection from the Christian population.

With their safety guaranteed by the ducal government, the Jewish community prospered in Ferrara, enjoying the rights of worship and ritual and special legal privileges. Jews could operate their own courts to adjudicate matters relating to their communal affairs, especially in regard to religious issues. Ferrara soon emerged as the major Italian center for the study of Talmudic law. One reason for the immense construction projects of Duke Ercole I was, in part, to accommodate the influx of Sephardic refugees from Spain after 1492. Whenever Sephardim in other Italian cities suffered persecution or faced banishment, the Estensi offered them asylum. Even Marranos who had earlier converted to the Christian faith out of duress felt sufficiently free in the Este realm to resume the open practice of the Jewish religion. Ladino-speaking Jews could operate their own printing press in Ferrara. Hebrews also benefited from the city's cultural institutions, since the dukes permitted them to attend the University of Ferrara and take doctoral degrees.[5]

That artificial era of openness ended with the Este reign, and an age of closure began in Ferrara, which has not completely vanished in present times. The cardinal legates who succeeded the Estense lords progressively revoked the privileges granted to Jews in Ferrara until by 1624 all Hebrews had to dwell in a sector of the old medieval southern district with sunless, twisting streets: the ghetto off Piazza delle Erbe along via Mazzini and nearby streets that is the setting for many of Bassani's tales. During the prolonged period of papal administration, the Ferrarese Jews had to wear the yellow badge of shame to signify their exclusion from the main currents of civic life. Existence in the ghetto, with all its constrictions, came as a favor granted by a hostile Christian community that might at any time further punish the Jews for refusing to convert to the true faith.

In that situation of perpetual accusation, the Ferrarese Hebrews, like Jews in ghettos throughout Italy during the seventeenth and eighteenth centuries, enacted their own constricting regulations, such as sumptuary laws to prohibit lavishness in dress and bans on holding masquerades. This self-censorship became a means of avoiding the easily provoked anger of both ecclesiastical authorities and the general populace.

During the last decade of the eighteenth century, in the aftermath of the French Revolution, a chaotic period began that disrupted the fragile though restrictive harmony of ghetto life while offering tantalizing promises of freedom that were realized for only a brief moment. With French invasions and the establishment of Cispadane and Cisalpine republics and finally the Napoleonic Kingdom of Italy, discriminatory legislation was replaced by a reign of liberty, equality, and fraternity not destined to endure beyond 1814. In Ferrara, the last years of the 1790s proved especially difficult for the Hebrew community because of the city's liberation by the French, then occupation again by papal and Austrian authorities, the return of French troops, and subsequent reestablishment of cardinal legates. With every French retreat, there followed a wave of reprisals against the Jews for collaboration in revolutionary activities. A very popular anti-Semitic song, "Gnora Luna," with its derisive story of an unfortunate Jewish wedding, inspired a successful play, *The Jewish Marriage* (*Il Matrimonio ebraico*), which was first performed in Ferrara in 1798. Judeophobe publications abounded to warn Gentile citizens about the Hebrew conspiracy with the French invaders.

With Napoleon's victory at Marengo in 1800, the French secured domination of the Italian peninsula for the coming fourteen years, which became an era of emancipation for Jews, who, as citizens, enjoyed perfect equality with Christians. Hebrews were able to serve in the civic and national guards as well as hold posts on municipal and regional legislative bodies. For the first time in centuries, Italians of the Jewish faith could prepare their children for professional careers other than rabbi or member of the Hebrew guild of merchants or for careers in service areas essential to ghetto life. Jews were free to acquire land wherever they chose. In *The Garden of the Finzi-Continis*, the family patriarch Moisè Finzi-Contini, took advantage of the freedoms granted by the French in order to purchase enormous tracts of farmland in the Ferrarese countryside.

Following Napoleon's defeat at the Battle of the Nations, reactionary regimes once again took control of the various Italian states. After the Congress of Vienna had established the principle of legitimist restoration, the ecclesiastic authorities reinstated the degrading barriers of past centuries. But although

Ferrarese Jews had to take up dwellings in the ghetto, they were able to retain most of the farmlands acquired during the French occupation. If the centuries before the French and Napoleonic invasions had been hopeless periods of resignation for Italian Jews in ghettos, the decades after legitimist restoration would be marked by rebellion to regain freedom.[6]

That state of confinement seemed to have ceased forever between 1860 and 1863 with the annexation of the papal territories into a unified Italy under a constitutional monarchy that guaranteed equal rights to all citizens without regard for religious belief or practice. In Italy, as in Austria-Hungary under Franz-Joseph, there dawned what Stefan Zweig called "the golden age of security." In the "The Walk before Supper," Dr. Corcos's father, Salomone, would remind his son of the glorious night when the last remnants of the gates to Ferrara's ghetto had been pulled down with popular acclaim. It appeared that there would be no more obstacles to social advancement.

Soon, however, the new era of emancipation began to compel members of the various Jewish communities to seek affiliation with, and assimilation into, mainstream Italian society while they were still struggling to free themselves from a ghetto mentality that had conditioned them to accept segregation. Being accustomed to ghetto restrictions in Ferrara had become so deeply ingrained that newly enfranchised citizens frequently continued the old ways of life. Unlike many Italian cities, such as Rome, Florence, and Turin, where members of Jewish communities gave their emancipated status a monumental expression by commissioning resplendent temples to replace the old ghetto synagogues that had housed several sects on different floors, in Ferrara, the Hebrews persisted in using the synagogue on Via Mazzini that appears throughout Bassani's writings.

A long tradition of shame and humiliation led some Ferrarese Jews to avoid rejection while others struggled to realize their longing for admission into society. But despite their tradition of apartness, the Hebrews of Ferrara did succeed within a few generations in integrating themselves into the city's professional circles. As a young Aryan character observes in *The Gold-Rimmed Eyeglasses*, by the mid 1930s, the Israelites in Ferrara belonged to the most distinguished levels of the middle class as physicians, educators, lawyers, and jurists. Jews had even played a far from inconsiderable role in the Fascist fighting squads of the early 1920s that brought Emilia-Romagna under control of the Fascist party. For in the economic turmoil following the First World War, with veterans returning to face unemployment in Ferrara and the countryside, the Socialist party at first seized political hold of the region. But the threat by Socialists to expropriate agricultural and industrial properties so frightened the urban and rural bourgeoisie that by early 1920, the tide of events turned in favor of the Fascists. Any party wishing to rise to power had to reach an agreement with the large landholders, who naturally opposed the Socialist policy of collectivizing farmlands. Leaders of the Agrarian Association in the Ferrarese province (several of whom were Jewish) soon accepted the moderate reform proposals of the Fascists, who demanded a token redistribution of some land parcels to peasants and veterans demonstrating patriotic and party loyalty. In the crucial years that determined the political destiny of all Italy, the Ferrarese Hebrews took a prominent part in the coalition of businessmen, shopkeepers, and landowners who lent their decisive support to the Fascist cause.[7]

That Fascist receptivity to the Ferrarese Jews resulted partially from the personality of the man who later became the leader of the terror squads throughout the region: Italo Balbo. Of all the future Fascist hierarchs, it was Balbo who proved a genuine and consistent Judeophile. That violent organizer of squadrist raids always appreciated that the well-to-do Jews of Ferrara and its countryside gave financial assistance and participated in his campaigns. Driven by a design for wealth and social position, Balbo felt at ease among the Hebrew bourgeoisie who only a generation before had also been parvenus in the upper strata of Ferrara's communal life. Balbo set out on a conservative political course of action favorable to landed proprietors, industrialists and merchants who wished to maintain the economic status quo.

Among the close comrades-in-arms who aided the ferocious leader against Fascists who supported social revolution were Jewish political activists like Renzo Ravenna. While intent on preserving the structure of provincial existence under Fascism, Balbo sought to incorporate the Nationalist and Republican parties into his own organization and to suppress Socialists, Communists, and the Catholic-based Popular Party. Punitive expeditions by Fascist squads rapidly crushed all opposition. With the consolidation of power throughout Emilia-Romagna, Balbo and his militant supporters joined the march on Rome, which resulted in Fascists' taking command of the Italian government in November 1922. During his later career as head of the nation's air force and then as the progressive governor of Libya, Italo Balbo remained the champion of Italy's Jewish citizens.[8]

Establishment of the Fascist dictatorship had no initial detrimental effect on the Hebrew minority, since many Jews continued to hold party membership and some even occupied high-ranking party and governmental posts, including some in Ferrara and its environs. Living in a totalitarian state did not at first alienate most Italian Jews, who felt no more deprived of freedom than did Christians. Although the emergence of a worldwide Zionist movement found sympathy among the Hebrews in Italy, it did not lead to large-scale emigration even after the advent of Fascism. From 1926 to 1938, only 151 Italians of Jewish background immigrated to Eretz Israel most of them from Florence and Trieste, which were the cities with the greatest interest in Zionism, rather than from Ferrara. While many Italian Hebrews contributed generously to the Zionist cause, their desire was to assist persecuted coreligionists from Central and Eastern Europe. In a country where even under a dictatorship all citizens had the same privileges and responsibilities without concern for religion, very few of Italy's Jews recognized the political need for another national home.[9]

Because of the Fascists' desire to transform Italy into a totalitarian society, it was necessary to bring all disparate elements into a single ruling system or to crush and eliminate them. Consequently, the government reorganized the various urban Jewish communities in order to impose uniformity on the nation. The new comprehensive Law on Jewish Communities of 1930–31 conferred official status on Italy's Hebrew institutions and established the means for funding their different religious, cultural, and charitable activities. Because of Fascism's emphasis on centralization, the law called for the creation of a Union of Italian Jewish Communities that would represent the interests of Jews when dealing with the government. The various articles of the comprehensive law put an end to the age-old lack of efficient organization within Italy's Jewish communities and led to cooperation among them.

Since Fascist Italy was an authoritarian society, the law quite logically recognized for the first time the authority of the rabbi in local religious issues. Except for the statute that Jewish children had to attend public schools on Saturday, in violation of their Sabbath, the legislation eased tensions immeasurably between Hebrews and the regime. With Rome as the headquarters for the Union of Jewish Communities, other centers for Hebrew cultural life, such as Ferrara, began to decline in importance. The grand Fascist dream of unifying all the religious and cultural associations of the country under imperial Rome was realized in the new laws regulating and administering Jewish communities.[10] A few years later, in 1933, the Fascist hierarchy opened party membership to those of any religious belief. Within the legal structure of the dictatorial state, Italian Jews seemed to occupy a secure position.

Official governmental disapproval of the Hebrew minority, however, became evident with a full-scale journalistic polemic during 1933 to 1934, the first of several anti-Semitic campaigns that were to culminate in the racial laws of 1938. In spring 1933, Fascist newspapers launched attacks on the dual loyalties of Italian Jews to their native country and Zionist-internationalistic movements. Most of the critical comments in Italian newspapers remained on the general level of finding fault with the vague "Jewish peril" to the nation. While Italy fought a war of conquest in Ethiopia from October 1935 to May 1936, the press refrained from attacking Jews, since the government hoped to rally the entire nation to the military cause. Along with most Italian citizens, native Jews showed their loyalty for the Ethiopian venture by enlisting in the armed forces or contributing to the war fund. With victory in Africa, the Fascist government began to pursue a policy of ever-increasing collaboration with Nazi Germany that included discrimination against Hebrew citizens. Mussolini's press began the systematic psychological preparation of the Italian people for an official change in laws regarding Jews. Italy's military involvement in the Spanish Civil War along side German troops battling for Franco's forces further intensified criticism of Hebrew citizens. By the end of 1937, the Fascist government had definitely moved to the offensive against Western democracies like France and

Great Britain, which were labeled along with the Jewish minority in Italy as common enemies of the Duce's empire.[11]

Already in June 1936, the mounting journalistic campaign against Hebrew citizens had encouraged the first supposedly spontaneous public attacks of an anti-Semitic nature when some unidentified secondary school students in Ferrara (always a city that set a trend for the nation to follow) scrawled the slogans "Long live the Duce—death to Jews" across the walls of various homes. Police investigations subsequently determined that an unusually large number of final examination failures had aroused the resentment of gentile students against school directors who happened to be Jewish. The police report added that there was an ever-growing bitterness in Ferrara against the town's eight hundred citizens of Hebrew origin because of their disproportionately powerful role in the area's official life. Jews did occupy the posts of *podestà* (Fascist director of municipal administration), head secretary of the provincial council, chief secretary of the provincial council for corporate economy, and judicial instructor of the local tribunal. Jews were also directors of two secondary schools (where the resented failures took place), directors of the local branch of the Bank of Italy, president of the provincial Fascist federation of commerce, and they were on numerous local political committees.

If one recalls the early support given by Jewish landowners and businessmen to Balbo and his squads, the strong representation by Hebrews in Ferrara's administrative structure does not appear surprising. But given the poisonous atmosphere that successive journalistic campaigns had contributed to creating, an incident such as failing examination grades sufficed to arouse a long-repressed hostility. The Ferrarese incidents illustrate the extent to which the dictatorial regime had succeeded in convincing the general public of the Jewish peril to the nation.[12]

The publication of an official "Italian Race Manifesto" on 14 July 1938 marked the true beginning of the end for Italy's Jews under Fascism. Supposedly written as a manifesto by several leading scholars but actually drafted by a young opportunistic anthropologist at Mussolini's orders, this document provided the theoretical basis for ensuing racial legislation. The manifesto defined the program of Italian racism according to certain pseudoscientific propositions, such as the purely biological concept of race, membership of the Italian people in the Aryan race, and the biological exclusion of Hebrews from the pure Italian race. To a certain extent, Mussolini had issued the race manifesto in order to counter the contentions by Nazi race theorists that the Italians were a Mediterranean people contaminated by African and Arabic strains. By declaring Jewish citizens to be a totally alien race, Mussolini hoped to establish the legitimate claim of Italians as Aryans along with Hitler's superior Germanic people. Even the Duce was to admit one day that the race manifesto was little more than a German document rendered in bad Italian. Roman imperialism had finally merged with

Nazi racism to prepare for the elimination of Jews from civic life in Fascist Italy.[13]

In order to declare to the world his spiritual solidarity with Hitler's Germany, the Italian dictator set into motion the passage of anti-Semitic laws. On 2 September 1938, the Italian Council of Ministers enacted statutes barring all Jews (whether native Italians or foreign residents) from teaching or studying at public institutions from the elementary through the University levels. Students currently enrolled at universities were allowed to complete their course of studies to receive terminal degrees. Bassani, for instance, was able to continue his classes at the University of Bologna that academic year in order to receive his diploma in summer 1939. Following on the momentum of the first racial laws, the Fascist Grand Council convened on 6 October 1938 to approve comprehensive discriminatory legislation. As a justification for the decrees, the new law began by stating that the Fascist government had always worked for the qualitative and quantitative improvement of the Italian race and consequently felt compelled to resolve the Jewish problem. To preserve racial purity, an Italian would no longer be permitted to marry a person from a non-Aryan race. The legal definition of a Jew included anyone born of parents both of whom were Jewish even though those individuals might profess a faith different than Jewish; anyone born of Jewish fathers and foreign (Aryan) mothers; or anyone born of mixed marriages if on the date 1 October 1938, they still practiced the Jewish religion. Although not so comprehensive as the Nazi Nuremberg race codes, the Fascist laws relegated the nation's Jews to a metaphorical ghetto.[14]

Hebrews in Italy lost the right to become members of the Fascist party, to serve in the military forces, to own firms employing more than one hundred people, or to possess more than 50 hectares of land. Through its decrees, the Fascist Grand Council sought to reduce Italian Jews to the level of nonpeople whose very names could not appear in telephone directories. Discriminatory legislation excluded Jews from access to the society in which they had worked to achieve prominence. As time went on, subsequent laws further restricted the liberties of Jews—denying them use of public libraries, ejecting them from membership in local chambers of commerce, barring participation in Aryan social circles like Ferrara's elite Eleonora D'Este Tennis Club. All the positions of importance that had caused the resentment behind the June 1936 racial incident in Ferrera were taken away from anyone fitting the definition of a Jew.

By classifying domestic Hebrews as "Italian citizens of the Jewish race," the law recognized certain inherent rights and privileges, such as freedom of worship and the cultural activities of the legally constituted Jewish communities. Since Mussolini explained that his purpose was "to discriminate, not to persecute;" the government continued to grant Hebrews some special privileges, such as operating their own private schools. Bassani taught for a while at the Jewish School of Ferrara. The Grand Council also provided exemptions for some Jews on the basis of meritorious, patriotic, or Fascist party service. But, in time, the bureaucrats at the recently created Department of Race and Demography began interpreting the racial laws so strictly that both the number of people exempted and the range of exemptions grew more and more narrow. Exempted status, even with the loss of party membership in March 1939, inspired a false sense of security, for the day was to come when Italy would fall into the hands of the Germans, who would recognize no exemptions.

Discrimination meant perpetual humiliation—loss of the right to hire household help, own radios, publish books, or deliver public lectures. Individuals who lost businesses like department stores received in exchange low-interest government bonds that eventually became worthless. Further restrictive laws denied almost every means of livelihood to Jews, even for families with a Hebrew father and a gentile mother. Around them, everywhere, Jews in Italy saw once again the walls of segregation rising.

Three members of the Fascist Grand Council openly dissented from the vote on the October 1938 discriminatory laws: Italo Balbo, Emilio De Bono (general of the army), and Luigi Federzoni (leader of the party's nationalist wing).[15] Balbo had even made a visit to Ferrara to express his indignation publicly over the racial statutes, for this fierce governor of Libya made the rounds to pay his respects to every leading member of the Jewish community there. Then Balbo invited his old trusted lieutenant from the squadrist days, Renzo Ravenna (by then the highest ranking Jew in the Ferrarese Fascist hierarchy), to be his dinner guest at the Italia Restaurant. Although a few chiefs of the party could dare display strong disapproval for anti-Semitic policies, the majority in Ferrara and elsewhere ran the risk of being labeled *pietisti* for sympathizing with Jews, associating with them, or assisting them in circumventing the racial laws. Penalties for *pietismo* were loss of the party card, dismissal from governmental jobs, arrest and police interrogation, with the threat of incarceration. With all the severity of a police state, the Fascists worked to achieve the complete social isolation of Italian Jews.[16]

The cherished illusion of being part of Italy ended when Hebrews found themselves betrayed, ostracized, and abandoned. Yet Italy's Jewish communities had assumed such a strong national identity that, except for a few militant Zionists who immigrated to Palestine, most failed to take advantage of the government's willingness to let them leave the country. Instead, the majority accepted the indignities of second-class citizenship and remained in the newly recreated ghettos of their homes waiting to learn their fate. One of the writers whom Bassani often quotes—Simone Weil—analyzes this attitude of acceptance before the state in her study *The Need for Roots:* "The State is a cold concern, which cannot inspire love; but itself kills, suppresses everything that might be loved; so one is forced to love it, because there is nothing else."[17]

In time, the state did decide the fate of Jews in Ferrara and other Italian cities. After Italy's entrance into the Second World War on 10 June 1940, the nation's

Jews became subversive agents who had to be rendered harmless. By autumn 1940, authorities began to send politically suspect Jews to different concentration camps. Many Ferrarese eventually went to a detention center at Fossoli di Carpi. At first, most of the interned were foreign Jews rather than native Italians, and camp conditions in no way resembled the Nazis' extermination centers. Because of increasing military reverses, public anger irrupted in acts of violence, with Jews for victims, as when a mob vandalized Ferrara's synagogue in October 1941. The final act in the tragedy of Italian Jews came in the aftermath of Mussolini's fall from power in a coup d'état in July 1943. After leaders of the provisional government of Italy signed an armistice with the Allies on 8 September 1943, Germans reacted swiftly to restore command of the country from Rome northward by rescuing Mussolini and placing the Duce at the head of a puppet state called the Italian Social Republic. The new regime ordered the arrest of all Jews and confiscation of their property. Beginning in fall 1943, in one city after another of central and northern Italy, including Ferrara, German extermination squads and Social Republican agents collaborated in rounding up thousands of Italian Jews for extradition to Nazi death camps like Auschwitz. Neither wealth, former patriotic service, nor prior Fascist party rank excepted any but a few especially favored individuals from arrest and deportation. The only possibility left to the nation's Hebrews was destruction.[18]

In his narrative writings, Bassani attempts to transcend the nightmare events of recent history by contemplating his characters and their forcibly closed world as if above and outside temporal bounds. In an essay that was first published in 1964, Bassani speaks of the need to find poets with insight into the era of the Fascist dictatorship. Otherwise, stories about Mussolini's government would be no more than "costume tales" about an artificial past.[19] The novels and stories that comprise *The Romance of Ferrara* do achieve that poetic insight into the tragic period of betrayal for Italy's Jews. But before turning to the individual narrative works, one should examine those intellectual and literary traditions that inspired Bassani with faith in literature and art as civilizing forces throughout history.

THE AUTHOR'S ARTISTIC AND LITERARY BACKGROUND

Giuseppe Raimondi, who was both witness to and participant in the artistic reawakening of Italy immediately after the First World War, called 1916 (the year of Bassani's birth) a mythic time when creative young Italians in cities like Ferrara, Bologna, and Rome became conscious of themselves and determined to restore their nation to cultural prominence.[20] Those young artists and writers, some of whom were serving on the war front in 1916, concluded that the only way for Italy to break with spiritual domination by France was to rediscover and reaffirm the remarkable Italian tradition of greatness in literature, painting, sculpture, and architecture. While art historians were endeavoring to bring to light Italy's creative contributions through the centuries, young painters and poets sought to renew the traditions of exclusively Italian schools of art.

Among the artists attempting to revive the "Italian principle" of expressivity was the Bolognese painter and etcher Giorgio Morandi (1890–1964), whom Bassani was later to admire for his absolute sincerity and total aversion to rhetoric.[21] Few artists have ever deliberately worked to overcome any sense of display by choosing a strictly limited and monotonous range of subject matter as did Morandi. Still life paintings and etchings with bottles, cups, pitchers, and bowls predominate over the years with an almost numbing repetitiousness. During some periods of the artist's productivity, the objects represented in Morandi's works almost lose form to achieve a painterly abstraction. He was trying to divert art from its manipulative possibilities and instead concentrated on the humbleness of everyday utensils or on a landscape of an unpretentious scene of a country house in a nondramatic setting. During the Fascist era, with its emphasis on Italy's destiny as an imperial nation, Morandi's work stood apart from officially approved art, with its rhetorical intent to impress viewers. Although for a short period from 1918 to 1920, Morandi did join other painters like Carlo Carrà and Giorgio De Chirico in the Metaphysical School in using a severe geometry while infusing objects like an old table clock with human emotions, the Bolognese artist spent most of his career as a provincial recluse experimenting in restricted creative bounds of his own choosing. Toward the end of the 1920s, a group of young writers calling themselves *strapaese* hailed Morandi as one of their own, since his canvases seemed to represent their longing to revere small towns, the countryside, and ordinary objects as opposed to the mechanized life of modern urban centers. But this painter–etcher selected his subject matter not so much for its content as for the opportunity to gain control over the work of art and produce a purity of representation. It is that integrity of expressive effort over an entire career of disciplined productivity that led Bassani to recognize Morandi as one of the unobstrusive masters of modern art.[22]

Doubtless, the painter of this century who did exert the greatest influence on Bassani's creativity was the Ferrarese artist Filippo De Pisis. Not only does Bassani refer in his narratives to works by De Pisis, but more importantly, Bassani describes certain locales in the Emilian countryside as if they were landscapes by that painter. Unlike Morandi, De Pisis soon left the narrow atmosphere of his native city to pursue a critically and commercially successful career in Rome, Paris, London, and Venice. De Pisis (1896–1956) also championed other artists like De Chirico for the ability to portray the mystery of objects in an enigmatic space. During that fateful year 1916, De Pisis escorted De Chirico through the streets of Ferrara, which appeared to them to be a marvelous metaphysical city, and in the bakeries and confectionery shops of the Jewish ghetto, they purchased cookies and candy to serve as subjects for metaphysical canvases. While Morandi's works display a draughtsmanlike linearity that perhaps finds best expression in etchings, De Pisis' paintings reveal him to be an artist of immediate impressions and sensations rather than precise delineation.

One area of De Pisis' productions that has a parallel in Bassani's word paintings of the seashore near Rimini and Riccione on the Adriatic is marine still life. The striking visual quality of the marine paintings comes from the reversal of normal proportions: Dominating the large foreground of opaque sand might lie mountainous seashells, a fish with metallic scales, or a glistening lobster; somewhat further back on the middle ground stand minuscule human figures; infinitesimal ships sail over menacing green-gray waves while seagulls fly across a tempestuous, cloud-swept sky. The unexpected juxtaposition of objects on the canvase results in a new style of seascape stressing the importance of the drama depicted on the shore.

In his city scapes, De Pisis reveals himself to be anything but a *strapaese* escapist. Although high horizons and the oppressive verticals of buildings in paintings depicting Ferrarese ghetto streets or Via Fossalta in Bologna create a sense of imprisoning urban space, frequently De Pisis' renderings of bustling Parisian boulevards, Italian piazze, and congested London traffic circles possess an explosive energy that seems to anticipate the later action paintings of Jackson Pollock. All the solidity of human-made structures dissolves into vibrating lines and strident colors. The artist's late Venetian canvasses try to recapture the city's luminous evanescence with palaces and gondolas alike floating over the shimmering lagoon beneath a Tiepolesque sky. Like certain passages in Bassani's narrative works that describe an idyllic twilight moment during a stroll on quiet streets, some of De Pisis's city paintings have a lyrical quality similar to Utrillo's views of Paris.

While an artist like Morandi always avoided frightening or surprising his viewers, De Pisis intentionally set out to make each of his canvases an experiment in the unforeseen. The still lifes of the Ferrarese painter, for example, often appear theatrical due to the motif of a picture within a picture: Atop a table sits some over-sized mushrooms alongside a crudely framed painting with a Cézannesque landscape. Perhaps the quality of De Pisis' canvases that most reflects Bassani's view of reality is the artist's ecstatic primitivism expressed in violent and cruel images. The dead game bird hanging from a hook in *The Butchershop* parallels the depiction of a lifeless St. Sebastian in a series of paintings done during the 1930s and early 1940s showing the martyr tied to a tree with arrows piercing his bloodied flesh. Similarly, the painting *Isaac's Sacrifice* (1940) and its preliminary sketches hold none of the solemnity of the biblical source nor the classical harmony of the Renaissance bas-reliefs of Ghiberti and Brunelleschi but represent a sadomasochistic episode.

Some of the works that also parallel Bassani's portrayal of enigmatic characters are several paintings of male nudes reclining on leopard skins like odalisques or standing defiantly with right arm akimbo and left elbow against a chest of drawers. The disturbing addition of shoes and hose on the nude figure deliberately deprives the paintings of classical sensuality and causes an unresolved homoerotic tension. As painters of a world in dissolution De Pisis and Bassani are kindred spirits working in different media.[23]

That year, 1916, also marked the death of Guido Gozzano (b. 1883), the leading writer among Italy's "twilight school" (*scuola crepuscolare*) of poetry. A few years before, in 1907, the other major twilight poet, Sergio Corazzini (b. 1886), had also died from the same disease, tuberculosis, that claimed Gozzano. Throughout Bassani's narrative prose, these appear twilight characters and situations recalling Gozzano and Corazzini and their cult of melancholy resignation to death and the end of a beloved, intimate world. Gozzano's bittersweet recollections of *fin de siècle* Turin and Piedmontese country villas full of "good things in the worst taste" have their literary echoes in Bassani's depiction of the interiors of certain Ferrarese homes whose treasured objects glow in the softened light of oncoming evening. The Decadentist mood of verses by Gozzano and Corazzini, nostalgic for a life of tender emotions cut short by fatal illness, are echoed in works like *The Garden of the Finzi-Continis* whose title characters attempt to retreat to an artifical paradise where death by disease becomes a state of grace. Another representative of the twilight school is the Ferrarese native Corrado Govoni (1884–1965), whose works were published by the local bookseller Taddei. Texts by Govoni such as *Armonie in grigio e in silenzio* (*Harmonies in Grey and Silence*, 1903) and *Fuochi d'artifizio* (*Fireworks*, 1905) recall the canvases of French impressionist painters in recapturing light and shade over rustic landscapes and familiar still life arrangements. The chief difference between the evanescent atmosphere in poetry from the twilight school, with its voluptuous surrender to decline and dispersal, and the pathetic vision of a community condemned to destruction in Bassani's prose is the presence of the social, political, and military nightmare of the Holocaust in Italy. While many of Bassani's characters seek a twilight refuge away from society and time, an inexorable historical reality transforms their sentimental desolation into an anguished awareness of their impending extermination.[24]

While Bassani gained from the twilight poets a sense of life enveloped in a gentle melancholy acceptance of fatality, his elegant, and disciplined literary style came from the theories and example of writers producing one of the most influential Itaian journal of this century—*La Ronda*, appearing in Rome from April 1919 to November 1922 and then in a special issue in December 1923.

Like many artists of the same period, the editors of *La Ronda* wanted to renew the *traditions* of Italian literature: to reestablish traditionalism amidst modernity without becoming reactionaries. The editor-in-chief, Vincenzo Cardarelli (1887–1959), lamented in the prologue to the first issue that none of the journal's contributors still felt young because of the disillusionment brought on by the war, but the Rondists displayed a desperate intensity and heroic energy in their defense of the Italian language.[25] Those authors sought to achieve complete understanding of national life and history through their literary projects. Admitting that the struggle for independence and unification had delayed Italy's becoming a modern country by half a century, the Rondists did not wish to sacrifice their nation's cultural heritage for modernization. In their profound conviction that the Italian language was suffering a crisis that reflected the postwar turmoil, the staff of *La Ronda* intended to reeducate the literate public in order to create a new elegance in style. For these Rondists, clarity of style expressed the spirit of an inquiring mind that sought truth, and writing in a language that was forever alive would reaffirm their cultural identity and civilizing mission. The outside world might be disintegrating politically and socially, but by using grammatically correct style, these authors would regain control over reality and reestablish equilibrium. Thus, a Rondists' program was a call for order at a time of extreme upheaval in Italy.

Because creating a superior literary style was a moral issue for the editors of *La Ronda*, they looked to an almost ideal time shortly before Italy's unification, finding their stylistic models in the first half of the nineteenth century in the works of the poet–novelist Alessandro Manzoni (d. 1873) and and especially the poet-theorist Giacomo Leopardi, (d. 1837). The journal devoted a triple issue in March, April, and May 1921 to *The Literary Testament of Giacomo Leopardi*, extracted from that writer's private notebooks, the *Zibaldone*, as the model for perfect Italian prose. It seemed to the Rondists that Manzoni and Leopardi were writing in an era when their works attracted European-wide attention, whereas national unification only isolated Italian authors in provincial backwardness. Leopardi's style offered an example for literary renewal to young writers who would undergo the necessary apprenticeship. The Rondists fervently believed that Leopardi's neoclassicism and harmonious historical conception of Italian literature and language would inspire a restoration in modern times. With Leopardi and Manzoni as models, the editorial staff of the journal set out to teach Italians the art of good writing.[26]

With proselytizing zeal, the Rondists began to destory the false idols corrupting Italian literary and cultural taste. In the issues of November 1919 to January 1920, the journal held a referendum on the popular poet Giovanni Pascoli (1855–1912), who was condemned for breaking with literary tradition by introducing simple-minded onamatopoeia, infantile language, jargon, and dialect into his verse. Any literature that could be enjoyed as a pastime came under vitriolic attack. Although the Rondists assailed the many imitators of the flamboyant poet–novelist–dramatist Gabriele D'Annunzio (1863–1938) for falling into florid bombast, they spared that highly seductive stylist from caustic criticism. Instead, the writers of *La Ronda* directed their polemics against the avant-garde movement Futurism, recognizing in its verbal experimentalism a serious menace to the proper syntax advocated by the journal. The deliberate grammatical anarchy of Futurist writers like F. T. Marinetti (d. 1944) and

Ardengo Soffici (d. 1964), who destroyed the logical structure of language by eliminating conjunctions, adverbs, conjugations, and punctuation, horrified the Rondists with their love for classical order and lucidity of expression. In the bewildering and often self-contradictory Futurist manifestoes, editors of *La Ronda* also beheld the frightening challenge to their program to renew Italian cultural traditions, for the Futurists considered Italy a land whose cities were dead museums of the past, to be leveled in order to build a glorious, modern era. The frequently combative nature of articles in *La Ronda* reflects the defensive attitude of writers who felt that formal correctness of style constituted a norm for civilized attitude and behavior.[27]

Along with their reverence for tradition, the Rondists also recognized the need for receptivity to new literary currents. Consequently, one of the journal's major policies was to review works by foreign writers and to invite guest submissions from authors outside Italy. The editor who most actively encouraged that openness to stimulating foreign contacts was Emilio Cecchi (1884–1966), who before joining the staff had written a history of nineteenth-century English literature. Cecchi not only wrote reviews of British and American literature but penned profiles of writers like Rudyard Kipling and Robert Louis Stevenson. Some of the foreign writers whose works appeared in *La Ronda* were G. K. Chesterton; Hilaire Belloc; Edward Shanks; the illustrator Charles Ricketts; the political theorist Georges Sorel; W. B. Yeats; E. Gordon Craig, with his fundamental essay on the actor and the ubermarionette; and Thomas Mann. The journal also introduced Italian readers to serious discussions on Gogol, Tolstoi, Dostoievski, Thomas De Quincey, and Henry Adams, among many other authors. Baudelaire and Rimbaud appeared as masters of a modern vebal alchemy. The fine arts received attention in articles by Carrà (on Cézanne and the Parisian postimpressionists) and by De Chirico on the linear harmony of classical painting.

Because the journal intended to provide models of creative writing in addition to critical essays, various issues featured original poems, novelle, brief examples of art prose, and plays. One of the founding contributors, Riccardo Bacchelli (b. 1891), published in segments his dramas *Hamlet* and *Spartacus and the Slaves*. Indeed, *La Ronda* constituted a school for innovative writers as the subsequent careers of its major authors indicate. Cardarelli carried his love of classical simplicity into poetry and narrative writings. Cecchi emerged as a master of the imagistic essay and Italy's foremost expert on Anglo-American literature. The historical novel found its most proficient practitioner in twentieth-century Italy with Bacchelli's *The Devil at the Long Bridge* (*Il Diavolo al pontelungo*) and the multivolume *Il Mulino del Po* (*The Mill on the Po*).

The journal's editorial secretary, Giuseppe Raimondi, produced incisive studies on De Pisis and Morandi, along with the autobiographical narrative *Joseph in Italy* (*Giuseppe in Italia*). All these writers illustrate the creative success of the Rondists in balancing the free play of imagaination with critical self-control.

Although editors of the journal did succeed to a great extent in combatting the abuse and careless use of language, their program possessed several obvious failings. Certainly, the Rondists proved themselves politically naïve. While Bacchelli defended the monarchy as an institution above corruption that had the poetic force and tradition to affirm freedom, many staff writers advocated a pragmatic liberalism similar to the policies of the long-time prime minister Giovanni Giolitti who had brought stability to the government before World War I though parliamentary maneuvering. The most outstanding example of political ingenuousness on the part of the Rondists is an article on Fascism by Vilfredo Pareto published in January 1922 (ten months before the march on Rome), where the author decried that party's use of violence but dismissed its danger as a transient phenomenom.[28] Remaining blind to the crisis exploding about them, the chief writers for La *Ronda* tried to reduce society's problems to literary and linguistic dimensions.

Despite its brief existence, the journal was an inspiration for two generations of authors—those who, like La *Ronda's* editors, were born before the turn of the century and others, like Bassani, who belonged to the Fascist generation. Although the periodical established the highest possible technical standards for writing, its fragmentary decadentism produced jewellike mosaics of formalistic or decorative literary purity. The preciosity that characterized many pages in the journal reflected a self-satisfying mannerism of style realized by almost flawless technique. Following a poetics of form, the Rondists sacrificed content to the pursuit of perfection. With their sterile cult of form, the journal's major contributors could never correct the disorder in Italian society through a conservative restoration of proper language. To the credit of its editors, rarely did their zeal for penning stylistically perfect pieces cause them to abandon human values.[29]

From the Rondists, Bassani learned not only a lesson in style and appreciation of many non-Italian authors, like Hawthorne, Melville, and James, but he also acquired an abiding faith in literature and a belief in the dignity of writers uncompromisingly dedicated to their craft. Largely due to the example of La *Ronda,* Bassani worked in the main line of Italian literary tradition rather than in avant-garde experimentalism. Exhibiting a Decadentist awareness of the difficulty that isolated human beings have communicating with each other, the young author would one day apply his Rondist quest for a disciplined style to create works of literature that even in their inability to alter a fixed and painful historical reality would yet transfigure it through eternity.

Bassani differs most from the writers of La *Ronda* in his perspective on history as a living process over the course of time. To a large extent, his attitude toward historical events came from the lectures and writings of Roberto Longhi (1890—1970), Bassani's professor of art history at the University of Bologna. So inspiring were Longhi's ideas that his student later wrote an essay, calling him *"un vero maestro"* ("a true teacher") for his lectures that recreated the developmental moments in the career of an individual artist or an entire regional school of painters or sculptors. Bassani also pays tribute to his professor in a passage in *The Garden of the Finzi-Continis* where the novel's young narrator praises Longhi's book *Officina ferrarese*, the fundamental study on the formation of the Ferrarese school of painting during the Renaissance. Longhi did not restrict his research to past artists like Piero della Francesca and Caravaggio; he also tried to assess the efforts of contemporary figures like Carrà and the Futurists. Morandi found in this renowed scholar a sensitive critic who confirmed that painter-etcher's contributions to modernism. Longhi's power as scholar and teacher was due to his success in making art history come to life by carefully relating the work of a painter or sculptor to the environment that offered patronage and encouraged a certain style. Bassani came to view art as a remedy for the transcience of human existence, a spiritual testimony of the life of a creative individual.[30]

Longhi expressed his thoughts on the cultural climates that gave rise to artistic movements in a vigorous literary style that fused precise technical terms, correctly chosen dialect phrases, and scrupulously conducted research on texts and works of art in order to convey the clarity of his insight. Longhi's *Officina ferrarese* is an exciting reconstruction of the drama of the human spirit in fifteenth-century Ferrara, involving artists like Cosmo Tura, Francesco del Cossa, and especially the dynamic Ercole di' Roberti, and also the sixteenth-century creation of a classical style that united various northern and central Italian painterly traditions. Bassani learned from his professor how to arrive at an ideal restoration of the original design for Renaissance polyptichs that had been dismantled over the centuries. Above all, Longhi communicated to his student a sense of historical responsibility toward an undying past.[31]

That concept of historical continuity which guided Longhi and all his students in their scholarly investigations found a theoretical basis in the writings of the philosopher Benedetto Croce (1866—1952), the most important Italian thinker during the first half of the twentieth century. Croce had influenced the editors of *La Ronda* by stressing tradition as an expression of historical development, and the Rondists attempted to use that philosopher's ideas on aesthetics to construct a poetics of form. Bassani would one day feel such a great debt to Croce for the courageous example of independent thinking under a dictatorial regime that he dedicated his volume of essays *Le Parole preparate* (1966) to the Neapolitan philosopher. While declaring himself a Longhian and an historicist, Bassani stated that the source for his literary writings was derived from Croce.[32]

By 1917, Croce had already formulated his thoughts on history in the text *History: Its Theory and Practice (Teoria e storia della storiografia)*, where he identified history with philosophy in motion across time. For Croce, the past is always with us in the present and future, and consequently history becomes our present reality. Doubtless the distinction of the most serious import for this philosopher and his followers like Bassani is that between history (*storia*) and chronicle (*cronaca*). Documents, records, and chronicles are the basis of history that a historian brings to light through a dynamic vision of reality. Because the past remains alive in us, the historian must use documents to interpret the enduring significance of history for us: Where the chronicle merely records, history interprets. Croce constructed his historiography in reaction to the Positivists who saw history as a scientific accumulation of facts verifiable in documents. This philosopher instead moved history to the sphere of the mind, of spirit on its dynamic course in time. All history for Crose is contemporary history where the past affects us now. There then exists a unity across time as historical events from the past reverberate in the present. The historian has to assume the role of philosopher in order to interpret the ethicopolitical nature of history as the mind's forever present activity. Thus, history, as a movement of spirit, always precedes chronicle, which resembles a lifeless recording. For Croce, the one reality is the individual act that makes itself felt throughout the ages. Names and dates appear as just so many meaningless details until the historian places them in the context of living experience. The thinking mind transforms chronicle into the vivid events of history.[33]

Croce's distinction between *storia* and *cronaca* has influenced various Italian narrative writers in their efforts to represent changes in society during the course of time. For his *Tales of Ferrara*, Bassani chose the title *Storie ferraresi*. His contemporary, Vasco Pratolini (b. 1913), used the term *cronaca* to designate some of his novels, such as the autobiographical story *Cronaca familiare* (1945), literally *Family Chronicle* but usually known as *Two Brothers*. Pratolini sees a continuity in the history of his native city Florence, and his choice of the designation *cronaca* refers to the tradition of such medieval Florentine chroniclers and storytellers as the thirteenth-century writer Dino Compagni. In 1946, Bassani produced a volume of verse en-titled *Storie di poveri amanti* (*Stories of Poor Lovers*); the following year, Pratolini published his novel *Cronache di poveri amanti* (*Tales of Poor Lovers*), where he chronicles the lives of the inhabitants of the Florentine street Via del Corno as they fall under full Fascist domination in 1925.

In those earlier works, Pratolini intended to compose "sentimental diaries" or "chronicles of the human condition." Between 1950 and 1966, the Florentine author wrote a trilogy under the general title *Una storia italiana* (*An Italian History*), a vast historical panorama of events in Italian society from 1875 to 1945: the aftermath of unification, with industrial growth, class strife, the First World War, the advent of Fascism, and its disastrous consequences. For Pratolini, the difference between *cronaca* and *storia* lies in the scope of the narrative, in both time and space, and his trilogy on Italian national history moves acrosss the proletariat and middle clases of Florence. The historical novel, from Pratolini's perspectives, must deal with individuals whose experiences typify those of all social groups in Italy.[34]

Of the Italian narrative authors in this century writing historical novels, the one who has adhered most faithfully to the tradition set by Manzoni in his masterpiece on seventeenth-century Lombardy, *The Betrothed* (*I Promessi sposi*), is Riccardo Bacchelli. In a 1923 article for *La Ronda,* Bacchelli also contrasted the narrative structures of Dostoievski and Tolstoi, declaring his preference for the historical objectivity of the latter novelist over the tormented subjective style of the former. Years later, in an essay that appeared in the volume *In the River of History* (1955), Bacchelli observed that the adoration for history arises from a deep-rooted human capacity for pity and sorrow born from our awareness of time and death. In *The Devil at the Long Bridge* (1927), Bacchelli recounts with compassion and irony the pathetic conspiracy of the Russian anarchist Mikhail Bakunin and his Italian disciples to organize a rebellion in Bologna in 1874. Tolstoi's *War and Peace* inspired Bacchelli's three-volume novel, *The Mill on the Po* (1938—1940), detailing the history of a family living near the Po River from the close of the Napoleonic area to the final battles of the First World War.[35] In that novel, the Po becomes the river of life and time. For Bacchelli as for Pratolini, the historical novel must recreate the events of a past time whose human drama touches the lives of future generations.

Bassani's *storia* of Ferrara differs radically from the historicism of Bacchelli and Pratolini. With one exception, all of Bassani's narrative writings cover the years from about 1937 to the beginning of 1948, and that one exception is a tale beginning in the early 1920s and continuing through the first decade of Fascism. There are frequent references to the emancipation of Jews after 1860 and the secure years before World War I. Although Bassani did not write historical tales and novels about the Fascist era, he produced human histories *(storie)* about individuals and groups (especially the Hebrews of Ferrara) living during that period. Here the term *storia* means truthfulness to social and historical reality at the particular moment represented in a narrative; tales and novels with a documented authenticity of facts illuminated by the author's intuitive imagination.

Bassani's descriptions of districts in Ferrara and sites along the Po valley are so accurate that a literary geographer could almost map the region from the author's details. Sometimes, Bassani mentions the names of actual people, often in the case of second-rank Fascist chiefs, or quotes from journals of the period in his desire to reinforce the sense of contemporary realism. But above any other consideration, Bassani studies the reaction of individuals to historical situations, since none of his characters can fully escape time. The many Jewish characters, too, discover their historical destiny as victims of persecution when unexpected political events interrupt their existence. While Bassani never renounces a historical vision, he constantly beholds the drama of the individual over-whelmed by unforeseen circumstances.[36] Within the literary text, a confrontation develops between history and story, inside and outside, light and dark, with the intensity of a shattering rupture. In a Crocean context, Bassani composes *storie* because his characters are a living reality for him although time annihilated them. The Ferrarese narrator shares Croce's view that since history dwells in all of us, its true sources are in our hearts. Bassani responds to that vital inner summons which recovers history from time's devastating power.

At the very moment in 1938 when political and military events were about to plunge Italy into an abyss, Croce published his most comprehensive treatise on the direction of history, *History as Thought and Action (La Storia come pensiero e come azione)*, where the philosopher envisioned liberty as the moral ideal and the explicatory principle of history. Disagreeing with Marxist historiographers, Croce felt individuals and not social classes determined history. While Fascist propagandists were attempting to persuade the public of the need for war against democratic nations, the Neopolitan philosopher affirmed that the practical law impelling one to action was liberty along with the necessity for truth. The struggle to achieve liberty would reestablish social and political conditions to strengthen individual freedoms. Croce's ideal of liberty inspired the youths of Bassani's generation, particularly during the dark days of the Second World War. Reading books like Croce's *History of Europe in the Nineteenth Century (Storia d'Europa nel secolo decimonono,* 1932), with its first chapter on the religion of liberty, persuaded many young Italians to join the resistance movement against the dictatorship.[37] With his redeeming theory of history as liberation, Croce became the spiritual guide directing his countrymen away from the myths of Fascism.

To awaken youth to Italy's new role in international affairs, Mussolini proclaimed, "Our myth is the greatness of the nation." In order to sustain that myth, the government required writers who would celebrate the spiritual imperialism of the Fascist cause. The regime seemed to be promising a renascence of art and literature. In order to encourage young authors, the state offered numerous prizes for poetry, plays, short stories, and novels that expressed the aspirations of the new society. Various anthologies of Fascist writers appeared, such as the series *Poets of the Time of Mussolini.* Theater critics like Corrado Pavolini declared that the stage of tomorrow had to appeal to the great masses by showing the problems of workers and explaining the responsibilities of employers. Eligio Possenti, writing in the Milanese newspaper *Corriere della sera* on 27 October 1935, defined the Fascist view of reality as "faith in life itself, consciousness of today, and certainty of tomorrow" (p. 3, cols. 1–5). The antiliberal elite running the country sought to pass off Fascism as a genuinely revolutionary movement intended to reform through decisive action the inequities of the old parliamentary order. A purely Fascist literature would inspire all Italians to participate in the moral and social labor of renewal.

Several already established writers who were in their fifties or closely approaching that age at the time of the march on Rome in 1922 generously gave their allegiance to the Fascist cause, not out of opportunism but from a sincere belief that the regime offered national redemption. Ugo Ojetti (b. 1871), a somewhat distinguished essayist who dominated the "third-page" articles that appeared in *Corriere della sera* from 1921 to 1938, served as the arbiter of literary taste for the Fascist era by directing journals like *Dedalo* and *Pegaso* in which every aspiring young writer wished to be published. The flamboyant author Antonio Beltramelli (b. 1874), whose literary career peaked in 1921 with the novel *Il Cavalier mostardo,* rallied to the Fascist camp by editing the weekly journal *La Rivolta ideale,* the organ for Fascist university students. As the government's quasi-official dramatist, Mussolini relied on Giovacchino Forzano (b. 1884), who collaborated with the Duce on bombastic historical plays like *Julius Caesar* to illustrate the dawn of another imperial era. One writer of unquestionable genius who joined the Fascist party in 1925 at the moment of its greatest political crisis was the playwright Luigi Pirandello (1867–1936). But although Pirandello received government sponsorship for his Art Theater of Rome (1925–28) and accepted membership in the newly formed Italian Academy, he voluntarily exiled himself from the country's repressive atmosphere. The overwhelming number of authors who became associated with Fascism never rose above the level of the conventional and mediocre.[38]

For a period during the 1920s, the regime approved of the modernism of the Futurists, since the party wanted to demonstrate that Italy had become an efficient twentieth-century nation. Futurism's founder, F. T. Marinetti, actually hoped to create with fascism a government of artists who would demolish all past monuments and erect on their ruins soaring edifices of strikingly innovative design. Marinetti extolled the vigor of Italian blood, which would assert itself in ultra-violent nationalism. Both Futurist and Fascist art would become one in being truly Italian in its virle, warlike, optimistic, and dynamic character. Another Futurist, Ardengo Soffici, advocated the expulsion of every non-Italian element from Fascism: the liberal, Jewish, Masonic, and democratic. But by 1930, the government abandoned modernism in favor of the ancient Roman classical tradition, which could truly express Fascisms's desire to revive the imperial spirit. Rhetorical monumentalism effaced Futurist syntheticism.[39]

In popular journalism, Fascism attracted the services of an opportunistic but highly gifted writer–publisher who definitely contributed to shaping the tastes and ideas of the youths of Bassani's generation, Leo Longanesi (1905–57). A Rondist in his sytlistic ambitions, Longanesi founded in 1927 the Roman journal *L'Italiano,* which he called "the weekly for Fascist people." While participating in the *strapaese* movement, Longanesi devoted an entire richly illustrated issue of *L'Italiano* in 1932 to Morandi. In his nearly cynical willingness to lend his talents to the Fascist cause, Longanesi created the slogan "Mussolini is always right." Yet, as frequently occurred with enterprising writers and artists under the regime, the moment arrived when Longanesi deviated too far from the spirit of conformity that every dictatorship eventually requires from its citizens. Only two years after Longanesi established Italy's first rotogravure magazine, *Omnibus,* in 1937, the authorities compelled him to cease publication. Originality of thought or even format could not flourish in that totalitarian society.[40]

Independence of will also brought official disfavor and imprisonment to the one writer who succeeded best in expressing the aims of Fascism; Curzio Malaparte (1898–1957), a one-time contributor to *La Ronda* and veteran of the march on Rome. Malaparte understood that the effort to build a new social order exacted discipline, sacrifice, obedience, along with fearlessness. In books like *Living Europe* and *Barbarous Italy*, this writer affirmed that Italian tradition once again was coming into its own time with Fascism, because the Duce's regime would free the country of its servile imitation of northwestern Europe. For Malaparte, there existed two European traditions: the rational, scientific, and modernizing tradition of Protestant northwestern Europe as opposed to the Catholic, dogmatic, artistic, and classic southeast. Fascism represented the counterrevolution of the Latin tradition that would rekindle in Italians the spirit of artistic intuition, irony, tragedy, and teach them the national duty of suffering. Almost alone among Fascist authors, Malaparte displayed an epic vision undistorted by rhetorical exaggeration.[41] From 1928 to 1932, he directed the rightfully prestigious journal *La Fiera letteraria* until his book *Coup d'État: The Technique of Revolution* caused his incarceration on the charge of antifascist activity. The Fascist state could not tolerate the candidly expressed reflections of a freely inquiring mind like Malaparte's. In creating a national literature, the government preferred to rely on noncontroversial pedestrian authors.

As a child during the Fascist period, Bassani had to take part in the juvenile rituals of a regime whose anthem was "Giovinezza" ("Youth"): Fascist youth movements required of all public school students and, later, membership in the Fascist University Group until his exclusion after the 1938 racial laws. Like many Italians of that era, Bassani equated patriotism with sympathy for the party in power. But unlike his contemporaries Pratolini and Giuseppe Berto (b. 1914), he never wrote for a Fascist magazine like the Florentine journal *L'Universale* nor joined the Black Shirt militia nor worked in any governmental ministry. Because of his family's comfortable financial circumstances young Bassani was able to dedicate himself to professional studies and remain apart from politics as much as was possible in a totalitarian regime until his religious background made him a pariah. Although he was less compromised by complicity with the Fascist cause than Pratolini or Berto, Bassani later recognized that his passive acceptance of Fascism's indolent traditionalism and belligerent imperialism was a form of collaboration. Bassani, too, had been an adherent of the ruling ideology, so that the shock of official rejection proved all the more stunning than if he had been a rebel. But because of the inspiring consolation that he discovered in the aesthetic libertarianism of the Rondist and Crocean traditions, Bassani survived the disillusionment of the empty Fascist dream.

THE GOAL OF THIS BOOK

This study will penetrate and explore the closed world of Bassani's narratives published in the 1980 edition of *The Romance of Ferrara*, with its chronological ordering of tales and novels according to their original date of publication. Frequently, I refer to earlier published versions of individual works in order to illustrate Bassani's effort to create a language of anguished alienation. The author's point of view in his romance about Ferrara is investigated in its major lines of direction: from third-person narration in the first tales, to first-person involvement in the three central novels, and then to refuge in the third-person in his final novel. As guides for my exploration, I turn to the writings on the poetics of space by the phenomenologist Gaston Bachelard, to Georges Poulet's studies on time and interior distance, to the research on human geography of Yi-Fu Tuan, to inquiries on the silent language of temporal and spatial communication by the anthropologist Edward T. Hall, and to Melanie Klein's psychoanalytical theories on childhood sexual identity and mourning. My book explores how the spiritual movement of Bassani's narrative writings leads his tormented characters beyond the time of history and chronicle to an eternal literary world.

1

The Community of the Excluded

A sentimental abyss separates the characters in the literary universe of *Within the Walls (Dentro le mura)*, the opening division of *The Romance of Ferrara*. The tales that comprise the section originally appeared together in 1956 as *Cinque storie ferraresi (Five Stories of Ferrara)*. Then four years later, Bassani reissued the stories along with two other tales and the short novel *The Gold-Rimmed Eyeglasses* under the title *Storie ferraresi*. In 1973, when the author gathered his narrative writings into *The Romance of Ferrara*, he regrouped the nuclear five Ferrarese tales in the volume *Within the Walls*, recognizing that the five stories do, indeed, constitute an organic unity in theme and point of view. The definitive title of the collection of tales expresses Ferrara's simultaneously protective and menacing encirclement of walls. Each edition enabled the writer to revise the tales by adding or deleting epigraphs from other authors and especially by altering the language from an originally Rondist art prose to an almost journalistic commonplace tone. For both lyricism of language and elegance of structure, the 1960 edition represents a moment of artistically achieved balance between Rondist preciosity and everyday prosaism. Bassani chose to frame the 1960 version with the brief opening tale "The Enclosing Wall" ("Il Muro di cinta") and the concluding story "In Exile" ("In esilio"), which reappeared years later under different titles in considerably altered versions in the volume *The Smell of Hay*. Even slight differences between the 1974 and 1980 editions of *The Romance of Ferrara* indicate that the author's narrative work demands to be studied as always "in progress." In this chapter, I shall examine the five nuclear tales of Ferrara.[1]

Throughout those stories, Bassani consistently represents existence as a state of exile where individuals remain forever excluded from the life of others. Exile for the writer also transcends geographical and political banishment as it comes to represent the psychological condition of being apart from others. This state of aloneness does not arise solely from one's ethnic identity, since Bassani views all human beings and not any particular religious or racial group as dwelling in exile.[2] Borrowing a term from the writings of Luigi Pirandello, the characters in Bassani's narratives are *esclusi*, the excluded ones, the outcasts. In one of the essays in *Le Parole preparate*, Bassani observes: "Dreams, visions, nightmares. Realty in fragments. For one who is excluded from life *(escluso dalla vita)*, for one who has chosen to stand outside of it, it is just and humane that life not give back other messages."[3] Those *esclusi* form a community throughout the tales in *Within the Walls* whose author attempts to rescue his characters from the torment-ing nightmares of destructive time.

In their time span, the five tales run from the late nineteenth century to the period of reconstruction following the Second World War. As could be expected from a disciple of Croce's historicism, Bassani's *storie* never appear as chronicles but as histories of individuals falling victim to time's devastation. Throughout the tales, Ferrara's Estense Castle clock continues to toll every quarter hour as the main characters become prisoners of the temporal process. Most of them seek to hold onto a cherished moment, which survives time's fatal passage only through memory. As such, these characters display that penchant for privileged recollection that Henri Bergson in *Laughter (Le Rire)* analyzes as an essentially comic attitude. The mental inelasticity of some of Bassani's characters recalls the Bergsonian situation of individuals who refuse to accept present reality in favor of the past.[4] But the Italian author does not try to arouse laughter as a comic corrective for mental rigidity in characters who reject the unavoidability of loss through time even at the expense of their own extermination. Bassani strives to create through historical occurrence, temporal process, and individual history an elegiac vision of loss and disillusionment. It is his characters' unwill-ingness in these tales to surrender cherished and privileged recollections that creates the pathos that envelops *Within the Walls* as its fictional figures are forced to come to terms with annihilation.

In those tales, the narrator's vision crosses all temporal barriers to redeem the characters from the physical and spiritual exile to which they are eventually condemned. Figures in those stories move in a world of light and shadow, so that the tales may be viewed as twilight reflections on a lost time. There is, indeed, no concrete time, only elusive temporal fragments to be reclaimed by memory for the barren present. Not only are characters imprisoned in certain past moments, but they do not even succeed in mastering the familiar space of their home town, since Ferrara does not serve them as a mediating force: The grim city divides rather than unites its inhabitants. Ferrara stands at the center of the author's imaginative universe as a totality of intensely lived experiences.[5] One of the outstanding changes that takes place from the earliest published versions of Bassani's tales in the 1940s to their collection in the *Storie ferraresi* is the movement from a vague allusion to environment (a city called F and streets referred to by initials) to the almost cartographic precision of naming the crooked medieval streets and Renaissance boulevards in Ferrara. Bassani represents what a particular city, his Ferrara, can do to shape, determine, and shatter the lives of some of its inhabitants. In an essay in *La Parole preparate* that deals with the theme of the city of Venice in literature, the author comments that a city is "something that lives, that palpitates as everything that belongs to the painful and glorious history of humans" (p. 16). The writer sees his task as penetrating his city in order to understand its life and history. To accomplish that task, Bassani had to recreate painful moments in Ferrara's recent past.

Recovering the past is the subject of the essay "Laggiù, in fondo al corridoio" ("Down There, at the End of the Corridor") that concludes *The Romance of Ferrara*. In that piece, Bassani discusses how he came to write and publish the tales that make up the *Storie ferraresi*. Acknowledging that the past is not dead, the writer describes the effort to reclaim life from the passage of time:

> To recapture the past is possible then. But if one truly wants to recapture it, one has to run down a kind of corridor that every instant becomes longer and longer. Down there at the end of the remote, sunny point where the corridor's black walls converge, there stands life as vivid and throbbing as once before when it was first experienced. Eternal then? Eternal, of course. But nonetheless farther and farther away, more and more elusive, more and more unwilling to permit itself to be possessed.[6]

Through memory, the writer tries to possess that past in all its undying intensity. Even though Bassani admits that the goal seems to move farther and farther away, the author has to overcome the destructive process of history to reconstruct the lost time. In his Ferrarese tales, Bassani rebuilds a world that political treachery and wartime atrocities radically disrupted and combats that destructiveness by evoking the sorrows of the community of the excluded.

That vital creativity of human memory transcending the past is evident in an epigraph from Blaise Pascal that prefaced the 1974 edition of *Within the Walls*: "A city, a countryside, at a distance are still a city and a countryside; but as you get closer, they become houses, trees, roof tiles, leaves, blades of grass, ants, legs of ants, ad infinitum." In Bassani, spatial and temporal terminology converge as the artistic perspective moves from distant past events to a detailed present recollection of cherished experiences that forever remain close to the human heart. Writing conquers the distances of time and space, transforming each previously lived moment of an intimate world that merely appears to be lost.

Bassani's approach to the recent past of Ferrara recalls the lyrical search for spatial and temporal depth by the eighteenth-century French author Joseph Joubert, who stressed the importance of distance: "Perspective or remoteness is necessary for events, in order for us to be affected (or touched) by them poetically, and in order for us to give them poetic treatment."[7] Bassani achieves the poetic re-creation of the Ferrarese community in *Within the Walls;* for him, as for Pascal and Joubert, the passionate resonance of intense feelings like love permits memory to preserve and prolong a time that has seemingly vanished.

Pascal suggested the timelessness of love with his observation that "love has no age; it is always born again."[8] Similarly, Bassani's narrative relives earlier instants of conflicting emotions, unreciprocated love, resentment, exclusion, pain, and disappointment. Both time as a loving aspect of existence and history as sociopolitically objective facts beyond individual control determine Bassani's literary universe. While historical events nullify human illusions of permanence, continuity, and identity, the artist's organizing memory surmounts temporal dispersion of the past.

Ferrara seems almost to address readers in a collective voice as the writer employs substitutionary speech or narrated monologue in these third-person stories to represent the anguished thoughts and frustrated longings of the townspeople. Although Bassani only occasionally uses snatches of actual Emilian dialect and Jewish ghetto slang, he most often adapts standard Italian to the speech patterns of the Ferrarese at home, school, synagogue, church, or fashionable café. To portray the restrictive mentality and mores of that urban milieu, the writer composed choral stories about characters whose futile attempts at communication with one another resemble the forbidden conversations of convicts. For as both a geographical entity and a psychological state, Ferrara in Bassani's tales is a prison city of red-roofed homes, desolate neighborhoods, or elegant districts that enclose its inhabitants within the deadening silence of confining walls. By resorting to standard Italian rather than recording the provincial voices of linguistic ghettos, the author succeeds in making Ferrara a microcosm of human suffering.[9]

Although Bassani presents these five nuclear tales through third-person narration, he has permitted his interpenetration as ultimate narrator, poet, judge, and historian of their events: The narrator who has survived the nightmares of historical reality can look back and reflect on the sense of what has occurred.[10] To explain his task as an author, Bassani included in the 1980 edition of *The Romance of Ferrara* an epigraph from the eighth chapter of Alessandro Manzoni's novel *The Betrothed*: "Certainly the heart always has something to say about what will be to whoever pays attention to it. But what does the heart know? Scarcely a little of what has already happened." Bassani, like Manzoni before him, rejects the godlike claim of authorial omniscience. Some of the characters in his tales and novels will be just as enigmatic to the narrator as to the readers. But as a witness to what happened in Ferrara during the Fascist era and its immediate aftermath, Bassani speaks from direct experience of the doomed world of his youth. Since the past for this writer will always remain alive in our hearts, the tales of *Within the Walls* represent a narrative quest to express across historical reality the timelessness of enduring love for that vanished world.

"LIDA MANTOVANI"

Closed, stuffy rooms where people strike out at each other in despair over the frustrations of a lifetime dominate the intimate space in the tale "Lida Mantovani" that opens Bassani's romance of Ferrara. No story better illustrates the author's habit of returning to earlier tales to rework them with elaborate revisions than this study about barriers erected by differences in social class. As the writer reveals in his essay "Down There, at the End of the Corridor," Bassani first sketched "Lida Mantovani" in 1937 when he was twenty-one. In 1940, he published it under the title "Storia di Débora" ("Debora's Story") in the book *Una città di pianura (A City of the Plains)*, which had to appear under the pseudonym Giacomo Marchi, taken from the maiden surname of Bassani's Aryan mother, since Fascist laws forbade publication by Jews. After the Second World War, the editor of the forthcoming journal *Botteghe oscure*, Marguerite Caetani, invited the author to submit a narrative piece, and in the opening issue in 1948, the tale was entitled "Storia d'amore" ("Love Story"). Eight years later, it figured as the lead tale for the *Five Stories of Ferrara* "Lida Mantovani." Although "Lida Mantovani" was to be the second tale in the 1960 version of *Storie ferraresi*, the piece regained its opening position in the 1973 printing of *Within the Walls*. With each successive publication, Bassani introduced variations in language, title, the date of major events, and in names of characters. One American critic has compared the task of studying the modifications over the period of more than thirty years to that of an archaeologist or geologist examining the chronological developments of strata to reconstruct the past.[11] Of all Bassani's youthful attempts at narrative composition, only this story has remained a witness to his abiding concern with certain themes and literary structures.

Throughout all versions, the plot of this tale remained essentially the same. An adolescent gentile girl from the lowest class of Ferrara's proletariat (those of peasant background) falls in love with a Jewish youth from the upper bourgeoisie, becomes his mistress, and later gives birth to his illegitimate son after her lover has deserted her and returned to his family. In the first two versions, the girl's name is Débora Abeti, and it was not until the 1956 version that the name Lida Mantovani replaced the original biblical and rather Hebraic appellation. In the version for *Within the Walls*, the Jewish youth David acquires the surname Camioli and an address on corso Giovecca as his family residence, since Bassani was seeking to tie together various characters in his literary world of Ferrara. In all these reworkings, the heroine has to return with her child to a slum neighborhood to live with her mother in a dismal basement apartment. By the printing of the 1948 revision, the author had already eliminated a long, lachrymose opening section with variations on the verb *piangere* (to weep) to describe the protagonist's feelings during and immediately after her pregnancy. The heroine's deliverance from social shame occurs in all editions through her marriage to a middle-aged bookbinder, Oreste Benetti, a shopkeeper in her mother's neighborhood, who eventually adopts her son Ireneo as his own child. In the first version (1940), the author continues the story beyond Oreste's death to discuss Ireneo's marriage, the relationship between Lida and her daughter-in-law, and Ireneo's enlistment as a volunteer for Italy in the Spanish Civil War.

Bassani concludes all later revisions, however, with the heroine's reflections on the loss of her husband. The movement throughout the versions of this tale is condensed as the writer concentrates on key moments in the lives of his main characters and their failure to close the distances separating them.[12]

This opening tale of *Within the Walls* demonstrates the influence of filmic technique on the author's narrative structure. Flashbacks continually carry the characters back to some special time in their existence when they still hoped to realize a particular dream. The flow of events at first moves forward but then turns back. Although in the essay "Down There, at the End of the Corridor," Bassani does not compare the tale's structure to any geometric form as he does with the other four nuclear stories, the continual repetitions over time initially suggest a spiral but then ultimately, a circle. From the 1948 version on, the story has a nine-part structure: Ireneo's birth; Lida's return to the apartment on Via Salinguerra; description of the lower-class setting and Oreste's visits to the apartment; the marriage proposal; a flashback to the affair with David; her mother's death and Lida's recollection of the period she lived with David; her mother's funeral; Lida's wedding and subsequent marriage until her husband's death; Lida's realization that she disappointed Oreste. Progression never follows a linear course. The story begins with an actual birth and closes with the heroine acknowledging that she never fulfilled Oreste's intense desire to have a son of his own. A physical birth and an unrealized birth round out this tale of regret, selfishness, anger, and desperation.[13]

Every act in this story has already occurred in the past, so that instead of witnessing events, the reader reflects on their significance across time. The first line of every revision from 1948 on includes the phrase *finché visse* (as long as she lived), indicating that the protagonist is no longer alive. Readers learn about events that are as irreversible as history itself. One passes from the remote past tense to the present perfect as the author juxtaposes heterogeneous temporal levels. A dreamlike imperfect tense characterizes flashbacks to the period when David and the heroine used to frequent out-of-the-way movie theaters. The text moves from narrated monologue to actual dialogue with supporting verbs like *diceva* (she was saying) and then to indirect discourse. All forms of discourse indicate the wall of incommunicability separating characters from one another.

Only once, in the eighth and final section of the 1940 version, does the narrator interfere, betraying his presence by the phrase *come dissi* (as I said); in all later reworkings, Bassani prefers to let the narrative present itself, especially through the thoughts of the protagonist and her mother who frequently seek to escape the immediate moment of narration through memories of precious and irreparable instants in their past. When characters imagine another turn of events in their lives, the past conditional is used. Unlike Pirandello, who employs the past conditional to represent his characters' lies to themselves about the outcome of their lives, Bassani permits Lida Mantovani and her mother, Maria, the freedom to muse over the possibilities irrevocably denied to them. For

Lida Mantovani does not attempt to cast off responsibility even for events beyond her control, such as never having presented Oreste with a child. Because of the author's narrative strategy, readers view these characters almost as victims of past time. The writer, in successive editions of the story, stresses that he is dealing with the interbellum period by specifically mentioning dates like the heroine's twenty-fifth birthday in 1928 at the time of Oreste's marriage proposal, her mother's death the following winter just around the occasion of the Lateran Treaty, and Oreste's death in 1938. To emphasize the historical period under discussion, Bassani reinserted in the revision for *Within the Walls* a description of the role played by local Fascist authorities in organizing ski competitions on the city's bastions during winter 1929, details that appeared in the original 1940 printing but not in those of 1948, 1956, or 1960. Another descriptive detail that the author introduced in the 1956 edition and continued afterward is the somewhat gratuitous reference to the municipal lamp lighter at work on the streets as Lida and Maria return home after having the baby baptized: gratuitous only if one does not appreciate the author's efforts to situate the tale at a definite time during the gaslight era. Thus, the reader is led to consider the tales of Ferrara in retrospect across history.[14]

Although the 1948 edition of this work is entitled "Love Story," Bassani deliberately deflates the Italian tradition of feverously impassioned love narrative as expressed in the novels of Gabriele D'Annunzio (1863-1938) and continued in sentimental movie romances during the Fascist period. Love is a disruptive force in this story for both the heroine and her mother, since Maria Mantovani gave birth to her daughter illegitimately as a result of an affair with a blacksmith in the village of Massa Fiscaglia. Intimate involvement with men who would not (or, as Maria claims, "could" not because of parental opposition) commit themselves to marriage led to banishment in the city for the mother and a return to a life of drudgery as a seamstress for Lida. The author here represents love as a master–slave relationship where Lida willingly permits David to reduce her to an object of his erotic desire and a means of scandalizing his bourgeois family. In scenes after the lovers have gone to the movies, Bassani emphasizes such unromantic details as cold, foggy nights in the Ferrarese autumn and the city's uninvitingly damp grassy bastions where Lida assumes a passive role by reluctantly surrendering to David. During the movie scenes, Bassani juxtaposes the petty, mean situation of the real-life lovers with the glamorous images on the screen on which Lida projects fantasies about David as her heroic angel or god. Love as a celluloid picture of tenderness and sweetness or a D'Annunzean extravagant passion is exposed as one of the sustaining lies of the Fascist era.

In this "love story," Bassani presents the seasons of the year as seasons of the human heart vacillating between optimism and despair. Because of its cyclical nature, seasonal time transcends chronological time and participates in eternity.[15] Spring in Bassani's fiction usually gives the world a spirit of evanescence charged with deluding hope in nature's renewal in its green loveliness. But for

Lida, in the 1948 versions on, the month of April 1921 is the uncomfortably warm time when she gave birth. [16] The shining leaves on the magnolia tree in the garden of the Ferrarese Maternity Hospital offer no consolation to the distressed young woman as she envisions a future of deprivation for herself and her baby. In the the midst of her hardships Lida returns to the memory of the two summers of her affair with David. That first summer of their earliest intimacy represented the young man's most intense rebellion against his family when he flaunted his association with the proletariat girl by taking her to the city's leading cafés. The following summer, when David decided to simulate the life of the urban working class by taking a top-story tenement apartment with Lida, the lovers used to escape their sweltering and airless rooms to savor the cool relief of Italian ices sold at kiosks near the city's gates. Late on summer nights, the two would join crowds of impoverished young couples stretched out on the turf of the bastions exchanging frenetic embraces. With the onset of autumn mists came disillusionment, boredom, and a total breakdown in communication. Bassani's characters frequently find in exterior nature an analogy to their private torment.

Memories of winters of a nearly Siberian coldness are a measure of comparison for Oreste Benetti over the years in his efforts to diminish the glacial wretchedness of a present moment. In all versions of the story, the bookbinder recalls the infamous winter of 1903 when the Po became frozen and heavy snow covered the streets until the beginning of April. [17] Having been educated by priests in a seminary, Benetti uses the language of religious reverence to describe the awesome river with its Arctic severity. The Po, so deeply frozen that itinerant carters from nearby villages crossed the river in safety rather than using the iron bridge of Pontelagoscuro, in its icebound fixity symbolizes timelessness rather than flux. People could rely on that wintertime river as a means of passage or an unchanging point of reference in memory. The frigid river represents continuance over time.

In the chaos of life's events, Bassani's characters turn to the fixed features of their homes or the city's architecture in order to preserve a precarious illusion of stability and continuity. Although in the story's first two editions, the author generally refrained from precisely naming the town and its boulevards, in every version, he located Maria Mantovani's basement apartment on Via Salinguerra in the decrepit medieval district. Yet, despite this street's location within the shadow of the city walls, it escapes from the oppressive enclosure to the large country gardens just outside town. Even Maria and her daughter in their subterranean apartment are occasionally comforted by the thought of the expansive countryside just beyond the end of Via Salinguerra.

While Bassani details how the two women are buried alive deep in a well (*pozzo*), in the revision for *Within the Walls*, a sense of peace and protection still welcomes Lida after she is deserted by David. The foyer of her apartment building suggests the dark dimensions of a hayloft, whereas the apartment at once recalls its original function as a coal bin. The author also describes how this building's design prevents easy accessibility to the Mantovani home because of a double stairway: one rising from the vestibule and the other descending into the dim apartment. Certain unchanging features of their bedroom, like two iron beds and the dusty floor, ambivalently inspire melancholy and a sense of permanence. The bedside carbide lamp with its bluish light and buzzing sound attests to the sleeplessness of tenants preoccupied with thoughts of failed relationships and unrealized dreams.

Contact with the outside world is through a manually controlled doorbell, whose ring had a vastly different significance according to the identity of the caller. Because David never entered the apartment and always refused to meet Maria Mantovani, his ring was an imperious summons for the girl to rush out to him. But Oreste's vigorous ring announced his cheerful arrival at the home, for the bookbinder, unlike the young Hebrew, truly wanted to become part of that family.[18] Ironically, the improverished apartment began to acquire amenities like electricity, a fresh coat of paint, and new furniture only in the last months of Maria'a life, following Oreste's proposal to Lida, as if the old woman were not destined to enjoy the comforts of a secure existence. Maria's release from the well would come only with death.

One way that Bassani's characters flee the oppressiveness of their surroundings is by enjoying the view from windows, which can become symbols of expectation or frustration.[19] Windows mediate between interior and exterior worlds, permitting one to ease briefly the anguish of the heart by looking beyond a troubled existence. Three windows symbolize the limits of Lida Mantovani's life. In the basement apartment, a high-placed window permits the two women quick glimpses of passersby. Oreste once stands like a beggar outside that window immediately following Maria's death when Lida drives him and sympathetic neighborhood women from the irreparably lonely apartment. The barrier forever separating Bassani's characters is symbolized by the frosted glass window through which Oreste tries to behold his distraught fiancée lost in memories of David. In the stifling garret apartment on Via Mortara that the girl shared with the Jewish youth, a window enabled her to turn away from David's peevish rejection of her affection: The view of red rooftops, the Emilian countryside, and the distant hills of Bologna relieved the pain of being forever excluded from his love. On marrying the bookbinder, Lida moves into a newly constructed home in a recently developed section of Ferrara, and there during the nine years of their life together, she watched Oreste pause every autumn to peer out the front window as if to determine the severity of the coming winter, reassured that his well-insulated and centrally heated home would protect them from the outside world. While the space behind windows can be one of loneliness and regret, the solitary watcher does overcome the imprisoning confinement typical of Bassani's literary world.

Complete liberation for many of Bassani's characters arrives only with death.

Here, in his earliest story the writer begins a meditation on the places of death, which reoccurs throughout his narrative works. Death appears as the supreme dividing force, marking off confining spaces of permanent exile in Ferrara's Christian municipal cemetery in this tale or in the Hebrew graveyard in other stories, concluding dramas of tacit desires, sterile waiting, and constant isolation. For the 1960 edition of *Stories of Ferrara*, the author balanced a Jewish burial ceremony in the opening tale, "The Enclosing Wall," with Maria Mantovani's Christian funeral in the second story. Lida's mother at last rounds out her existence of exclusion and poverty with honorable burial in a tomb under the newly added porticos of the Church of St. Christopher in the city cemetery, thanks to Oreste's generosity in paying for the costly gravesite. In dying, Maria Mantovani finally finds a secluded zone of repose away from the shame and humiliation that haunted her life.

A search for unattainable peace and enduring human contact motivates characters in this tale about the inability to establish bonds of companionship. Lida's self-loathing—she considers herself unattractive in physical appearance and personality—conditions the girl to accept without protest and almost with pleasure her abject role as David's mistress. She is always prepared to settle for next to nothing, so deeply ingrained is her sense of social inferiority before the youth from the high bourgeoisie, with its exclusive clubs admitting only attractive and fashionable members totally unlike that illegitimate working-class girl. Just as Lida permitted David to exploit her, she submits to Oreste's benevolent manipulation when the bookbinder brings her respectability through Catholic marriage and legally adopting her son Ireneo. In no way can their marriage be "an human symbiotic associaton" of kindred spirits from the same class.[20] Because of their similar background, Lida adapts easily to Oreste's habits and religious viewpoints. Feeling somewhat guilty over not bearing him a son, she gives her husband respect and even affection; but she never shows Benetti the passionate devotion of slave to master as in her earlier relationship with David. Only time serves to modify Lida's passion and causes her to develop a degree of maturity to adjust present realities and future expectations with past disappointments, as expressed in the epigraph from *La Princesse de Clèves* that first appeared in the 1948 printing but has disappeared from *Within the walls*: "Finally, after entire years had passed, time and absence allayed his pain and extinguished his passion." Like Nemours at the loss of the company of Mme. de Clèves, the heroine here must learn to contain her suffering over a separation that she can never change. Reconciliation must occur with oneself before it can extend to others.

To a large extent, Lida can never reconcile herself to living with her mother. Throughout the variations of this story, Maria attempts in vain to stand with her daughter in front of a wardrobe mirror in order to demonstrate to Lida how their fates mirror each other's because they were abandoned with child. Not only did the mother do nearly nothing to resist the girl's affair with David, but she seems to have rejoiced at the doomed relationship, since Lida's eventual fall would give her a companion in disgrace. One cause for Lida's resentment toward her mother arises whenever the elderly woman reminds her daughter that the blacksmith from Massa Fiscaglia loved Maria and wanted to marry her. That feeling of superior advantage over her own child prevents them from ever forming close bonds of affection and frequently disrupts the laconic association of two women united in rejection. In one regard, the daugher suffers less than her mother because Maria had to flee the prejudice of country society and take exile in Ferrara, whereas no one on Via Salinguerra shuns Lida, and Oreste in time redeems the young woman.

A need for certainty and stability motivates Oreste Benetti in his relationship with the Mantovanis. Because this usually kind bookbinder believes in establishing a hierarchy in dealing with others and keeping them at a proper distance, he sometimes resorts to insulting vulnerable individuals like Maria Mantovani to prevent excessive familiarity. Benetti, always searching to gain prestige, combines the formal manners of his seminary education with a military stiffness acquired during service on the frigid Carso plateau during the First World War. This gentleman of advanced age appears grotesque with his large head and robust chest and short legs and in his amorous pursuit of a woman a quarter century his junior. In political views, Benetti reflects the values of his class in uniting piety to patriotism by joyously welcoming the rapprochement of the Vatican with the Fascist regime in the Lateran Treaty of February 1929. Domestically, Benetti shows himself to be an enlightened despot indoctrinating his wife in the Catholic faith and making Ireneo his apprentice at the bookbinding shop after having sent the boy to a seminary school. All that Oreste does is for the welfare of his artificial family, but it is that very artificiality that forever gnaws away at him until death releases him. Benetti never wins the adoration that his wife reserved in memory for David. The unlikable Ireneo, weak in character and lacking industriousness, never once responds to his adoptive father's unspoken but obvious plea for love and instead persists in calling him only Uncle Oreste as a form of rejection. It is, of course, the longing for a son of his own that sustains the bookbinder during the brief period of his marriage. For although Oreste Benetti succeeded in entering the Mantovani home from a winter's cold and eventually transferred that family to a place of warmth and security of his own creation, he did not penetrate a space of loving warmth and reciprocated generosity in the hearts of others. Like all those in exile, the bookbinder remains an outsider.

One character stands voluntarily apart from the others in his own aura of hostility: David, the outsider by choice. In this Catholic world of proletariats, the young Hebrew, with his upper-class family, is a stranger who refuses to condescend to join the small society on Via Salinguerra even though he intends his liaison with Lida to offend his relations. As a Jew, David acknowledges that religious differences separate him from members of his class and obstruct his marriage to a young lady of one of the town's leading families. Bassani carefully situates David's petulant resentment in the era before Fascist legislation reduced Jewish citizens to outcasts. David yearns to escape from a world that officially did nothing to discriminate against him. But his simulation of working-class life goes no further than taking an apartment with Lida in a tenement where he continues to evade his existence by reading French novels, talking of flight to America, and sleeping for hours on end. In most versions of the story, reading French novels and wearing a blue fur overcoat become leitmotives for the remote young man. Because Bassani never attempts to account for David's innermost motives, the young Hebrew is the first of the major enigmatic characters in the author's fiction. One Marxist critic has accused the writer of superficiality for raising questions about certain characters but failing to penetrate their spiritual core, for Bassani asks, "Who was David, what did he want?"[21] But in David and other characters enveloped like him in oblivion and incommunicability, the writer depicts the opacity of otherness, the "impenetrable shadow of secrecy" that makes every individual a mystery to all others.[22] Bassani does not pretend to invade the heart's mysterious depths. David's unexplained rage toward life and his cruelty to an adoring victim like Lida also place him in a state of perpetual exile from his family and the one person offering him unlimited love. In David, the author represents what another Italian novelist, Alberto Moravia, calls in *The Empty Canvas* (*La Noia*, 1960) the "unseizability" of the beloved one.

Unlike other characters in this story, David does not dwell in a time of his own; he exists solely in Lida's memory of the past. Time as a dimension of the soul in the triangle of characters Maria, Lida, and Oreste dominates this tale. Maria Mantovani repeatedly slips away from the present to the fateful period of the youthful error that caused her ostracism from rustic society. Oreste continually reproaches Lida for ruminating on the past that she can change only by agreeing to make a new life with him. Although the bookbinder recalls ferocious winters of earlier years during his seminary education and military service, it is to a glorious future golden age that the artisan looks when the concord established by Fascist and Catholic authorities will guarantee undisturbed peace and happiness for couples like him and Lida hoping to bless their union with children. Here, the unsubstantiality of past memories merges with the irreality of future hopes in a spiritual barrenness. Past loss and impossible future miracles form a continuum as the heart comes to know and value absence and disappointment.

"The Walk before Supper" ("la Passeggiata prima di cena")

In the second tale in Bassani's collected narrative writings, "The Walk before Supper," time more than space is the dimension that segregates people. Of all the author's fiction, this story surveys a greater expanse of time than any other piece, moving from 1888 to the final phase of the Second World War. The writer first published this tale in 1951 in the seventh issue of *Botteghe oscure*. Two years later, it reappeared in a volume entitled after the story. Since that time, Bassani has included "The Walk before Supper" in every edition of the Ferrarese tales. Although important changes do occur from edition to edition, it would be erroneous to speak of an evolution in the various versions.[23] During the period that Bassani originally composed the story, from 1948 to 1951, the author admittedly had in mind motion picture technique, as he has stated in one of the essays for the volume *Le Parole preparate*. The tale opens as with a filmic long distance shot viewing Ferrara's main street, Corso Giovecca, in the blurred light and shadow of the magical twilight hour in May twelve years before the close of the nineteenth century, when every hope for civilized progress seemed about to be realized. Here, the scene is from a fin de siècle postcard representing buildings that Fascist authorities later ordered demolished in 1930—a past whose monuments would be lost except for the writer's efforts to capture moving images along that thoroughfare. As the author's imaginary camera approaches the setting, certain figures emerge from the luminous dust of the street: especially a man in frock coat and bowler hat approaching a young woman dressed as a nurse. From that fateful encounter would result the controversial marriage of the Jewish physician Elia Corcos to the gentile Gemma Brondi. Throughout this tale, the writer presents sequences similar to those in a silent movie: pantomines of the lovers strolling home from the Municipal Hospital to the Brondi house opposite the city's bastions; smiles of tacit understandings between Gemma's mother Dolores and the girl's elder sister Ausilia trying to discover the physician's identity.[24] Rather than employing flashbacks as in "Lida Mantovani," Bassani brings into close focus individuals from Ferrara's recent past—from the optimistic time following Italy's unification to the disastrous regime of the fascist Social Republic. Bassani's explicit intention is to achieve a definitive portrait of the enigmatic Elia Corcos. For the author comments that the only film image of the Hebrew physician was an indistinct and incomplete picture cut out of a group photo of medical colleagues and nurses at the city's main hospital, a photograph that was eventually lost. This story becomes the author's attempt to preserve the image and memory of a physician who perished in the Holocaust.

Among the barriers dividing the characters in Bassani's world must be included differences between rustic and urban cultures, as demonstrated by the inability of the Brondi family, of peasant background, to communicate with the bourgeois Corcos clan. In this tale, the groups never reach accord with one another but remain separate despite the bond of marriage. It is not so much religious difference or economic class that matter here but the cultural values of urban versus rural groups. In the glowing postcard world of late nineteenth-century Ferrara, a Jew of professional training like Corcos could win social acceptance and entrance into the otherwise exclusive and elite memberships of the Merchants' Club and the elegant Circolo dei Concordi. But the same

Ferrarese society that greeted with approval Corcos' rise to prominence as chief physician of the Municipal Hospital and personal doctor to the Duchess would never reconcile itself to his having taken a wife from the class of urban peasants like the Brondis. For although the Brondi family had lived in town for more than a generation, its habits and manner of speech betrayed that the family had never fully assimilated the ways of the city. Although no one reproached Elia for marrying a gentile, townspeople felt the young physician had disappointed them by taking a wife from beneath his station. Common gossip quite accurately accounted for this gross social mistake by supposing that at the time of their engagement, Gemma had been pregnant. From the period beginning with Italy's unification until after the first fifteen years of Fascist government, Ferrarese society made outsiders of its peasants, not its native Jews. Part of the structure of this tale is the opposition between *inside* and *outside,* with Elia Corcos occupying a privileged position within the city until racial laws prescribed his exile and destruction. In the contrast of rustic and urban environments, there never once develops authentic communication between the Emilian peasant and the Ferrarese city dweller. Each remains merely a visitor in the other's territory, even in town.

As the phenomenologist Gaston Bachelard has suggested,[25] homes are a psychological state. In Bassani's literary world, several homes reflect the schizophrenic divisiveness of Ferrarese social life. Representative of the division between rustic and urban worlds is the house on Via Ghiara where Elia Corcos eventually settles with his bride. From the street entrance, which the physician and his Jewish relatives always use, the building resembled other rather austere townhouses used for a residence and a place of business, as announced by the brass medical nameplate on the front door. Intimidated by that main entrance, Gemma's relatives preferred to take a roundabout path from their in-town farm house in order to reach the back entrance, where the three-story structure looked like a country home with its welcoming garden gate left open for them. The men of the Brondi family spent entire days down in the ground-floor woodshed, only coaxed by Gemma in the evenings to sit in the kitchen: Those town peasants steadfastly refused to enter the impressive drawing room where they never felt at ease.

With the stark contrasts of light and shade that invaded the house's shutters, the structure acquired a nearly human life that indicated the gulf of incommunicability between its peasant and city-bred visitors. Gemma Brondi alone (and then to a limited degree) succeeded in penetrating the circle of withdrawal and contemptuous irony with which her husband used to surround himself to keep away gentile and Hebrew relatives alike. Even the wife regarded the enormous number of learned volumes in her husband's study with resentment because the physician would use them to retreat from her and all others, no matter what religion or class. Elia's sister-in-law, Ausilia, who became his housekeeper in 1926 after Gemma's death, never once pierced the wall of reserve around the physician to enjoy the light and warmth that Corcos had shared with only his wife. Time one day worked an ironical reversal of roles at the home on Via Ghiara, for the moment was to come when Ausilia, the perpetual peasant outsider, would be the social superior in the house. Indeed, Elia lived too long, into his eighties, and in 1943, the Fascists sent him and his son Jacopo to annihilation along with other Ferrarese Jews. Every door closed to the once prominent physician except that of a gas chamber. Protected by her Aryan, Roman Catholic background, the city peasant Ausilia Brondi became the solitary survivor in the empty townhouse that was a tomb of hopes and dreams.

An unbreachable wall of misunderstanding forever separated the bourgeois Hebrews and the Emilian town peasants, as dramatized at the 1902 funeral of Corcos's eight-year-old younger son, Ruben, who died from meningitis. Although the ceremonies surrounding death unite mourners, Elia's decision to bury his child according to strict orthodox tradition alienated not only his wife's gentile relatives but also made Gemma an intruder among her Jewish in-laws. In one of the few examples of Bassani's use of dialect, Gemma throws herself on the freshly covered grave site screaming in Emilian that she did not want to leave her boy there. The assembled Hebrews interpreted Gemma's unrestrained grief as an insult to the officiating rabbi and an admission of the woman's desire to bury the child in the city's Christian cemetery rather than the Jewish graveyard. What further aggravated that unfortunate intercultural encounter was the demeanor and appearance of the Brondis' relatives, who offended members of the Corcos clan by openly expressing their sorrow as well as standing bare headed in ignorance of Hebrew custom. As the author demonstrates, between the two groups, not even the rites of death provide a meeting ground and an opportunity to establish bonds of community. From this situation of interethnic incomprehension, there can arise no possibility of lovingly shared experience, even here when everyone adored Ruben. Grief that could have created a bond ended by only further reinforcing the spirit of divisiveness.

Among the Hebrew characters, there was one whose boundless optimism and cheerfulness sufficed to overcome differences in attitudes and beliefs: Elia's father, the grain merchant Salomone, the Italian patriot who worshiped Garibaldi as the hero about to usher in an age of equality for all citizens. Within the nuclear family of Elia, Gemma, their children, and Ausilia, the elderly Salomone radiated a sense of trust in the future that would unite gentile and Jew alike. Although the merchant in appearance recalled the ghetto era in his exuberant outlook, he expressed confidence in a new civic identity. To Gemma and Ausilia, that elderly man always showed a courtesy so sincerely given that it caused mannerisms and ghetto slang to vanish in his aura of good will. Like the city peasants, Salomone Corcos did not quite fit in with the professional class of post-Unification emancipated Jews who regarded him as a relic of the past. And in the years of solitary exile that Ausilia Brondi suffers after Elia's deportation to a Nazi death camp, the unloved woman finds consolation in the memory of the congenial merchant. In what is Bassani's closest approximation to Marcel Proust's idea of sensory remembrance, Ausilia associates the figure of Salomone with the aroma of grain, dried hay, and citrus fruits that used to cling to the merchant's clothing. Long after the old man's death, Ausilia renewed that olfactory sensation by leafing through Salomone's Passover devotional texts, whose pages were redolent from the "fruits of the earth" that recalled his comforting presence. In the despair of the Holocaust that took Elia from her, Ausilia rediscovered in Salomone's enduring spirit the lost promise of a golden century.

Unfulfilled promise seemed to be a common destiny for both Elia Corcos and the town of Ferrara, whose citizens recognized a parallel between the provincial limitations of the physician's renown and the industrial backwardness of their community, resulting from political blackmail that gave Bologna the largest railway center south of Milan. Bassani begins his tale by pointing out the hopefulness emanating from an individual like Corcos as well as from the very physical structures of his city, like the Communal Theater, whose spur resembled a prow advancing boldly toward the future and freedom. As a young man, the physician used to measure his ill-fated ambitions according to the massive scale of the Este citadel: "Power, Glory, Happiness . . . Oh, the great, eternal words . . . capable of stirring in the imagination beyond the Castello's four towers that rise in the town's center and give the city's first greeting to whoever arrives from the country, wondrous skies marvelously glowing."[26] The man and his town existed in a dynamic, reciprocal relationship, but instead of moving toward a glorious future of liberty, the city and the physician were to come to know the disastrous consequences of Fascism and its alliance with Nazi racism. Although Elia Corcos did become an institutional symbol for the city, he never succeeded in escaping the municipal obscurity that deprived Ferrara of a luster like that of Bologna. Both the physician and his native town fell victim to political decisions beyond their control, first in being relegated to a minor part in the nation's commercial life and then by being plunged into the nightmare of the Italian Social Republic.

Corcos appeared to take a perverse delight in astounding the Ferrarese citizenry, especially his coreligionists who feared that achieving local fame might lead to conversion to Christianity. At the height of his imperious withdrawal, the physician almost confirmed those fears by refusing to pay dues to the Jewish community and maintain a pew in the Italian synagogue. But then he contradicted those acts by permitting his sons to be circumcised—as if to declare to the *goyim* that he would not desert his own people. Doctor Elia Corcos wished to preserve his autonomy from all realms of Ferrarese society, whether urban or rustic, professional or nonprofessional, Jewish or gentile. This chief surgeon often treated his wife like a beloved servant, as shown in the lines from the opera *Aida* that in earlier versions Elia mockingly addresses to Gemma and becomes the epigraph for the tale's edition in *Within the Walls*: "Come, beloved one, draw near / you are neither slave nor handmaiden." Corcos established an invisible and protective wall around himself to maintain his personal distance by preventing others from drawing close to him. Like so many of Bassani's characters, the physician shielded himself and his private domain from intruders. As long as his father's crepuscular age of postcard dreams endured, Corcos could persist in his aloofness. But in autumn 1943, hostile invasion irreparably destroyed Elia's illusions of separateness. While the physician had always struggled to avoid identification as a Jew, husband, or local surgeon, an alien force marked his destiny with hatred. [27]

Detachment from the life of others also occurs when various characters gain a sense of control over their circumstances by establishing observation posts behind windows. For a person like Ausilia Brondi who chose to remain on the sidelines of life, never confessing her love for Corcos, an observation post first permitted her to behold the young physician from a protective cover behind the shutters of an upper-story window at the Brondi home. Bassani here employs a technique common to Joseph Conrad: limited point of view as Ausilia attempts in late spring and early summer 1888 to determine the nature of the stranger's relationship with her younger sister. Glimpses of formal gestures like hand kissing, passionate embraces on the heights of the bastions on a level with the shuttered window, and a tense, tear-filled farewell slowly complete the picture of Elia's growing emotional involvement with the exuberant peasant nurse. Since Ausilia is unable to listen to the lovers, all her impressions must be visual, like details of Elia's rather shabby suit, his pocket watch, and his bicycle. From physical details and gestures, the observer hopes to satisfy her curiosity about the extent and sincerity of inner motivations. At the very start of her acquaintance with her future brother-in-law, Ausilia assumes the role of a witness to the intimate experiences of others instead of partcipating in a romantic relationship. The distance before the shuttered window symbolizes the elder sister's inability to enter into the life of the beloved stranger. After Elia's eventual deportation years later, Ausilia still remains the observing outsider on her frequent visits to the empty townhouse on Via Ghiara. For her, the window post of her initial view of Elia Corcos represents a lifetime of exclusion from love. [28]

Window scenes also indicate changes in the mood and attitude of characters over the years. On that decisive night in August 1888, after Dr. Corcos became engaged to Gemma, he returned to his father's home in the ghetto toward dawn. From the lofty dormer window of his own room, the young physician watched the sunrise and resolved on what was never to be a fully realized mission to advance medical science. Bassani places this window sequence in the sixth, brief final section of the tale, as recollected by Ausilia from her dinner-time conversations with Elia during the years after Gemma's death. The last impression is the strange gaze of Corcos's piercing-dark eyes trying to see reality above and outside time—the exact perspective of Bassani. She would always be haunted by that intense expression of Elia's mocking eyes when he sat at the kitchen table strategically placed at the window farthest from the door by which his wife's relatives used to enter. From the privileged observation post of the kitchen window, Corcos could look up from his medical texts and escape the room crowded with servants and relatives except when his scrutinizing gaze fell on his easily intimidated sister-in-law. But the moderately successful man at the table had already lost the sense of youthful enthusiasm that once inspired him by the dormer window in his father's house. Disillusionment with time transformed his window post into a peaceful retreat.

A rare instance of reciprocal communication in Bassani's narrative occurs when Gemma Brondi would stand by the second-floor window of her home that faced the back-garden entrance. For once, a window permits the outside and the inside to greet each other in the welcoming wave that Gemma used to throw to members of her family approaching the house. The window framed the young wife as if in a portrait. Bassani comments on the similarity in gaze between Gemma's joyous expression and the house's beckoning appearance at the countryside entrance. Usually, however, a window in Bassani's romance of Ferrara offers a solitary inscape for an observer who has grown accustomed to an existence apart.

As this story's title suggests, the writer seeks to recapture the chiaroscuro atmosphere of an evening stroll at a time of waning light and advancing shadow, when thoughts shift between the fully familiar experiences of daily life and vague sentiments arising in the twilight. Such indistinct moments seem almost outside of time, but the tale demonstrates that no one can escape temporal and historical changes. The opening mood of mysterious recollection becomes painful acknowledgment of social forces that devastate individuals and nations. Bassani provided a key to understanding the destructive power of history through the epigraph that appeared in earlier editions but that he removed for the version in *Within the Walls*. The quote is from Henry James's *Notebooks*: "Why does my pen not drop from my hand on approaching the infinite pity and tragedy of all the past? It does, poor helpless pen, with what it meets of the ineffable, what it meets of the cold Medusa-face of life, of all the life *lived*, on every side. *Basta, basta!*" (italics James's). Life's Medusa face smiled derisively at Corcos on the day of his deportation, which deprived Ausilia of the beloved companionship that illuminated the late years of her life. Some critics see Medusa as a symbol of a haunting past that authors could overcome through writing.[29] Bassani writes to evoke a vanished world of light and darkness. Through this story of unreturned and undeclared love, he presents what Honoré Balzac has called "those supreme points that bind the future to the past."[30] Here, the lonely survivor, like the victim condemned to extermination, dwells in exile from a past of unrealized hopes and dreams.

"A Plaque on Via Mazzini" ("Una Lapide in Via Mazzini")

From the second tale's elegiacal harmony, the text passes to the nightmare realities of the twentieth century in "A Plaque on Via Mazzini," which originally appeared in the tenth issue of *Botteghe oscure* in 1952. Here, time serves as a principle of discontinuity, for its passage must be felt as a painful absence without any possibility of renewal for the protagonist Geo Josz, the sole survivor of 183 Ferrarese Jews who in autumn 1943, suffered deportation to Germany. In the essay "Down There, at the End of the Corridor," the author notes that in composing this story, he had in mind the geometric figure of two spheres of equal dimensions suspended in air at the same height and slowly revolving at identical speeds in opposite directions on their respective axes. Two worlds set near to one another but forever isolated. Geo Josz considers himself a closed individual, a universe unto himself that can never move in harmony with the world of Ferrarese society. Less than two years of internment at the concentration camp of Buchenwald left Josz a temporally displaced person, unable to reclaim the present and future in his native city that demands deliberate forgetfulness of him.

In the earlier editions of this tale, Bassani quoted a line from Arthur Rimbaud's *Le Bateau Ivre:* "And I have sometimes seen what men thought they saw!" The adolescent Josz witnessed and fell victim to all the horrors of the Holocaust, losing both his parents and his younger brother in extermination chambers. That banishment and annihilation came all the more as a shock to the Josz family because they were exempted Hebrews due to the patriotic service and Fascist loyalty displayed by Geo's father, Angelo, as a squadrist who had joined the march to Rome in 1922. Arrest by local officials of the Italian Social Republic and initial confinement at the camp in Fossoli not only shattered the sense of privileged exclusion but also obliterated a cherished illusion of civic identity. After having passed a season in hell, Geo Josz never succeeds in communicating to those persons he once believed to be his fellow Ferrarese citizens the gruesome facts of his deportation because they refuse to acknowledge a reality they were guilty of creating or condoning. Even the Jews in Ferrara who managed to escape internment wish to forget the time of persecution by petrifying the past.

This tale's title refers to a plaque that the Hebrew community had hung outside their synagogue on Via Mazzini in summer 1945 to commemorate the town's victims of the Holocaust. Everyone hopes the dust of time will obliterate those names, but Geo's unexpected return irrevocably undermines the monumental effort to consign the past to an easily forgotten memorial. As Josz soon suspects, his coreligionists would have preferred to see him on the list of victims on the marble slab; his arrival disrupts the citywide attempt to restore an atmosphere of prewar normalcy. To everyone else, Geo belongs to the dead past. His very physical appearance on repatriation indicates that Josz is a man without time because hunger edema has transformed him into a creature of indefinite age. Most townspeople reject the idea of starvation edema and attribute Geo's swollen condition to favorable circumstances in the concentration camps.

When Josz first arrives on scene to interrupt the mason who is setting the plaque in place, Bassani, like a film director, attracts attention to the grotesquely distorted figure by turning toward him gradually. First, a mocking voice calls out the name Geo Josz from behind the young peasant mason, who wheels around to behold from his scaffold a strangely clad individual in a leather jerkin and fur hat despite the August heat. Geo resembles a large water-swollen creature from the sea, an *annegato* (drowned man), washed up on shore. Although the mason interprets the stranger's frequent laughter as an effort to put others at ease, it betrays Geo's resentment at seeing himself inscribed among the dead. Bassani emphasizes his narrative sound track by describing Josz's antiquated eloquence, highlighted with the German word *bitte* (please), all of which is inappropriate to a streetside conversation with the stone cutter but indicative of the survivor's spiritual displacement. While most of the angle of direction in this sequence takes place at middistance from the scaffold down to the sidewalk, at its conclusion, the author achieves a close-up of the stranger's hands to reveal the calluses of hard labor and then just over the right wrist, the identifying tattoo of concentration camp inmates. That close view extends from the first narrative section to the tale's second division, as one glimpses Geo's coldly staring water-blue eyes. Filmic technique here introduces Josz as a troubling presence in early post-war Ferrara.

Geo's return creates not only an embarrassment for those who would like to forget the war years but also poses a threat to those involved in war crimes. Participation in auctioning the confiscated property of Jews, service on tribunals that condemned people to the firing squad as reprisal for partisan raids—such activities compromised a large segment of the professional and land-owning middle class who were attempting to retain political control over Ferrara immediately after the restoration of peace. Those Hebrews who succeeded in eluding the various round-ups for deportation also resented Josz's return, which caused them to feel guilty for having escaped the torture camps. Bassani accumulates verbs and nouns of fear (*paura, temere*), anguish (*angoscia*), and self-torment (*torturarli*) to represent the dread that Geo Josz's reappearance arouses in his fellow townspeople.

Instead of bringing about the arrest and subsequent execution of those Ferrarese who were most prominent in the massacres of the Social Republic, Geo ironically becomes responsible for saving the lives of Fascist war criminals. During the internment and supposed extermination of all members of Angelo Josz's family, the Black Brigade appropriated their home on Via Campofranco and used its cellars as a prison. After April 1945, officers of the partisan Committee for National Liberation turned the large Josz residence into their headquarters and a jail for deposed Fascist leaders. In describing the shift in power from the "blacks" to the "reds," irony borders on cynicism as war and politics appear to be a sinister game claiming victims for abstract and inhuman causes. The only space in the house that the committee concedes to the not especially welcome refugee is the attic of a tower that dominates the street and the inner courtyard. Soon the faint glow of an oil lamp behind the window in Geo's tower observatory becomes a warning to members of the Liberation

Committee not to pursue summary executions of political prisoners. The mere knowledge of an enigmatic presence behind the window suffices to cause the usurpers of the Josz home to reflect on the rapidly changing circumstances of the postwar period and the need for flexibility to adjust to unexpected realities. Here the space behind a window gives the observer a degree of control over the observed. But Josz ends up protecting the lives of individuals who committed atrocities against Jews and anti-Fascists.

As in "The Walk before Supper," where a parallel develops between Corcos's fortunes and those of the city, so here the efforts of the Ferrarese to restore the bombed ruins to their prewar condition of order and cleanliness find a correspondence in Geo's attempts to fall in line with the general desire for normalcy. As time passes from autumn to winter in 1945 to 1946 to early spring, Josz ceases to resemble a grotesque figure as his swollen body gradually deflates. Along with other townspeople who endeavor to resume their careers, Geo begins to plan reopening his father's cloth wholesale business. It seems as if the youth and his city were competing to return to the past:

> one might imagine that between Geo Josz and Ferrara there existed a kind of secret dynamic rapport. . . . Everything was turning around, then. Geo, on one side; Ferrara and its society (not excluding the Jews who escaped the massacres) on the other side: everything and everyone ended up at once caught in a vast, unavoidable, and fatal motion. In harmony like that of spheres connected by gears linked to a single invisible pivot, so that nothing would ever succeed in stopping or resisting that motion. (P. 84)

A rejuvenated Josz orders the town's leading tailor to make him a new suit so that he can stroll in the evening along streets recently cleared of rubble. But as the author's highly mechanical simile suggests, Josz in his olive gabardine suit resembles an automaton parading in a farce of postwar peace and understanding. The dynamic harmony established between the man and the city proves to be superficial, for as Ferrarese society slips back into the decadence, lethargy, and pettiness of earlier times, the refugee must express the tormented consciousness of his exile in the Nazi inferno.

Human beings are not buildings of concrete and steel that can be torn apart and put back together again without leaving a sign of damage; human beings possess memory. All the agony that Josz briefly manages to repress surges forth on one of those enchanted twilight moments in Bassani's narratives, in mid-May 1946. The mainspring controlling the automaton of social conformity in Geo snaps forever when he sees a former Fascist Secret Police informer standing on a street corner and whistling a painfully familiar tune. The past, that anguished yesterday that the sight of the Fascist agent reevokes in a deceitful, hypocritical present time will not die in Josz, who is compelled to strike the spy. This incident is one of the decisive moments that the writer represents as determining the course of a life. The scene becomes intentionally theatrical as the author refers to the setting on Via Mazzini as a little stage offering its spectacle of springtime renewal of life's promise of happiness. Symbolically, the one-time spy, Count Lionello Scocca, from one of the city's oldest, though long-impoverished aristocratic lineages, leans against a marble shaft that once supported a gate to the ghetto—as if that representative of the privileged nobility who chose to sell out to Fascism and its German alliance were once again watching over excluded Hebrews. And the tune that the former director of the local Italo-German Culture Institute is blissfully whistling is none other than "Lili Marlen," the song most popular with German troops during the Second World War because of radio braodcasts from the Arctic Circle on the Russian front to the deserts of North Africa. The count's charming nonchalance and seeming innocence cause something to explode within Geo's psyche.

The two slaps that Josz administers with the brutality of a black-shirted squadrist from the early days of Fascism communicate all the agony in him that will not succumb to the demand of postwar Ferrarese society for silence.

To expalin the finality of that event, which takes place in the tale's fourth section, Bassani returns in the extremely short epilogue of the concluding sixth division to reflect on the enduring significance of that incident. According to the writer, a calm twilight evening can provide an instant of lightning-flash illumination of truth. In the author's order of artistic calculation the epilogue works like a mirror of the key incident that occurrred in near silence but whose meaning deserves to be heard in a terrifying shriek. All the falseness, all the pretense of Ferrarese society that the town's sole survivor of the Holocaust attempted to imitate collapse totally before the resurgence of the past.

From that moment of reawakening, Geo Josz begins a campaign to compel the people of Ferrara to acknowledge that time of betrayal and annihilation to which all the townspeople in varying degrees were accomplices. By dressing in his tattered concentration camp uniform and turning up at public gatherings to show photographs of his dead relatives, the youth intends to force the past of suffering onto the insensitive Ferrarese public. Throughout the city, the immediate reaction is to reject the uncooperative reminder of an era best forgotten. To the public, the man in the ragged camp uniform is a *travestito*—someone in disguise or costume. But in truth, the actual masquerade was Josz in his newly tailored suit strolling at dusk and smiling at lovely girls on bicycles as if nothing had ever happened to him and his family; or the frightening scarecrow figure taking a seat in the town's center at a table in the Caffé della Borsa to stare critically at the well-dressed old-line Fascists enjoying their afternoon aperitif. One critic has compared Josz in his deportee disguise to that specter of tormenting conscience, Banquo, in *Macbeth*.[31] But the people of Ferrara fail to display the gnawing sense of guilt evident in the usurper to the Scottish throne, for they merely find Geo to be a somewhat disgusting intruder into their present search for amusements to obliterate the hardships of the war years.

That moral examination of personal and collective complicity in crimes by

the Fascist dictatorship, which occupied some Ferrarese at the immediate end of
the war, by summer 1946 had vanished. The consequence of Geo's attempt to
instill the lessons of "yesterday" is exlusion from a serene "today" rich with the
promise of a fulfilled life. To the townspeople, the living enigma posed by Josz's
exhibitionism arises from his unwillingness to permit time to heal his spiritual
wounds. For the Ferrarese, one must not resist time by dwelling within a past
that recent reconstructions have nullified. But reconstruction is confused with
covering up the atrocities of the Social Republic, as when workmen plaster up
bullet holes on the Castello's parapet that resulted from a massacre on 15
December 1943, which is the central concern of another Bassani tale.

Bassani specifically marks the time of incidents in Geo's campaign against the
spirit of oblivion while noting the result of the young man's exclusion from the
city's life. In August 1946, Josz disrupts the festive mood at a popular dance hall
recently opened near the site of the execution of five leaders of the National
Liberation Committee in 1944. While everyone else tries to dissociate place
from time, Geo, with his macabre pantomime, insists on making that tragic
connection. Symptomatic of the new era of exclusion beginning in mid-1946 is
the change in the name of the Friends of America Club to its old designation as
the Circle of the Union, where in February 1947, the ragged Josz finds his way
barred into the elegant company of aristocrats like the Scoccas even though he
has paid his dues. During that same winter of 1946 to 1947, the proprietress of
the town's most fashionable house of prostitution also denies entrance to the
tattered beggar. Membership in Ferrarese society, from its elite circles to its
brothels, requires conformity in behavior, dress, and perhaps most importantly,
attitude. With his rotting uniform, Geo Josz tries to become a haunting presence
but succeeds in suffering social banishment.

Unlike Bassani's other narratives, there is no meditation here on Ferrara's
cemeteries. Because death in concentration camps prevented burial in the
Hebrew graveyard for Geo's family, not once does the protagonist reflect on the
place of ultimate retreat. His program consists of imposing death on life among
the insouciant townspeople. By summer 1948, following the elections of the
preceding April, which seal the restoration of normalcy, Josz disappears from the
city without leaving a trace. Unable or unwilling to repatriate himself in the
present world, he must flee to an evanescent zone of shadows and memories
where he will remain merely a name on a dust-covered plaque.

In distinguishing between picturial representation and dramatic scene, the
author reveals the influence of writers like James.[32] The dominant tendency here
is to alternate between a descriptive summary of events and a scene characterized
by substitutionary speech rather than direct dialogue, although dramatic enactment does occur at key moments. Bassani's careful distribution of narrative space
and emphasis is disturbed briefly by the obtrusive involvement of a first-person
narrator in the singular *io* early in the story's opening section who comments on
the seeming irreality of Geo's return to Ferrara. First-person viewpoint also

appears with the use of the disjunctive pronoun *noi* (us) in the objective case to indicate the relationship between Josz and the social collective. The narrator is still far from the intervention found in later writings where the first-person expresses his direct participation in the story.[33] Whether presenting actual dialogue or summarizing parts of conversation, Bassani carries his readers beneath the surface of speech into the minds of his characters.

This tale begins in the sultry silence of an August afternoon with the mason at work on the plaque while observers gather on the street. Through interior monologue, Bassani penetrates the stone cutter's thoughts: the peasant's typical resentment toward city folk, his need to avoid reading the plaque's inscription to shield himself from recent political events and possible future revenge by the Fascists. The author twice records the mason's name by inverting the order of surname and given name, as on an identity card—Podetti Aristide from the village of Bosco Mesola. To protect himself from the significance of history and the alien contact of urban residents, the mason remains "enclosed in his rough dialect" of the Po delta. Not even the directly reported exclamation by an elderly civilian about the number of Jewish deportees to Germany succeeds in breaking the stone cutter's willful silence. Only Geo's politely insistent remarks disturb the mason, demonstrating that life and time intrude on the desire for evasion.

Ironic overtones of address, with a nearly threatening emphasis, distinguish Geo's interview with Nino Bottecchiari, the provincial secretary of the Partisans Association housed in the Josz residence. Although the presence of the refugee's impoverished uncle, Daniele, at first keeps the conversation on a cordial level, one mocking observation by Geo about Bottecchiari's beard—the only comment in direct discourse in the entire passage—shatters the feigned good will of the meeting. Josz also immediately establishes an adversarial relationship with the partisan leader by deliberately ignoring the familiar pronoun *tu* addressed to him and instead answering in the formal *Lei,* which under the circumstances is anything but polite. On a non-verbal level, Geo gives Nino's typist such a menacing glance that she actually jumps away from the machine. Every look, every gesture by Josz stresses that the house is *his* and to be returned in due time. From the street come the words of a partisan song about marching forward to a reformed world through life's storms. But the reported-speech technique focuses on the tense drama between the ambitious provincial secretary and intimidating refugee determined on the restitution of his property in the confrontation between political pragmatist and political casualty.[34]

Bassani's narrative technique resembles instant video replay in the section that reports the slapping incident. There are so many versions by townspeople claiming to have witnessed the scene that the authenticity of the event almost comes into question. Each version of what happened, reported in rather tortuous clauses relying heavily on the passive voice proceeds like a filmic sequence in slow motion. As in films, each report moves in for a close-up of the faces of the two participants: Geo's initial bewilderment, then the furious hardening of his features at the moment of attack; Scocca's lordly expression of ease that masks his spy's sense of careful observation until the slaps knock him into incredulous silence. The multiple reports and consequent distortions of facts underline the irreparable significance of the incident, which marks the *ne plus ultra* in the protagonist's attempt to integrate himself into Ferrarese society.

Time in this story possesses the terrifying depth of a past of such agonizing loss that Geo Josz can define himself merely in terms of deprivation. The present and future hold no urgency for the refugee, who values time as only an opportunity to impress the living with the horror that took place among them and with their consent. With his family photographs and his camp uniform, Geo constantly tries to return the townspeople to the stopping point in his life where he lost his youth and ceased to age. But as the text insists, Geo's campaign is at a disadvantage (*svantaggio*), because of the climate of deliberate complacency that began in 1946. While Josz finds comforting reassurance in such signs of continuity with his life before deportation as the great magnolia tree in the garden of his family home that remained untouched by the war, he resents the changes that occurred during the last months of the Social Republic, like men growing long or thick beards in order to disguise themselves for fear of arrest by Fascist or Nazi authorities. When Geo sees for the first time his ultra-Fascist maternal uncle, Geremia Tabet, who never suffered persecution or discrimination, he screams hysterically with joy at beholding that man's Mussolini-era goatee. Tabet's beard evokes a time of security and acceptance from which the war forever exiles Geo. Count Scocca's Hitler-style mustache, on the other hand, provokes an assault because it recalls treachery. Josz can never share the optimism of his paternal uncle, Daniele, that the post-war period will realize the heroic idealism of the Resistance movement. Although the townspeople initially misinterpret Geo's "masquerade" as part of a Communist plot to combat control of the government by rightist and centrist parties, Josz has frozen his life in an immobile past that no political group could ever alter—to the regret of Bassani's Marxist critics.[35] Geo finds no hope in a society that believes history will fade into oblivion, because for him, the historical past coincided with his personal past. Since memories constitute Josz's sole present and future realities, he can have no permanent place in a city that renounces its past.[36]

In this tale pervaded by irony, Bassani has described the actions of a man who returned from what the real-life Holocaust survivor David Rousset called *l'univers concentrationnaire*: "a universe apart, totally cut off, the weird kingdom of an unlikely fatality."[37] Because Bassani never experienced the moral and physical chaos of a concentration camp—unlike his Piedmontese contemporary Primo Levi, author of *Survival at Auschwitz*—he would not presume to write about that brutally regulated world of constant abjection. Instead this writer dwells upon the aftermath of the season in hell, on the survivor's sacred responsibility to bear witness to the horrible truth. The Ferrarese people were reluctant to correct their past mistakes because such acts would have made them think about a painful time that no one wanted to confront. Bassani's irony in this tale works to make the text almost seem to agree with the natural desire of the townspeople to forget the war years and resume their normal lives, but the tortuous style of the syntax turns on itself to affirm the validity of Geo Josz's revolt against indifference and complacency. Unlike other postwar Italian authors, such as Natalia Ginzburg, whose enigmatic characters remain minimal presences, Bassani gives central importance to this refugee by his rejection of the present and the material comfort that the future promises him. The enigma behind Josz's supposedly baffling behavior and unrelenting attitude is his desperate determination to expose the great lie corrupting Ferrara after the war. With its underlying irony, this tale at first shows Josz's campaign and subsequent flight to have been futile since his absence causes the eventual transfer of his considerable estate to the executorship of his ultra-Fascist uncle, Geremia. While this narrative clearly represents the Ferrarese attitude of disapproval for Geo's actions, its ironical technique ultimately reinforces a feeling of moral outrage at the violence inflicted on Josz, his family, and the other victims of the Holocaust. Geo's attitude toward the past and its anguished bearing on the present and future becomes part of literature's extra-artistic dimension, creating an ironic portrait of a society founded on deceit, which attempted to cast into oblivion a time of genocide and rigorously organized inhumanity.

"THE LAST YEARS OF CLELIA TROTTI" ("GLI ULTIMI ANNI DI CLELIA TROTTI")

An aura of death hangs over the characters in "The Last Years of Clelia Trotti." The last years of the Fascist dictatorship, corresponding to the final years in the life of the socialist activist Clelia Trotti, mark the death throes of social order in Italy. First published in 1954 by the journal *Paragone,* this tale, according to the author, was modeled on James Joyce's "The Dead," the concluding piece in *Dubliners.*[38] In both stories, not only do their titles affirm the motif of death and finality, but from their opening sentences, a funereal mood prevails. The Italian tale begins with a description of the Ferrara Municipal Cemetery. Some earlier versions of Bassani's story bear an epigraph from Italo Svevo about a dying man who refuses final visitations from people mistakenly trusting in his love for them. Also, the last words in the first part of the Italian story are *fosse morta* (she had died), reinforcing the irrevocable sense of life's end. A graveyard atmosphere predominates from the beginning of Bassani's tale about the death of human hopes and illusions.

As in its Irish model, there are three levels of dead among the characters: those already deceased; the *passés* surviving beyond their proper time; and the disenchanted whose past experiences prevent them from fully participating in the present life of Ferrara or planning a part in its future.[39] Clelia Trotti, who perished in a German prison in the Emilian provincial town of Codigoro late in the war, and the Ferrarese Jews who suffered deportation to concentration camps figure among those dead before this story begins with Clelia's official funeral in autumn 1946 by municipal authorities. The orator for that occasion is the city's foremost anti-Fascist, Mauro Bottecchiari, once a Socialist deputy in Italy's parliament until the Fascists removed him from office. But Mauro and several of his former opponents in the Republican and Catholic Action parties have ceased to be a determining force in the present political reality that belongs to Communists like Bottecchiari's young nephew, Nino. Twenty-three years of a dictatorial regime have made those old-guard politicians relics of a bygone era. Death, too, has deprived some of the young of the spontaneous will to assume a role in Ferrarese society, as in the case of the tale's disillusioned protagonist, Bruno Lattes, who lost his parents in the Holocaust. Bruno's disenchantment with his country runs so deeply that he is making an academic career for himself in the United States. A deadening feeling of waste and destructiveness has corroded the vital spirit of the social world depicted in this story.

Bassani's tale begins in a deceptive mood of serenity and consoling openness in the square of the Certosa, the former Carthusian monastery where the city cemetery is located. Nothing grim or menacing oppresses the square, unlike much of Ferrara. Open meadows, nearby vegetable gardens, a red fifteenth-century portico, two pairs of attractively molded terra-cotta angels, all contribute to an impression of sweet solitude that sets the soul at ease. Death appears almost comforting in the Piazza della Certosa, which has even become a favorite meeting place for lovers to carry on the drama affirming life in a site reserved for the dead. To express the peaceful sense of unrestricted vastness in this gentile graveyard, the author employs variations of the past participle *aperto* (open): *prato aperto* (open lawn), *braccia aperte* (opened arms), *fossa aperta* (open grave), *volto aperto* (open face). Thus, death loses its frightening aspect in the inviting spaciousness of the cemetery. Constant references to Clelia Trotti's funeral and its expensive hearse, coffin, and an honor guard of peasant women in red tunics displaying Socialist hammers and sickles create a festive rather than mournful scene of public celebration.

Despite the beguiling sense of unrestricted openness at the story's onset, images of perpetual closure dominate the tale. In contradiction to forms of the verb *apire* (to open), the key word becomes *chiudere* (to close), with the double meaning of shutting out from the lives of others or closing within a domestic prison. Bassani uses phrases like *porta socchiusa* (half-closed door), *si richiudeva* (it was shutting again) to suggest the constriction of Italian society in fall 1939, the time to which the second part of the story returns, describing the moment when Europe entered the Second World War. In this tale, doors are constantly being shut, not slammed violently but slowly closed in order to spy on others or to whisper forbidden messages. During that period, many homes in Ferrara took on the appearance of prisons and jails as the secret police placed the dwellings of political subversives like Clelia under surveillance and recruited relatives to supervise and report their movements. In that world of suspicion and intimidation infinite spiritual ghettos arose to maintain impassable barriers.

This story focuses on an unusual and emotionally unsupportive relationship among three people that developed after fall 1939: Clelia Trotti, an involuntary recluse forever watched by her sister and brother-in-law; Bruno Lattes, a Jewish youth of the upper middle class trying to flee the stultifying despondency of his home on Via Madama, where his officially exempted father, a lawyer, was retreating into the emptiness of his study because racial laws barred further legal practice; and Cesare Rovigatti, a middle-aged shoemaker and Socialist who helped lead Lattes to Trotti. Cautionary gestures, all-knowing winks, and a guarded codelike language characterize the difficultly sustained relationship among the three suspects who never appear together at the same time until Clelia's belated funeral in 1946. Rovigatti never grew close to Lattes, whom the shoemaker always saw as a member of the superior class that looked down on him as a lowly artisan. Although the clandestine meetings between Bruno and the elderly Trotti woman possessed the excitement of games between fellow convicts, differences in political ideology prevented a genuine meeting of minds. In this tale, banishment from society deprives individuals of dignity without conferring the glory of martyrdom until that day in 1943 when the Nazis liberated Clelia from the boredom and idleness of her sister's home to a martyr's death in the Codigoro prison.

Unlike what Joyce in "The Dead" calls a spacious age, the Fascist era was one of minds closed in pettiness and meanness. And in Ferrara, the atmosphere of constraint actually preceded Mussolini's regime, which merely reinforced the sense of closure. For members of the city's professional bourgeoisie, bonds of class inspired an attitude of respect that crossed political lines. But living in a totalitarian society brought about a degeneration of values that corrupted even a politically independent individual like Mauro Bottecchiari, who compromised himself by serving on the local board of directors of the Fascist-backed Bank of Agriculture. In doing so, the former Socialist deputy not only collaborated with the government but profited from the association. In order to endure daily compromises, people lied to each other with chauvinistic and militaristic rhetoric that even before the establishment of the regime had become part of the Italian scene, as illustrated by the bombastic Bulletin of Victory that hung on the wall of the Pensioners' Home in the ghetto street of Via Vittoria, proclaiming the communiqué of General Armando Diaz about the glorious triumph of Italian troops in defeating Austrian forces late in October 1918. Ironically, even after the Pensioners' Home was converted into a Jewish school because racial legislation expelled Hebrew children from public schools, the Diaz proclamation continued to hang in the hallway along with the busts of Italy's three kings since national unification, almost mocking the local Jewish community for its misguided patriotism, voluntary service in the First World War, and early adherence to Fascism as a means of saving Italy from anarchy. The nationalistic rhetoric that attested to the Ferrarese Jews' love for their country after the fall of 1938 eventually expressed the empty promise and betrayal that left them without a civic identity. In place of spiritual spaciousness, an oppressive social narrowness enclosed Ferrara.

As Bassani demonstrates in this tale, no one completely escaped the contamination of soul inspired by that regime. Although public legend associated Clelia Trotti with a nearly heroic age of socialism before the outbreak of World War One, she revealed to Bruno her all too human and disillusioning prejudices by admitting that she had never read any of Croce's books simply because of the philosopher's opposition to her political beliefs. A similar closedness of mind determined Rovigatti's literary tastes in favor of foreign writers like Victor Hugo as opposed to Italy's age-old tradition of elitist authors who ignored the needs of the masses. As the shoemaker sarcastically observed to Bruno, the Ferrara Municipal Library did not provide the proletariat with a public service, since it closed before the end of the work day; racial laws, of course, forbade Jews to enter public libraries. Books and the buildings that make them available to the public express a society's attitude about the free diffusion of ideas, while an individual's choice of reading matter indicates an intellectual and emotive openness to challenging thoughts. Thus even the original opponents to Fascism fail to show the breadth of spirit that forever renews the vitality of intellectual inquiry.

Two worlds opposed each other in Ferrara's narrow confines—that of outsiders officially and unofficially banned from the mainstream; the other a beautiful, inaccessible realm of welcome insiders. An exiled individual like Bruno yearns with a prisoner's delirium to enter the resplendent world of blond boys and girls on their bicylces and Vespas who under any regime enjoy acceptance and adoration.

Bassani, like Joyce, portrays the different realms of an urban society. Within the shadows and light of Bassani's customary chiaroscuro style—which here reaches its conclusion at the story's close in an Autumn sunset viewed by Clelia and Bruno from the height of the town's Wall of the Angels sometime during the Second World War—color depicts attitudes of superiority and inferiority, moods of elation and dejection. Red banners at Clelia's funeral represent the sanguine emblem of the workers' movement, but the red ribbon binding the hair of a blonde adolescent symbolizes an insouciance and insensitivity to the disastrous events of Italian history and the oppressiveness of Ferrarese society. The green plush decor of Attorney Lattes's study as well as the pretentious green cloth covering the dining room table in the home of Clelia's sister and brother-in-law indicate defeat, withdrawal, and despair before a political order that cannot be overthrown. Blue eyes, whether those of a nonchalant youth with a tennis racket or of an elderly recluse like Clelia, radiate an exuberance that asserts itself despite restrictive circumstances. The absence of all color, white, symbolizes death, defeat, and despair: These are represented by the white snow that fell on Ferrara one night during the winter of 1939–1940. Bassani here carefully follows the final paragraph of "The Dead" where the protagonist Gabriel Conroy looks out from the window of the Dublin hotel on the snow covering the city and the whole country. For Joyce's character, the solid world of everyday experiences dissolves in the snow's deadening whiteness. In the concluding paragraph of the third section of Bassani's tale, Bruno Lattes opens the shutters over the window of his room on Via Madama to behold the frigid spectacle of a wintry Ferrara: "The snow continued to fall. In a few hours it would be deep, it would spread over the whole city, the common prison and ghetto, its oppressive silence" (p. 122). Snow buries life and hope in its cold absence of color. [40]

In that prison city of silent oppression, two conflicting emotions occupy the hearts of its urban inmates: attachment to place and the need for escape. Clelia once explained to Bruno how prison was a school teaching her how to live with herself. According to her, one grew most attached to the places where one has suffered most and found the inner strength not only to endure but transcend the ordeal. The elderly political suspect made her prison home and city a kind of protective enclosure within the hostile environment. Trotti mistakenly thought that Bruno would never willingly leave Ferrara because of a similar need to withdraw into a sequestered retreat. Just as Charles Dickens in *Oliver Twist* describes personal prisons with black corridors of increasing depth, Bassani also speaks of narrow hallways closing in on his characters. But in this story the protagonist can glimpse a light at the end of the corridor beneath the door to his father's room, which symbolizes Lawyer Lattes's desire for his young son to leave Italy for a new life in Palestine or America. [41] Ironically, Bruno's parents relied on their exempted status to guarantee them a safe place in their beloved Emilian homeland only to discover, along with 181 other Ferrarese Jews, that all the dark corridors and narrow winding streets of their city led to extermination. But in summer 1943, Bruno chose the way of light and hope by leaving his city for Rome and later the United States. The tragic situation for many of Bassani's characters rests in the impossibility of ever creating a circle of security within the surrounding danger.

With the loss of private space comes the destruction of personal time. When Bruno returns to Ferrara for Clelia's funeral, he notes to his surprise, the rapid physical restoration of the town. Only the broken companile of the Certosa bears witness to the devastation of the recent past, otherwise, most people, like Rovigatti, do not appear to have suffered the ravages of time. The postwar era in Ferrara combines reconstruction from an earlier period with an American-style modernism. Members of the municipal band performing at the funeral cere-monies have new uniforms with broad caps in the style worn by American policemen. An adolescent couple who noisily interrupt Mauro Bottecchiari's graveside oration resemble "teenagers" (Bassani uses the English word) stepping out of an illustrated American magazine. The two carefree adolescents seem to exist in a timelessness beyond war and changes in regimes. While the older generation, like Mauro and Rovigatti, finds identity in a past preceding the dictatorship of 1922, young adults either seek an extremely vague future in the political programs of communism and Christian democracy, or like Bruno, they can abandon Ferrara for a genuine American existence. For Bruno, a change did occur in Ferrara from autumn 1938 to the war's end. Although authorities returned the Lattes home to him intact from bombings and street fighting, the confiscated furniture and his deported parents represent the irreparable loss that denies Bruno the hope of future life in the Italian city. Only a distant foreign society with no century-old traditions can offer him the promise of renewal.

As in Joyce's *Dubliners*, Bassani adds a dimension of fairy-tale narration to his otherwise realistic story. The quest to penetrate the prison home where Clelia's sister and brother-in-law have incarcerated her makes Bruno a prince liberating a princess in distress. At the beginning of the story's third division, Bassani explicitly compares Clelia's zealous jailer and sister to monsters in fables. When Bruno does succeed in breaking the spell that separates Trotti from him, his own disillusionment begins. The Fascist Secret Police (O.V.R.A.) also appear at first as a sleeping beast that has almost forgotten its prisoner until one day in late September 1940 (a few months after Italy's entry into the war), the monster suddenly awakens to begin again its vigilance over the troublesome maiden. Here, the monstrous dictatorial regime brings about an unhappy ending for the imprisoned princess. Just as Bruno once sought Rovigatti's aid in entering the marvelous realm of Clelia's private world, the Italian Jews, after the enactment of discriminatory laws, long to reclaim the wondrous kingdom from which a monstrous ruler expelled them.

Although Bassani planned this tale's structure in broad blocks of distinct experiences, its temporal dimensions reveal an underlying, connecting structure. In the article "Down There, at the End of the Corridor," Bassani remarks that this story's four divisions seemed to him to resemble rigid, vertical elements of an opaque substance like paper or cloth rather than stone or metal: broad and flat in surface, separate but parallel. But as in "Lida Mantovani," time spirals back on itself, especially in two key episodes that appear to repeat each other. The incident in section 1 with the two blond teenagers who distrub Mauro's speech is paralleled toward the story's close in the sunset scene near the square of the Certosa when Bruno Lattes sees a blond couple meeting and walking toward the city walls. The enchanting girl from the second episode has also bound her hair with a red ribbon just like the uncaring adolescent who drowned out Bottecchiari's words with the noise of her Vespa's motor. Both incidents occur in the autumn, the season of decline. In both instances, Bruno Lattes comes close to experiencing what Joyce would define as an epiphany, not an ultimately violent insight into his life, as happens to Geo Josz on hearing Count Scocca whistle the German song, but a saddening realization of the impossibility of continued existence in Ferrara. At the end, by the Wall of the Angels, Lattes at last perceives that Clelia's dreams of a future Socialist utopia have blinded her to the realities of her prison city. That understanding permits the youth to accept his aloneness and later to flee the circle of oppression and death in Ferrara.

This tale moves in a circle of frustration and futility, beginning on that golden afternoon in autumn 1946 when Lattes returned home for Clelia's funeral only to realize that it was a politically staged affair rather than a spontaneous expression of respect for Trotti. Disillusioned, Bruno resigns himself to his destiny of exclusion in also recognizing that Clelia in death has become a tool of the postwar socialist party. As the person who grew closest to the Socialist exile in her last years, the Jewish youth appreciates the irony that Trotti in that funeral with all its meaningless pomp achieves her wish to be buried among the illustrious freethinkers and heretics in the unconsecrated soil by the Piazza della Certosa. The common hope of belonging proves only a prisoner's dream on a radiant afternoon. Death itself marks the final segregation, raising barriers that will never be scaled. Like the protagonist in "The Dead," young Lattes knows in his epiphany that he must make a journey westward, to America and a new time.

An additional conclusion that might be drawn from "Gli ultimi anni di Clelia Trotti" is that even those who are tightly allied in the face of a common persecution remain separate from one another at a deeper personal level. The shoemaker, Clelia, and Bruno—despite their shared status as enemies of the regime—really have nothing in common as individuals. As the funeral proves, expressions of solidarity, such as the parade and accompanying orations, are often empty gestures that can only underline that fundamental solitude. This solitude and alienation in the face of death is also an important theme in Joyce's "The Dead."

"A NIGHT IN '43" ("UNA NOTTE DEL '43")

An atmosphere of disease pervades "A Night in '43," which originally appeared in *Botteghe oscure* in 1955 and a year later figured as the concluding piece in the first edition of *Storie ferraresi*. Here, the autumn melancholy of Clelia's story is submerged by a nocturnal nightmare of Fascist murder squads executing eleven victims on 15 December 1943 in reprisal for a political assassination. Once again, the author returns to the perspective of an observation post behind a window; here, the window is in the second-floor apartment of the pharmacist Pino Barilari, who witnesses the massacre during the sleepless winter night. Paralyzed by a venereal disease that he most likely contracted during an incident on the way home from the Fascist march on Rome in 1922, Barilari retreated to his apartment above the pharmacy in the center of Ferrara, on Corso Roma to sit as immobile as a sentry while gazing down on the bustling street. Perhaps the motif of the theme characterizing this story is the gaze, for all that the pharmacist can do is to look upon the theatre stage of life in Ferrara. But in the political tension prevailing throughout Italy from summer 1939 onward, that gaze is sufficient to arouse the suspicion of several perpetually insecure Fascist officials who interpret it as an accusation against them. Here, Bassani portrays the situation of Ferrara's middle class: People largely interested in their private affairs but forced by historical circumstances to declare allegiance to a regime founded in terror.

Although the constant stare of a cripple from an upper-story window might have caused Barilari's arrest as a subversive, the direct intervention of a ruthless party boss known as Sciagura (disaster) rescues the pharmacist from incarceration. One of the few instances of shared solidarity in *Storie ferraresi* is the relationship between Barilari and Sciagura. It was during the boredom of a train transfer from Bologna to Ferrara on return from the Roman march that the Fascist leader thrust the seventeen-year-old Pino at gunpoint into the arms of a prostitute. Years later, Sciagura interpreted Barilari's gaze as an expression of oneness with the Fascists rather than criticism.

The correctness of Sciagura's interpretation becomes evident at the postwar trial when Liberation authorities summon Pino to testify to the identify of the executioners. Exchanging a conspiratorial wink with the arch murderer similar to the wink that Sciagura had directed to him at the Bolognese bordello in 1922, the pharmacist lies to the court, stating that he slept through the entire episode. That act of nonalignment with the new ruling coalition not only absolved the former political boss of guilt but hastened return to the status quo of the prewar period. Barilari believes that since everyone is guilty of some sort of evil in their lives (he himself, for example, has literally been contaminated by his acquiescence to Fascism), he is reluctant to cast the first, self-righteous stone in the postwar trial. Behind the enigmatic gaze is an attitude at variance with those of the municipal chorus.

Pino's testimony illustrates the discontinuous relationship between an event and its personal meaning. Although disease abstracted Barilari from history, he remains subject to the temporal process. For on the night of the massacre, just after 4:21 A.M. according to the Castle clock, the precarious reality of the invalid's existence disintegrated as the pharmacist witnessed his young wife standing over the victims' bodies on her way home from a rendezvous with a lover. After that night, whose political and historical significance held no interest for Pino compared to the personal drama of his wife's infidelity, a total solitude encompassed his life—one so oppressive that his wife left him to survive on the streets rather than risk losing her sanity. Thanks to the protection afforded by Sciagura, the pharmacist succeeded in exiling himself from history, but not even physical immobility could exempt him from suffering the effects of time on his domestic life. Pino wanted to divide his private existence between gazing from the window and solving crossword puzzles while his beautiful wife, Anna, attended to the shop and his needs. As the pharmacist eventually learns, human beings are far more enigmatic than puzzles or rebuses. If Barilari had told the truth about the shooting, he would have had to acknowledge the emptiness of his marriage. Like many members of his class, Pino believes he can remove himself from political and military realities in order to preserve a domain strictly his own. Illness prevented his direct participation in the world, while his one-time eroticopolitical connection with Sciagura shielded his home from invasion. But although Barilari could spy on the townspeople with his binoculars, he failed to observe the betrayal in his midst until the moment when history and private life coincided.

Bassani states in his essay "Down There, at the End of the Corridor" that the pharmacist in his window-side chair is the story's focal point within the smallest circle of a series of concentric circles encompassing the world of Ferrara. In its outward structure, the tale falls into five divisions. The prologue, which occurs sometime during the mid-1950s, uses a literary device of Henry James: hypothetical spectators sitting at the Caffè della Borsa on Corso Roma watch strangers in town strolling along the parapet of the Castle's moat at the very spot where the December 1943 massacre took place. Instead of employing the hypothetical observers to achieve a sense of objectivity as did James, Bassani describes the grimaces on the faces of the spectators who, as insiders, always avoid walking by the moat with its dreary memories. A piercing cry from above—like an off-stage call in the theater—draws attention to the street's grim past, for the voice belongs to the main character—Barilari at his window. To explain his disturbing presence, the second division moves to the immediate prewar period in 1936 when Barilari inherited his father's shop and then surprised the envious townspeople a year later by marrying a local beauty. His paralysis in 1939 and subsequent assumption of the observation site are revealed to be the outcome of Pino's adolescent participation in the march on Rome. It is only in the third and central division that the narrative turns to the dreadful afternoon and night of 15 December 1943. Even then the tale never directly represents the violent events.

Reference to forthcoming events first occurs during the afternoon in a radio broadcast of an angry session of the Social Republic's Constituent Assembly in Verona calling for revenge for the assassination of Ferrara's Fascist regent. During the evening and night, the rumble of armored cars and snatches of war songs about death and graveyards precede by agonizing hours the actual shooting sometime after midnight. Bassani's technique resembles that of classical tragedy whose spectators never witness violent acts but learn of them by later reports. The author takes readers into the homes of terrified citizens who occasionally dare to peer into the street from cracks in their blinds or pass the time by playing cards. The following morning, anguished speculation over the extent of the executions end with the gruesome news about the eleven victims. Here, at the crucial moment, Ferrara's world belongs to Sciagura, but the political boss almost shudders before the one window illuminated in the city's wartime blackout: Barilari's upper-story post.

Bassani experienced enormous difficulty in writing the start of the fourth section, because as he comments in "Down There, at the End of the Corridor" he had to exercise the collective imagination of the Ferrarese townspeople to describe a place that none of then had ever entered: Barilari's apartment, whose rooms and furnishings are represented down to the details of Pino's collection of adventure stories by Fenimore Cooper, Dumas père, Verne, and Poe's tale about Gordon Pym with a ghost on its cover anticipating the spectral figure the pharmacist becomes in time. After section 4 closes with the unsuccessful trial of the accused, the final division is devoted to Barilari's wife, Anna, and her inability to endure her husband's persistent silence about having seen her on the sidewalk near the bodies of the victims.

In several respects, this story parallels that of Geo Josz: Both Pino and the concentration camp survivor have seen what others imagine to have seen. In both tales, physical place awakens painful memories of the past: the Hebrew temple with its plaque and the parapet by the Castle moat. With his horror stories and photographs of dead relatives, Josz tried to counteract covering up the bullet holes on the parapet with plaster. Anna's life of prostitution begins just after the elections of April 1948, around the same time as Geo's disappearance. But unlike Josz, the pharmacist steadfastly refuses to speak out. Except for his puzzling cries of admonition to bewildered visitors to town wandering by the moat, Barilari encloses himself in the frightful silence that occupies the heart of this tale.[42]

With its very title, the concluding story of *Within the Walls* suggests the nocturnal blackness of wintertime. Even during the peaceful postwar years, the dark Castle parapet casts a sinister shadow over the massacre site. Fascist officials associate light with defiance of their authority, since they require the obscurity of the night to carry out their plans of vengeance. Terrified citizens huddle by the light of chandeliers listening to the echoes of firearms in the streets while wondering if death troops will knock down their door. The dawn of 16 December 1943 reveals the truth about the atrocity. Bassani's chiaroscuro art depicts in the fifth section the climatic moment that forever shatters the Barilari marriage. For at the instant that Anna Barilari stood over the bodies, the brilliant light of a full moon was shining over the crystaline white snow along the sidewalk. As the unfaithful wife immediately realized to her unending regret, that moonlight exposed her to the gaze of her husband in the darkness behind his window. Here, the dynamic contrast of light and darkness recaptures the painful drama of truth and falsehood, loyalty and betrayal, deception and loss of illusions.[43]

This story indicates how Ferrara was unlike a vast metropolis full of faceless crowds where individuals lead an existence in relative privacy. In the tale's early versions, but not in the one for *Within the Walls*, the author comments that the city was like an extended family and in a family everyone knew each other intimately. Only an insider like Sciagura could have directed the Fascist squads from Verona and Padua to ferret out some of the victims from hiding places in their homes. Evidence also indicated that a Ferrarese was responsible for the choice of the political martyrs: former Socialist and action party leaders removed from the city jail, two Jews discovered in their attic, a turncoat Fascist deputy in sympathy with the king and the Badoglio government after Mussolini's arrest in July 1943. The bonds of urban kinship in Ferrara do not join individuals together in mutually reinforcing relationships; instead, the ties that develop from years of growing up close to each other inhibit freedom of action and thought.[44] In this story, the constricting bonds can be deadly, since there seems to be no way of escaping from the community, which acted like a negative force. Living in such a community also requires striking certain attitudes in order to command respect; Sciagura's political career illustrates that need. At his trial, the fallen boss contends that he was always "a soldier in service of an Ideal." That ideal involved using violence to exact the conformity of his fellow citizens. To Sciagura and his deputies, the Fascist march on Rome meant an inglorious end to the revolutionary phase of their party's struggle for power. In their disillusionment, those anarchic Fascists made the march a pathway of debauchery in brothels along the railway line. Consequently, the collapse of any social stability and normalcy with the establishment of the repressive Republic of Salò caused Sciagura to rejoice, and it is a rejuvenated squadrist who presides on 16 December 1943 at the funeral of the assassinated regent. Sciagura's success depended on the complicity of townspeople, and in the third central section, Bassani uses a choral effect to indicate the passive submission of the Ferrarese to the executioners. In representing the mentality of the terrorized citizens, the author used drawn-out clauses with numerous indirect questions as the townspeople pass a seemingly endless night trying to mask their fear by playing cards. In their attempt to dismiss feeling fright, the Ferrarese try to justify the Fascists and thereby diminish thoughts of possible reprisal. Here, as elsewhere in his narratives, Bassani shows the complicity of intimidated citizens crowding the streets for the regent's funeral and then rushing the following day to enroll in the Fascist party. Sciagura strategically selected victims for the firing squad to prove to the Ferrarese how vulnerable they would all be if they did not demonstrate loyalty to the new regime. Although Bassani explicitly states that History (the capital is his) consecrated those martyrs as the first victims of a civil war, his writings do not focus on the struggle for national liberation. Instead, the writer puts the Ferrarese on trial for cooperating with the brutal rulers and after the war, absolving the executioners of blame.

Throughout this tale, Barilari's disease is a metaphor for the moral corruption and weakness of spirit affecting Italy under Fascism. In preparing the version of the story for *Within the Walls*, Bassani overcame the sociolinguistic taboo of the 1950s by substituting the word *sifilide* (syphilis) for the earlier *malattia* (illness).[45] Only a demeaning and vulgar disease would be appropriate for the black-shirted troops of the march on Rome. Syphilis necessitated Barilari's seclusion from life while giving meaning and structure to his existence. Exile as an invalid withdrew the pharmacist from the hell into which political events precipitated other members of the town's middle class. Disease marked a line, a point of interruption in the pharmacist's life and transformed him into a privileged being in time but outside of history. That physically debilitating illness which left Barilari a cripple for submitting to Sciagura's gunpoint command at a Bolognese bordello also seemed to infect the regime in its very core with a venereal poison.[46]

Although, as the author observes in "Down There, at the End of the Corridor," this story's center is Barilari's little prison room, from whose window he watched the murders, Anna Barilari, after her voluntary exile from the marital madhouse, occupies a parallel window post. Behind the shelter of protruding grilles over the two ground-floor windows of her apartment on Corso Giovecca, Anna could chat with male clients or slam shut the window in their faces if any of them spoke too familiarly to her. Even though Anna's domestic life and reputation suffered permanent damage from the events of 15 December 1943 from her window post she exercised a degree of control over others and compelled them to treat her with a semblance of respect.

Bassani points in this tale to the need of the Ferrarese to find safe hiding places. From the opening page, the town's inhabitants are huddling in the semidarkness of the porticos at the Caffè della Borsa while only outsiders walk along the open parapet at the site of the killings. Neither attics nor studies on remote streets could preserve the life of an intended victim. A sense of life's horrifying possibilities predominates in the story, as suggested by the epigraph from Tchekhov: "What should I say to you? Visions are frightful, but life is also frightful. I, my dear, do not understand life, and I am afraid of it." Pino Barilari alone witnessed the massacre, but because that public event meant nothing to him except the disintegration of his private existence, the pharmacist was merely a witness and accomplice to an atrocity. He did not become the conscience of his fellow citizens pointing out their common responsibility for collaborating with the agents of terror.

Pino Barilari *did* admit to himself what happened on the street outside his room. It is because of the private betrayal that he felt disqualified (not frightened!) to testify about the public betrayal of community represented by the group assassination. For Barilari, someone who is himself infected cannot denounce the sickness of others. Bassani would seem to suggest that a more humane attitude toward these matters—at least for a writer, though perhaps not for a citizen—is one of compassion rather than of self-righteous denunciation. For Bassani, there are no righteous selves in Ferrara anymore—and none elsewhere either. Thus, in this story of hiding, no one escapes the corruption of evil.

CONCLUSION

Through the tales that comprise *Within the Walls*, Bassani develops oppositional structures to reveal situations of closure in his literary world of Ferrara. On almost every page of the five tales, the writer stresses opposition as a fundamental structural relationship. He dwells on such basic binary opposites as inside and outside, inclusion and exclusion, light and dark, illness and health, constraint and freedom, presence and absence. Those oppositions create the tension characters experience as they struggle to define their identity and their role within Ferrarese society. Although the author frequently emphasizes the period of the Fascist dictatorship with its denial of individual liberty and its official legislation of ethnic identity, the painful polarities oppressing his immured universe are continuous elements throughout the history of Ferrara. Since the writer observes the events in the stories from the vantage point of the era following the Second World War, it is obvious that the opposing tension will never be resolved.

Because of the persistent development of basic opposites, the tales gain coherence and unity. Even though readers may treat each story as a separate entity, just as they were originally published in journals, the pieces form a whole where each one reinforces the thematic features of the others. The stories reflect and comment on each other, thus overcoming the decadentist tendency of fragmentation that Bassani had acquired from the writers for *La Ronda*. Indeed, he succeeds here in reconciling his art prose with documentary precision of historical realism. Throughout his variations, Bassani displays an ever-increasing need for accurate details, as shown by his precision in naming such objects as bicycles and motor scooters. It is almost as though Bassani had undertaken the semantic conquest of the past. From the numerous revised editions of these tales and from essays on their genesis, one can see the extent to which Bassani is a writer of "self-conscious fiction" directing readers' attention to technical and theoretical aspects of his works.[47]

The meticulous attention to detail has earned Bassani the criticism of being a writer of "still-life" word pictures lacking historical vitality. Marxist critics have compared him to writers of neorealism and socialist realism with a faith in historical evolution as opposed to class struggle, faulting his pessimism about the renewal of postwar Italy.[48] In the Ferrarese stories, the only proletariat protagonist is Lida Mantovani, who despite victimization by the bourgeois David, finds security in Fascist society thanks to an artisan of ultra-Catholic sentiments. According to Marxist critics, the burden of failed historicism makes Bassani's characters enigmatic because of the author's admitted inability to understand life and, consequently, sociopolitical processes. Unable to penetrate the human mystery to its depths in social conflict, Bassani cannot find solutions for the problems created by Fascism. But in actuality his attitude toward the Resistance and national reawakening is similiar to his contemporary, Carlo Cassola (b. 1917), even though the Ferrarese writer would resent the comparison. Cassola and Bassani both recognize the moral and political failure of the Resistance movement. While Cassola focuses on the destructive nature of resentment stemming from the era of partisan struggle, Bassani emphasizes the short-lived moment of spiritual recovery that soon succumbed to a longing for prewar normalcy and stability. The Ferrarese writer's awareness of the power of evil becomes ahistorical as it crosses all temporal periods and political regimes, afflicting Fascists and anti-Fascists, Catholics and Hebrews, bourgeois and proletarians alike.

Within the agonized soul of Bassani's characters in the Ferrarese tales is the same kind of wound torturing the fictional figures of two foreign writers most admired by the Italian author: James and Joyce.[49] Not only does Bassani emulate the parenthetical qualifications and syntactical compression of James to intensify the duration of his characters' suffering, but he also seeks to render in his own Italian manner certain persistent themes of the American writer: the conflict between two cultures (Europe versus America for James, Catholic versus Jewish as well as urban versus rustic for Bassani); the sense of wasted time and lost opportunities; the failure to defeat isolation by never successfully communicating innermost feelings. From Joyce, Bassani learned to represent an epiphany of total awareness that illuminates the individual's consciousness. Lida's exploitation by David, Ausilia Brondi's exclusion from Elia's affections, Geo Josz's direct experience of the Holocaust, Bruno Lattes's disenchantment with Fascists and Socialists alike, and Barilari's discovery of his wife's infidelity all exemplify spiritual wounds that never heal. Bruno Lattes reaches that epiphany on a glorious autumn afternoon when he sees beyond Ferrara's constrictions.

Exile in *Within the Walls* results from division. Community exists for neither the ruling majority, with its prejudices of caste and class, nor the excluded ones relegated to the periphery of society. Whether the excluded resist time and historical process or passively submit to the will of rulers, no one succeeds in vanquishing exile through the sustaining love of another. Each lonely individual must become resigned to the inevitability of permanent separateness, relinquishing a brotherhood of affection and suffering. Ironically, time possesses little true urgency here, since all is in the past. The tragedy of many of Bassani's characters is that they have no future, certainly not in Ferrara. Those who have physically survived betrayal must build a life elsewhere or withdraw into solitude. While the author presents the past discontinuously and fragmentarily to reflect lives that were shattered by history, memory does counteract time's desolation. By creating tales of remembrance, the writer defeats the deliberate attempt of his fellow citizens to impose oblivion on past injustices.

In these tales, Bassani explores Ferrara's confining world, but to continue his narrative work, he requires another mediating agent among the opposing structures inspiring his fiction. Since memory offers the opportunity to discover an enduring identity in time, in the three following novels of self-investigation, the writer turns to first-person narration. Although Bassani never seeks selfless contemplation as a way to painless acceptance of time and history, in the next three novels, he represents the development of personal identity despite temporal displacement. The anguished psyche of the first-person narrator comes to reflect all the characters and classes of Ferrara's restrictive society.

2

The Time of Persecution

Narration and the Ontological Fallacy

Surrender to the will of the majority who hold the power to classify certain categories of humans as outcasts and undesirables leads the central character of *Gli Occhiali d'oro* (*The Gold-Rimmed Eyeglasses*), to suicide rather than endure exclusion from his society. First published by the Einaudi Press in 1958 in a separate volume, it became book 2 of the expanded edition of *Storie Ferraresi* in 1960. Although this work is usually referred to as a brief novel, Bassani achieves here a nouvelle in the tradition of Henry James, who once described that intermediate genre between tale and novel: "Its main merit and sign is the effort to do the complicated thing with a strong brevity and lucidity—to arrive, on behalf of the multiplicity, at a certain science of control. . . ."[1] Aesthetically, Bassani endeavors to realize control as he pictures a world and its inhabitants on the verge of losing all control.

In this work and *The Garden of the Finzi-Continis* and *Behind the Door*, Bassani commits the ontological fallacy of confusing the first-person narrator of explicitly fictitious though highly autobiographical works with himself. The author does not label those three compositions as *ricordi* or *memorie* (memoirs) recording with documentary accuracy the events of his own life but instead permits himself the considerable latitude of inventing fictitious, composite characters and settings in Ferrara. It is almost an axiom of literature that the author is never the same as any character, no matter how closely the two might resemble each other.[2] Bassani's confusion between the self-portraying author and the autonomous narrator differs from the practice of his contemporary, the Italian novelist Alberto Moravia (b. 1907), who at a critical moment in his literary career abandoned writing novels in the third person in preference for first-person narration, not through any impulse to tell "his" story but to escape the God-like pretensions of omniscient narration. Although one critic has described Bassani's three extended narratives in the first person as an attempt at a spiritual auto-biography or a novel of the self,[3] an aesthetic imbalance results from the tension between the autonomous work of art and authorial intrusion into the literary world. So persistent is Bassani's confusion that in criticizing Vittorio De Sica's motion picture version of *The Garden of the Finzi-Continis*, the author objected to the film's misrepresentation of some facts of his life rather than its violation of the novel. For what De Sica and Bassani both ignored was that a literary text possesses its own wholeness, identity, and uniqueness.[4]

In this work, Bassani has created a secondary first-person narrator to witness the disintegration of the life of the protagonist, Dr. Athos Fadigati. The young Jewish narrator, whose life story also appears in *The Garden of the Finzi-Continis* and *Behind the Door,* is an *escogido*, a creature chosen for pain, who grows increasingly aware of the parallel between the ostracism of the homosexual physician Fadigati from Ferrara's middle-class society and the fate of Italy's Hebrews in a climate of increasing anti-Semitism.[5] From being a fairly detached and somewhat disapproving observer, the narrator of *The Gold-Rimmed Eyeglasses* undergoes an apprenticeship in suffering so similar to that of the central character that some critics have regarded the narrator as protagonist or consid-ered Fadigati and the Jewish youth protagonists of equal importance. The "eye" of the "I" (Italian *io*) who witnesses the physician's decline must achieve an insight into the hero's experiences by undergoing his own fall from grace. For even though Fadigati wears the gleaming gold-rimmed spectacles in the title, the myopic physician sees nothing of the danger menacing him. Here, the narrator acts as both observer and an experiential center for filtering the hero's movement to self-destruction. What the narrator shows his readers is perhaps not so much Fadigati as his own view of the indiscreet physician. Through the relationship between the narrating *self* and that anguished *other* person, the emotionally maturing youth in time comprehends the depth of desolation that an individual suffers when rejected by society.

One of the writers with whom critics frequently compare Bassani is Marcel Proust, and this particular work holds numerous parallels with that French writer's *A la recherche du temps perdu*. In neither this narrative nor the following two first-person novels does Bassani ever name the narrator, in contrast to the film adaptation where the young Hebrew is called Giorgio. Certain critics have even erroneously referred to the narrator in those three works as Giorgio. Throughout Proust's seven-volume novel, he calls the narrator Marcel only twice, since the author was striving to create a narrator existing beyond time and within the world of the text itself. Both Proust and Bassani explore the mysteries of the self in their narratives, with their texts of the French and Italian authors becoming reflexive works with the self as the tormented subject. In both Proust's novel and Bassani's story of Athos Fadigati, there is a search to recover personal identity.

Bassani noted in *Le Parole preparate* that the structure of *The Gold-Rimmed Eyeglasses* recalls the dramas of Corneille and Racine by gradually building to a fifth-act catharsis of violent emotions. As one critic has commented,[6] the work opens with an air of fatal suspense: Dr. Fadigati . . . "he ended so badly, poor fellow, so tragically, indeed someone who when he came as a youth to settle in our city . . . had appeared destined for the most normal, tranquil and therefore the most enviable of careers" (p. 167). The sense of the dreadful ending is already evident. The author constructs his Racinian drama in four acts. Part 1 covers the first three chapters recounting Fadigati's arrival in Ferrara in 1919, his early success in establishing a medical practice within six years (chap. 1); the gradual invasion of Athos's privacy by curious townspeople eager to see him married and settled in the middle class until the first rumors of his sexual deviancy (end of chap. 2); the realization of the physician's erotic inclinations and the town's tacit acceptance because of Fadigati's discreet behavior (chap. 3) through 1936. The second act consists of fourth through the seventh chapters recounting the early morning commuter train rides from Ferrara to Bologna where Athos compromises himself during the academic year 1936 to 1937 by establishing a liaison with a handsome but unprincipled university student. For the first time in Bassani's narratives, the scene moves from Ferrara in Act III (chapters 8–12), which relates the physician's definitive disgrace before prominent Ferrarese vacationing at the resort in Riccione during August and September 1937. That third section also introduces the parallel between the medical practitioner's fall and the exclusion of Jews due to the government-inspired journalistic campaign of anti-Semitism. Chapters 13–18 mark the catharsis during the foggy and rain-swept Autumn of 1937, culminating in Fadigati's suicide and the narrator's unshakable despondency over the threat of racial persecution.

One critic has noted the plurality of narrative levels accompanying shifts in pronouns: In the opening chapters, *loro* (they) predominates as the Ferrarese community peers into Athos's unconventional private life from a distant time (expressed by verbs in the imperfect tense) in the narrator's infancy; then, with the train rides to Bologna, the narrator emerges as an *io* that is part of the *noi* (us) of commuting university students; finally, during the Adriatic resort vacation, the observing *io* becomes a major figure as he identifies with the persecuted *lui* (he, him), his alter ego, Fadigati.[7] Here, the secondary first-person narrator almost becomes the primary figure, for both the Jewish youth and the scandalous physician appear for ethnic and sexual reasons, respectively, to be victims of exclusion succumbing to a world without hope.

The Unhealing Wound

In the epigraph to some early editions of this work, the author quotes from Sophocles's drama *Philoctetes* to express the agony of an unhealing wound: "This is the end, boy! I shall no longer be able to hide the affliction from you. Oh! Oh! How it pierces me! Oh! How it pierces me! How wretched I feel! How miserable! I am lost, boy! That horrible affliction is devouring me. Oh, Oh, Oh! Take a sword and cut off my accursed foot! Quick, cut it off! Do not fear for my life! Go on, quick, boy!" Fadigati, because of his sexual inversion, and the narrator, because of his religious background, bear afflictions just as offensive to others as the loathsome sore on the leg of the Homeric Greek warrior Philoctetes, whose shrieks from pain caused his companions during the Trojan War to abandon him on the island of Lemnos. In the Italian work, the protagonist fails, however, to display the strength of will before treachery that characterizes Philoctetes's endurance of his wound. With his sensitive appreciation of ancient Greek culture, Fadigati quotes the opening of the *Iliad's* first canto to the narrator: "Sing, goddess, the wrath of Achilles the son of Peleus, the ruinous wrath that brought on the Achaians woes innumerable. . . ." By throwing caution to the wind and daring to come out openly revealing his sexual orientation to other Ferrarese of his own class staying at Riccione, the physician attracts the wrath of the townspeople.

Among the characters in Bassani's literary world, Dr. Athos Fadigati is one of the most decadent. The narrator describes the physician as seeming never to have been young, a quality of timelessness resulting from an innate process of decay. During his early years in Ferrara, the medical practitioner succeeded in balancing his Dionysian and Apollonian tendencies. Like a true Decadentist, Fadigati attempted to transform life into a work of art. He revolutionized the decor of Ferrarese medical suites by introducing comfortable furniture and paintings by promising contemporary artists into a generously lit and well-heated setting. Although the text does not elaborate on the paintings decorating the different waiting rooms, the choice of artists provides insight into the physician's tastes: De Chirico, with his haunting sense of melancholy; De Pisis, whose name signals homoerotic tendencies; and the Turinese painter Felice Casorati (1886–1963), who united classical harmony with the free rhythms and structures of abstractionism. In associating facets of a character's being with attitude toward works of art, Bassani recalls James, who often defined his characters by their reactions to certain paintings or schools or art.[8] In this work, the narrator also reveals an aesthetic approach to life when describing an adolescent girl who joins him in tennis matches at Riccione as resembling a blond angel musician by the Umbrian Renaissance painter Melozzo da Forlì (1438–1518). This use of visual art in literature links aesthetic attitudes to moral responses in both the physician and the young narrator who seek to possess in flesh and blood the incarnation of ideal beauty achieved by great painters. The university student, Eraldo Deliliers, for example, who precipitates Athos's fall from respectability, exploits his admirers through a physical attractiveness recalling an ancient Greek athlete or god.

Dr. Fadigati longs to construct a private enclosure for powerful aesthetic and sensual stimulation in his life. His profession as a medical specialist for the ear,

nose, and throat indicates his concern for those parts of the body most responsible for sense stimulation. Athos enjoys the fierce arousal of his senses by strong
aromas. In the evening, the physician frequents Ferrars's crowded market districts to savor the acrid aromas of fried fish, salami, salted foods, and wines, his
face glowing with satisfaction. His memory of Padua, the university town where
he took his medical degree, has an almost Proustian sensual quality without the
French writer's irrational spontaneity of experience: Fadigati recalls that city
from the smell of boiled beef that used to invade its gloomy arcades. An
individual attempting to mask homosexual inclinations has to find other outlets
for his passionate receptivity to physical stimulation. Thus, the repressed
Fadigati responds with a Gidean *disponibilité* to the olfactory experiences offered
by urban environments.

Music more than any other art arouses the physician's hyperrefined sensitivity
to beauty. Discreet visitations to his apartment by middle-aged lovers of former
athletic distinction are always accompanied by playing recordings by Bach,
Mozart, Beethoven, and above all, Wagner. During the winter 1934, Fadigati
rushed to Florence to attend a performance of his favorite opera, *Tristan and
Isolde*; the physician was, in fact, always unconsciously seeking a *Liebestod* where
the consummation of sensual desire in a deathlike rapture finds its eternal night
in the endless waves of Wagernian melody. Describing the performance to some
Ferrarese townspeople, Fadigati half-closes his eyes in ecstasy, recalling the
opera's second act and the lovers' bench symbolizing the nuptial couch of
forbidden love.

In this extended narrative about homosexuality, Bassani follows such twentieth-century authors as Gide, Mann, Proust, Forster, and D. H. Lawrence in
recording the contradictions in behavior, the deceits and subterfuges, the
tension and disorder, finally leading to scandal that characterize an invert's social
existence.[9] To the residents of Ferrara, Athos Fadigati leads a paradoxic
chiaroscuro life of a daytime existence as director of the ear, nose, and throat
department of a new hospital and unconventional nighttime wanderings along
back streets. Townspeople view the medical specialist as resembling the title
character of the 1932 Hollywood film *Dr. Jekyll and Mr. Hyde* because of his
schizoid existence. But as long as no one ever observed Fadigati making an overt
homosexual gesture, his dignity remains intact and his irregular nocturnal
pursuits ignored. Athos refers to a literary character in Nathaniel Hawthorne's
"Rappaccini's Daughter" when describing his lonely life as a medical student in
Padua. But instead of resembling the young student Giovanni Guasconti in the
American tale about a quest for illicit knowledge, Fadigati suggests the enigmatic
Dr. Rappaccini, who poisoned the lives of those around him and even destroyed
his daughter's chance to experience love. And Fadigati discovers that his highly
refined life possesses the poisonous quality of the artificial plants in Rappaccini's
Paduan garden.

Along with Athos's need for self-protective isolation there exists a desire for affiliation and integration. Professional success in Ferrara brings Fadigati membership in elite social clubs, and the local Fascist hierarchy forces a party card on the physician despite his claims of being apolitical. Yet on those very few occasions when Athos visits his clubs, he avoids joining card or billiard games and instead segregates himself in the libraries. While he belongs to cultured society, his deviancy sets him apart. Belonging requires him to honor social obligations and maintain appearances. Fadigati's loss of respectability begins when he decides to take postgraduate courses at the University of Bologna, which require him to use the same commuter train taken by Ferrarese students. At first, the doctor keeps to himself in a second-class coach while the students occupy third class. Behind his coach window, the physician looks like a political prisoner on his way to confinement. Passage from one class coach to another is prevented by locked communicating doors, which a disagreeable conductor, resembling a jailer more than a public servant, only reluctantly opens. When Dr. Fadigati finally does join the students in their own space, he descends to their level and through familiarity loses their respect. Proximity brings the physician taunting remarks and actual insults from the two students whom Athos wants most to like him: the intellectual leader Nino Bottechiari and the athlete Deliliers. Space in Bassani's world shields people from ridicule, and intimate contact bears with it the danger of betrayal—especially for a deviate who must never trespass certain limits—but Athos's desire to participate in the lives of others cause him to abandon the safety of his compartment.

The vulnerable Fadigati seemed to enjoy involving himself in relationships that were both degrading and destructive. And in the handsome Deliliers, the physician found his ideal torturer. Their relationship is, in fact, described in terms of victim and executioner. Athos so idolizes the youth that he even imitates Deliliers's manner of smoking cigarettes from the end with the trademark. As the narrator observes, it is doubtless the university student who maliciously persuades his willing slave to vacation at the Adriatic resort when the two could have easily avoided any scandal by traveling to the Tyrrhenian coast. But Athos's cooperation (no matter how apparently reluctant) in his self-destruction indicates his readiness to undergo public disapproval and rejection. The medical specialist actually glories in his pain on the day following the disgraceful scene in the ballroom of the Riccione Grand Hotel where Deliliers slapped him before all the vacationing guests. Fadigati also delights in relating to the narrator how his beloved vanished with all the physician's loose cash, watch, and clothes. Athos seems to enjoy being misused and actually exaggerates the extent of Deliliers's theft. A double crack across one lens of Fadigati's gold-rimmed eyeglasses symbolizes his fall from respectability as he at last experiences the torment he desired.[10]

Athos's true crime lies in betraying the Ferrarese society that has politely ignored his anomaly, since during the Fascist era, it was an act of social deviation not to marry, and bachelors even had to pay a celibacy tax. Although

homosexuality undermined the institution at the heart of the Fascist state—the
family—it is the physician's decision to end his charade of normalcy and openly
exhibit his sexual preference during the Adriatic holiday that irretrievably ruins
him. At once, the distinguished doctor becomes a pariah, wandering among the
beach umbrellas and awnings at the Riccione shore in hope of being readmitted
to the company of the cultured Ferrarese families who once constituted *his* world.
As would befall Italian Jews within a year from that fateful summer of 1937,
Athos found himself a nonperson. The shaken man in a Panama hat keeping
score at tennis matches among the narrator's friends is reduced to a shadow of his
former dignity. Condemned to exclusion by all who would never forgive his
breach of proper conduct, Fadigati loses his hospital post and his patients. With
his medical training and experience, he could easily move to another city and
resume his practice, for no authority takes official action against the physician as
with some homosexuals who suffered banishment to remote regions of Italy. But
the idea stressed in this story is that certain individuals (sometimes an entire
religious group) passively permit others to determine their existence and fate.
This inwardly defeated physician could no longer bear to behold his mirror
image because he saw himself as his fellow citizens regarded him: a despicable
degenerate. Reduced to a status more abject than that of a stray dog he once
befriended, the discredited physician does not rebel against those relegating him
to the margins of society. Here, Bassani follows the thesis of the Self and the
Other, where the individual abandons every chance of self-determination by
allowing others to mediate value judgments of the most vital nature. Following
the masochistic inclination to fondle his own pain, Athos destines himself to
self-annihilation.

   In this work, the author associates his protagonist with the deathlike qualities
of water, as Bachelard has noted in his treatise *Water and Dreams*. As in the
writings of Poe, water absorbs darkness, immobility, and silence to become "the
matter of despair."[11] Fadigati is from Venice, the city of canals—the supreme
urban image of death: The physician's beloved composer, Wagner, began to
write *Tristan* in Venice and later died in that city. Athos settled in Ferrara to
escape the painful memories of his family's townhouse on the Grand Canal
where his parents and sister had died within a few years of each other. The
doctor's disgrace takes place during his summer vacation on the Adriatic coast.
After their separation at the end of summer, the narrator and the physician met
again on a damp, foggy night in November 1937, just after that festival of death,
All Souls' Day, outside a brothel. As one critic has observed, fog creates a sense
of being lost and acts as a force separating people in its cold envelope.[12] The
narrator's last view of Athos alive is through that sea of fog as the young man
slowly closed the street door of his family townhouse. The physician ominously
hints about future communication between them: "Chi vivrà vedrà" ("he who
will live will see"). A few rain-swept days later, Dr. Fadigati drowned himself in
the flooding Po River. The all-absorbing water of despair claimed its self-

sacrificial victim. As Bachelard has commented, in the purity of water lies its fatal danger.

Like Proust, Bassani parallels the situation of homosexuals and Hebrews as the book's narrator comes to recognize that he, too, belongs to a *race maudite*. Because of the political circumstances, the banishment of Jews and inverts alike is reinforced by dictatorial decree. Both Fadigati and the narrator undergo an identity crisis as their society rejects them. Just as Signora Lavezzoli, the arbitress of Ferrarese society, excludes the doctor for his vitiated behavior, she insults the narrator's family by quoting an article by the Jesuit Father Gemelli in the journal *Civiltà cattolica* on the historical role of the Israelites to suffer the wrath of God. The article, of course, provided a justification for persecuting Hebrews and an excuse for the Christian majority to accept the inevitability and necessity of that oppression. The bond of sympathy that the narrator extends to Fadigati is the only kind of solidarity possible in Bassani's world: people recognizing one another as outcasts. Exclusion, in fact, becomes the ultimate form of social identity.

THE UNYIELDING SOCIETY

Bassani's *The Gold-Rimmed Eyeglasses* is not so much about homosexuality as about being different in a repressive society. Although homosexuality is central to this work, the true subject, is how bourgeois society in Ferrara destroys the lives of those individuals who happen to deviate from the norm. One of the novels that deeply moved Bassani is Nathaniel Hawthorne's *The Scarlet Letter*, with its theme of a pitiless society condemning an individual for succumbing to passion. Because Ferrara possessed a markedly structured society that emphasized outward appearances, Fadigati enjoyed numerous advantages for success until he abandoned discretion. Social hypocrisy is apparent in the fact that most townspeople continued to treat Athos with respect while in their homes, they obliquely discussed his "case" at the dinner table before their children and then openly with each other late at night. People refuse to recognize that Fadigati's homosexuality does not result from an act of his will but is just as much beyond his control as the narrator's Jewishness. For Fadigati to give up being homosexual or for the narrator to give up being Jewish would mean for each of them to give up their identities—identities that they may not have chosen but which nonetheless define them and without which they would be nothing. Signora Lavezzoli embodies middle-class hypocrisy in the novel. Her Pisan background sets her off from other members of her class, who recognized her as a natural leader with a cutting Tuscan wit and linguistic facility, which she uses to approve or condemn the acts of individuals like Fadigati, whom she labels a degenerate. Accepting assassination as a necessary political expedient for dictatorial regimes in Italy and Germany, Signora Lavezzoli relegates the Jewish question to a religious plane where cruelty toward the children of Israel finds justification in God's inscrutable design for human history. From her husband, one might have expected tolerance, since Signor Lavezzoli, a university professor and civil attorney, had once served in parliament and joined Croce in opposing Fascism. Bassani depicts the attorney passing his time at Riccione immersed in the twentieth-century picaresque novel *Anthony Adverse*, a story of slave-trading and fortune building. In the once liberal professor of law, the author reveals the corrupting compromise with Fascism, for the attorney praises the Duce for giving the Italian people an empire. This avid reader of romantic novels can reconcile himself to adventurous Fascist imperialism. A family holding the social prominence of the Lavezzolis could use its authority to declare others undesirables to be shunned.

Even if the events narrated did not take place under Fascism, Ferrara would still resemble a police state because of the way its citizens invaded each other's privacy. During the long period when Dr. Fadigati attempted to conceal his sexual anomaly, his lack of female acquaintances, his nocturnal strolls, and close friendships with older but still attractive men alerted his bourgeois patients to the physician's true inclinations. Because no one could avoid accusing stares, sensitive individuals tried to make their homes places of solitary retreat. During that oppressive autumn 1937, with its fierce journalistic campaign of anti-Semitism, the narrator's father would return to his townhouse crushed in spirit like an innocent schoolboy falsely accused of a misdeed and hoping to be recognized as guiltless. That desperate man found an illusory sense of peace by retreating for an afternoon nap to the seclusion of his living room where he would sleep "separated, shut away, protected" as if in a luminous cocoon. Yet even in their homes, Italian Jews had to speak in whispers before their gentile servants. Phone calls were received and made in closetlike alcoves as if one were afraid to reveal something forbidden.

At times of frustration, many of Bassani's characters seek the consoling view of a courtyard garden, as in the case of the narrator:

> From my room, I was looking through the window at the trees in the garden. The torrential rain seemed to be unleashing its fury expressly against the poplar, the two elms, the chestnut by stripping off their last leaves. Only the black magnolia tree, in the center, intact and incredibly dripping, apparently rejoiced in the downpour. . . . (P. 239)

At first, this passage seems almost serene, tranquil in the midst of the agitation over the new wave of anti-Semitic propaganda. The sight of the garden offers release from spatial and emotional restriction. But instead of identifying with the magnolia proudly rising above the storm, the narrator relates intensely to the rain-stripped trees. This is the season of melancholy resignation for the Jews as well as Fadigati, who will never know another spring. In that prison world, not even the window view of an inner garden can provide relief from oppression.

The passage has political overtones in the torrent of persecution about to strike Italian Jews.

Whenever disappointments or recriminations added to the already strained atmosphere of households in turmoil, frustrated individuals like the narrator took to the streets on foot, bicycles, or trolley in a vain attempt to flee their problems. Sometimes the pattern of Mediterranean streets did free one from the feeling of being hemmed in: After wandering for blocks along dismal winding streets, one would all at once enter a spacious, radiant piazza with imposing public buildings and sheltering porticos. Before the heavy November rains struck Ferrara, early autumn 1937 was a time of festive crowds under the arcades of Corso Roma. Public life in the city functioned as a spectacle, reducing church attendance to social ritual, with groups gathering together in squares outside churches like San Carlo and the Duomo di Ferrara on leaving Sunday's noon mass. Until the beginning of official anti-Semitism, Jewish citizens used to participate in that ritual by mingling with the noontime crowds leaving church. But in the climate of persecution beginning in late 1937, the open street ceased to protect individuals from the gaze of Fascist hierarchs sitting outdoors at the tables in the Caffè della Borsa in the civic center, pointing out undesirables and subversives. In *The Gold-Rimmed Eyeglasses* as in earlier stories like "A Night in '43," no Ferrarese could enjoy the anonymity of a large city.

If the streets proved too oppressive for troubled individuals, then the darkened interiors of movie theaters occasionally offered a brief retreat. But even there, the Ferrarese social structure persisted, since respectable people of financial means always purchased seats in the balcony to turn it into their private middle-class drawing room as they peered down from the railing, not just at the spectacle on the screen, but on other members of the audience in less expensive orchestra seats. Dr. Fadigati had started to arouse suspicions because he always sat in the back orchestra rows usually frequented by penniless young soldiers. In that dark, smoke-filled back section, one could, from time to time, discern the golden glint of the physician's eyeglasses until at intermission time light flooded the theater and revealed him among the "underworld" of inexpensive seats. As always, Bassani portrays Fadigati as pursuing a chiaroscuro life that in Ferrara became open to public scrutiny whether on the street or in a darkened movie theater.

At times, the atmosphere in Ferrara grew so restrictive that those who had the financial means attempted to escape the circuit of its walls. University students in *The Gold Rimmed Eyeglasses* had the advantage of daily flight from the prison city with their train commute to Bologna where, as outsiders in a fairly large city, they could leave behind their town's inhibiting spirit by gathering in reasonably priced restaurants, frequenting popular pastry shops, or arranging erotic assignations. For summer vacations, well-to-do citizens left to visit family farms, mountain resorts like Cortina d'Ampezzo, and especially the beach resorts along the Adriatic. However, the Ferrarese reconstructed their confining society at the large hotels and rented villas at Riccione and Rimini: All the conventions of the urban world were carried over to the beach resorts. Despite the seemingly unlimited horizon and open spaces of the seashore retreats, vacationers had to maintain their guard and beware of breaking the taboos of Ferrarese society. A destroyer of reputations like Signora Lavezzoli was constantly on hand to determine the correctness of decorum observed by the Ferrarese vacationers. A lapse from propriety, such as Fadigati's, would result in perpetual condemnation and exclusion at home. All the cruelty of urban prejudices permeated the apparent spatial freedom of the Adriatic beach world.

Aside from fleeing the city forever and avoiding its favorite vacation resorts, there was no escape from Ferrarese society and its unyielding oppression. After Dr. Athos Fadigati surrendered to the judgment of his class and definitively removed himself from their accusing stares, that same society refused to acknowledge the true nature of his actions or to assume any responsibility for his suicide. Here, the hypocrisy behind Ferrarese society fully triumphed, for during the Fascist era, newspapers used to report suicide by drowning or similar means when no note was left as accidents. Even the reasons for death had to be masked behind journalistic falsifications. Official language in newspapers reflected the prison-house spirit of that world which never forgave social transgressions, never pitied the dishonored, nor recognized its own aggression against individual freedom.

THE EPIPHANIC VISION

Benjamin Constant has spoken of individuals who become so isolated that they appear to be strangers in their birthplace and lose contact with their past.[13] The young narrator in *The Gold-Rimmed Eyeglasses*, on returning to Ferrara after summer vacation 1937, comes dangerously close to that state of estrangement from his home city, which rejected him as a subversive alien. Even after members of his family eagerly accept the assurances of Fascist party officials that the anti-Jewish campaign is no more than a political stratagem intended to deceive Western democracies about Italy's alignment with Hitlerite Germany, the narrator still gives way to despondency over the future as he realizes he has lost his past. The trauma of rejection causes an identity crisis so that the youth no longer knows who he is except for the label of treacherous Jew that the press has assigned to him and his coreligionists. The narrator has previously lived in a secure sense of his relationship with the bourgeois society to which he belonged. Now, he finds the very foundation of his life collapsing beneath his feet. His mental state resembles psychic suicide; he is as a walking and breathing corpse without contact with others except for his fellow pariah, Fadigati.

Yielding to his sense of despair, the narrator yearns for only the peace offered by death. Paradoxically, a Sabbath visit to the Ferrarese Hebrew Cemetery reawakens him to vital links to his own past. Standing at the heights of the city's bastions overlooking the Jewish graveyard, the young man at once overcame his alienation:

> And then . . . all of a sudden I felt penetrated by a great sweetness, by a very tender peace and gratitude. The sun in setting, piercing a dark blanket of clouds low on the horizon, brilliantly illuminated everything: the Hebrew cemetery at my feet, the apse and campanile of San Cristoforo a little farther on, and in the background, high above the dark expanse of rooftops, the distant hulks of the Castello Estense and the cathedral. It had sufficed for me to find again unchanged the *maternal* face of my city, to have it again once more, all to myself, so that the atrocious sense of exclusion that had tormented me in the past days suddenly fell away. . . . (P. 222; italics my own)

Perhaps this panoramic sequence is the supreme moment in all of Bassani's fictional writings, the epiphanic vision that permits the narrator to reconcile himself to a future of persecutions and massacres. Although the youth is not alone in the cemetery—there are two other visitors apparently not natives of Ferrara—only he truly belongs to the place and its past as he recaptures his identity as a Hebrew communing here with "his dead" on the holy day of the week. He feels part of that precious walled space as if in his own nuclear family. For the first time, Ferrara seems almost limitless in this downward gaze at Bassani's characteristically magical twilight hour, and for a brief moment, one of the characters is able to transcend the city's oppressiveness. Buildings like the Castello and the cathedral link the youth to the town's long history to which he also belongs. In the outer world, the narrator discovers a scene that corresponds to his innermost soul. The young man realizes as he looks from the parapets at his native city that he is both a Jew and an Italian. The church-bell that he hears ringing is a sign of his difference, since he is not a Catholic, but it is also a sign of his identity with other Ferrarese since he is and has always been a part of that city. The sound of the bell, then, marks both his inclusion and his exclusion. Bassani's larger point would seem to be that all of us are alone though part of a community.[14]

Even though the almost positive certainty of future persecution awaits the narrator, the sunset vision in the Jewish cemetery releases him from the spiritual desolation that has assailed him after returning from Riccione. Contemplating the graves of his people, he acknowledges another identity: that of victim, not one to be accepted passively as a defeatist already dead before death itself but as recognition of historical fact. For the narrator and his parents have been living in the illusory ideals of the Italian Risorgimento and the short period since national unification brought emancipation to Hebrews, but the long-term view of Jewish history in Ferrara in particular and in Italy at large includes a past of persecution and exclusion from which the era between 1870 and 1938 was an interval of relief. Unlike his parents, the narrator realizes that hatreds do not die but continue. Jews can not hope to become free from their *storia* of persecution, no matter how much they try to resist and deny the long centuries of oppression. The betrayal of the Jews by Fascists and bourgeoisie of a city like Ferrara was part of a duration of atrocities rather than an interruption of a well-established condition of assimilation. This visit to the Hebrew cemetery represents the narrator's breakthrough to maturity as he surmounts despondency by abandoning illusions of political freedom and confronts a heritage of hatred with love.[15]

FATAL TIME

Just as this work continues in the Proustian tradition by establishing a parallel between the social destiny of Hebrews and homosexuals, *The Gold-Rimmed Eyeglasses* also resembles the writings of the French author in its preoccupation with the force of time in human lives. This book is, in fact, an effort to resist the oblivion that time brings, for its first words are "Il tempo" that threatens to efface the memory of Dr. Fadigati unless the narrator undertakes the task of rescuing the physician from temporal succession. Memory in the Italian text does not, however, operate like Proust's irrational and sensory process that causes the past to live again. The poignancy of the situation in Bassani's book is that for the physician as for the narrator, everything is lost toward late summer 1937, never to be recaptured except through the work of art that is the fictional text. While the young narrator does succeed in discovering at the Jewish cemetery an enduring tradition in which he can participate, the doctor's humiliation and isolation can be resolved only through suicide. In a state of spiritual emptiness, the narrator concludes this work by announcing to his family, "Dr. Fadigati is dead." Thus, desperation obliterated a lifetime of discipline to medical science, service to community, and devotion to an aesthetic ideal of beauty.[16]

Time weighs so heavily on the provincial society of Ferrara that characters in this work are constantly trying to ease the conditions of their life. Part of Athos's initial success in his career is due to the relaxing atmosphere of his waiting rooms where the doctor seemed able to control time with attractively chosen furnishings and decorations to the delight of patients who visited the suite quite often on the slightest pretext of illness merely to enjoy its ambience. The idea of the efficient use of time frequently obsessed public officials during the early years of the Fascist regime when the government was trying to demonstrate to the world the modern, futuristic progress that the Duce had introduced to Italy. It was during that period that digital clocks came into wide use in public areas like railroad stations as proof of Fascist efficiency. But in this book, the symbol of the lateness and corruption of Fascism in the mid thirties is the morning commuter train between Ferrara and Bologna. Bassani's intention here goes far beyond exposing the old Fascist myth that Mussolini made the trains run on time to the admiration of Italians and foreigners alike, for in modern Italian literature, trains are symbols of alienation.[17] The late-morning arrival of the commuter train at the Ferrarese railroad station in defiance of government timetables signifies the progressive inefficiency of Fascist bureaucracy, lazily moving with the nation toward disaster. Through the symbol of the train, images of temporal process come into line with its representation as spatial constriction and exclusion. Fadigati's ruinous liaison with Deliliers develops during the physician's twice weekly trips to Bologna when he decides to move from his second-class compartment to join the university students in third class. Thus, time and space coincided to mark the fall of an individual just as it does to seal the fate of Italy's Jews.

Bassani's *The Gold-Rimmed Eyeglasses* testifies to the loss of an illusion of permanence in life. From its opening line, the book sadly acknowledges time's destructive power over memories of earlier periods and people. The narrator's record of his apprenticeship in pain to the doomed protagonist illustrates one of Bassani's favorite themes: An individual sometimes has to die more than once. Political betrayal exhausts the narrator's vital will until he regains contact with his authentic past. By entering the artificial paradise that is the subject of the author's following work, *The Garden of the Finzi-Continis,* the narrator once again experiences the spiritual death that renews life.

3

Transformation in the Garden of Love and Death

The Land of Motionless Childhood

Bassani's novel *The Garden of the Finzi-Continis* realizes the journey to the land of Motionless Childhood that Bachelard affirms in *The Poetics of Space* to be the cherished zone where an individual relives memories of protection and renews moments of happiness. Bassani has described his work as the heart of the novelistic poem that is the romance of Ferrara. First published in 1962 by Einaudi Press, this novel enjoyed such widespread public and critical acclaim that it received the Viareggio prize. By evoking memories of the palatial home and estate of the aristocratic Finzi-Contini family, the first-person narrator recaptures a world that vanished during the nightmare of Fascist collaboration with Nazi racial policy. While a political storm of anti-Semitism gathered outside the seemingly unassailable garden walls of the Finzi-Contini estate, its *magna domus* was a haven in the center of the tempest: a refuge and redoubt apparently resisting all outside pressures.

As Bachelard has suggested, a home is a psychic state;[1] and in the Bassani novel, the elegant mansion and its immense garden represent a self-protective inscape where the Finzi-Continis create a private universe, a luxurious ghetto, to avoid the devastation of time and to ward off intruders. This novel's structure rests on its spatial terminology, as if a door were opening in the narrator's mind onto past memories. The methodology of this chapter applies Bachelard's principles of topoanalysis to the various treasured sites of the Finzi-Contini cosmos to show how the novelist transforms human space by causing it to withdraw before meditation on the past.

Two numinous forces lived in conflict in the artificial paradise of the garden: the *genii loci* of Thanatos and Eros. A crepuscular sense of lateness prevailed in the garden space as the will to life and creativity yielded inexorably to a spirit of resplendent decay: that special "esprit" of the Finzi-Contini family that had fascinated and attracted the narrator from his earliest childhood. Before 1850, the family had lived like other Ferrarese Jews in the wretched heart of the ghetto, at number 24 Via Vignatagliata, until the nouveau riche Moisè used the income from his extensive farmlands to acquire a mansion and surrounding estate in the city's northern Herculean addition. The home's private park with its hundreds of exotic trees that Moisè's heirs had planted on the grounds reflect the determination of the Finzi-Continis to subordinate nature to their own will. Since many of the estate's original trees were over five hundred years old, the park testifies to the new owners' desire to create an impression of permanence. Just as Kipling used the carefully tended garden as a metaphor for the greatness of the English nation, the Finzi-Continis assert their magnificence through the beauty of their estate. One could attribute to the aristocratic Jewish family the same longing expressed by Kipling for his country:

"And the glory of the Garden, it shall never pass away!" [2] (Kipling's italics)

But pride in possessions could not safeguard the garden's trees from destruction during the last two winters of World War II, when they were cut down for firewood. Nothing remained intact before the devastation of physical time, and the fate of those trees that symbolized organic continuity through the created timelessness of the garden reveals the fundamental vulnerability of the Finzi-Continis' world. That family who styled itself as quasi–medieval feudal lords with vast holdings in the reclaimed Emilian plains was not destined to see the final eradication of its elegant garden, for in fall 1943 the remaining members of the Finzi-Continis joined the Ferrarese Jewish deportees to Nazi concentration camps.

Eros reigned not only over the plant life of the city estate, the Barchetto del Duca, but also over its many solitary retreats that were kind to love: the harbor bench at the embarcadero by the Po, the cowshed beside the butler's farmhouse, the coach house redolent with grapefruit and lubricating oil, the point outside the garden wall where the narrator and his beloved Micòl Finzi-Contini held their first true conversation as children, and the alpine refuge, *Hütte,* where in the narrator's imagination, Micòl used to receive her lovers. The strong olfactory sensations offered by both the plant life and buildings on the grounds aroused a powerful emotional response in the narrator beyond rational control as he sought in vain to become a permanent participant in the garden's world. But while the garden favored Eros with the rectilinear configurations of its sheltering walls, the estate's park expressed the conscious design of the Finzi-Continis to surround their existence with the same isolation that usually characterizes cemeteries. Their garden became a cemetery for the living, a space of secluded repose away from political realities. A sense of fatality permeated the park, which seemed to be awaiting annihilation by the woodsman's axe. The narrator's recollections communicate an awareness of death-in-life in the garden's recesses. [3]

Even as a schoolboy, the narrator longed to penetrate the Finzi-Continis' world, to take part in its mysteries, and share its spirit of disdainful apartness. Whereas the land of Motionless Childhood described in *The Poetics of Space* is usually the home of one's own childhood, here the narrator rejects the middle-class space of his comfortable but stifling home on Via Scandiana in favor of the Finzi-Continis' paradise. Perotti, the majordomo with the Hitlerian nose, and Jor, the family's Great Dane with cold staring eyes (one dark blue and one pale blue), stood as guardians barring entrance like Charon and Cerberus. But when Micòl first invited the narrator as a thirteen-year-old boy to scale the wall one afternoon in June 1929, in typical vacillation, he hesitated and missed his opportunity. In the novel's concentric structure, the episode by the wall represents the first failure to breach barriers and move to the vital center, but having just failed a course in mathematics, the narrator was so preoccupied with his feelings of inferiority that he could not ascend in time to the promised paradise. After having descended into the dark recesses of a Renaissance-era underground storehouse near the wall in order to hide his bicycle, he first yielded to childish fears of darkness and then wasted precious minutes imagining a romantic adventure with Micòl. When he resurfaced, the girl had disappeared to answer Perotti's summons to the mansion. Years later, on their pilgrimages around the estate, the narrator and Micòl refer to their first meeting place, the "vert paradis des amours enfantins," a name taken from Baudelaire's poem "Moesta et errabunda" about the intense yearning to reach a remote and fragrant paradise of innocent love and joy. With their literary culture, the couple heighten every experience, transposing it to an aesthetic plane. Another literary reference, from Dante's *Inferno*, III, 60, provides Micòl's nickname for the narrator (his only name in the novel): "Celestino," not just for his sky-blue (*celeste*) eyes, but in remembrance of Pope Celestine V, who in Dante's words "made the great refusal on account of cowardice." The schoolboy Celestino in 1929, indeed, made his own great refusal by not accepting in time Micòl's invitation.[4]

In the numerical tradition of Dante's love for Beatrice in the *Vita Nova*, it takes *nine* years after that summer afternoon encounter between schoolchildren before the narrator succeeded in entring the Barchetto del Duca, not surreptitiously over the wall but through the wide gate at the family's invitation. The oak gate represents the gateway to the knowledge of Eros and Thanatos that the narrator gains within the Finzi-Continis' universe. Because racial laws in autumn 1938 caused the expulsion of Hebrews from the Eleonora D'Este Tennis Club, the Finzi-Continis opened their estate so that Jewish youths could take advantage of their private court. Unable to use the public library, the narrator avails himself during the winter and spring 1939, of the Finzi-Continis' vast library to complete his doctoral dissertation. But writing his thesis is not the only phase of Celestino's education completed at the estate. In Micòl, he contemplates the lovely yet sad image of inaccessible truth: a portrait of Nordic blond beauty with rainbow-flashing irises in her blue eyes. A mystic amulet falls over her full breasts, giving the young woman an almost magical power that cast its spell over the enchanted Celestino. In Micòl's brother, Alberto, the narrator beholds the countenance of death, and in her father, Professor Ermanno, he witnesses the firm resolve to withdraw from the compromises of the outer world. To a great extent, Bassani's novel might be considered a Bildungsroman in retrospect, where the narrator relates the story of his development through the knowledge that came with learning the secrets of the garden and the pain he experienced on having to leave its world.

VOLUNTARY SELF-EXILE VERSUS FORCED EXCLUSION

Above all, the entire universe of this novel is one of the enclosures and barriers that the characters, especially the Finzi-Continis, erect to guard against intrusion. The primary structural principle arises from the dialectic between inside and outside, which creates an atmosphere of hostility and alienation. A major distinction must be drawn between the voluntary self-exile of the Finzi-Contini family and the official exclusion of Jews from Italian society. The Finzi-Continis consider themselves superior and thus willingly elect to remain apart from civic life. Young Nino Bottecchiari in *The Gold-Rimmed Eyeglasses* observes that it would be difficult for the Fascists to conduct a sweeping racial campaign in Ferrara because of the extensive role Jews have in the professional middle class, with the exception of the Finzi-Continis, whose voluntary isolation would easily make them victims of an official program of segregation. To the youthful social commentator the Finzi-Continis constitute an aristocracy replacing the extinct noble lines from the Middle Ages and Renaissance.

But the Finzi-Continis, by stubbornly refusing to accept assimilation—even as far as not joining the Fascist party, to which the wealthy family made large donations—shield themselves from the shock of rejection that stunned the Ferrarese Jews after the central government approved discriminatory legislation. The inner strength of the Finzi-Continis is their willingness to accept life structured in private enclosures where families or individuals lead isolated existences. Much like that other prominent character in Bassani's literary world, Dr. Elia Corcos, the Finzi-Continis keep others at a greater distance than normally occurs in Ferrara. Behind the fixed architectural features of the Barchetto del Duca, the lordly family screens itself from others, making domestic space a refuge from the outer world. Whenever they have to leave their estate, the Finzi-Continis are protected by their very exclusive and expensive chauffeured DiLambda limousine. Their weakness, as the narrator discloses, consists in obstinately ignoring the dangerous outer forces that may attack their walls and violate their sanctuary. Unlike most members of the Jewish community, the Finzi-Continis can not be ejected from a society to which they have never wished to belong, but they can easily be exterminated. In the eyes of the goyim, the only difference between the Finzi-Continis and other Ferrarese Hebrews is the wealth permitting the former its pretentions to exclusiveness: they were *judim*. That affiliation is fatally noted in their arrest and deportation. The Finzi-Continis never denied their Jewishness but sought to preserve it by shunning contact with the gentile world and those Jews who adopted gentile ways. The aristocratic family wished to maintain the purity of their Jewish identity untainted by gentile contact. Part of the narrator's sentimental education involves mediating between the pathetic helplessness of assimilated Jews like his father before the trauma of segregation and the sterile insularity of the Finzi-Continis.

Bassani's vision of human existence, however, goes beyond documenting a single period of discrimination in recent history; for he sees human beings as creatures who constantly seek to avoid alien contact. Despite the century-old traditional emphasis among Hebrews of communal solidarity in face of discrimination and physical persecution, this novel shows that even the different segments of Ferrara's Jewish community were divided against each other. The narrator emphasizes this division, by remarking that the Italian gentiles—those *negri goyim*—could never appreciate the subtle barriers that the Ferrarese Jews had constructed to compartmentalize their sects. In the same building on Via Mazzini (the temple with the plaque on which Geo Josz saw his name inscribed among the victims of the Holocaust), there was a German synagogue on the first floor and an Italian synagogue on the second. The two groups regarded each other with condescending tolerence: the severe, nearly Lutheran members of the German synagogue in their Homburg hats and the well-assimilated members of the Italian temple, who celebrated their rites with the theatrics of Roman Catholics. Both groups considered themselves superior to the Hebrews of the separate Levantine synagogue on Via Vittoria, who seemed to belong to a remote past when Jews practised a clandestine cult in the darkness of the night. According to the narrator, only a Jew brought up *intra muros* could understand the traditions that separated the Israelite community into distinct sects with their own temples.

Division among the Hebrews continued in the interiors of the individual synagogues, where each family held its own pew and women were segregated upstairs behind gratings that resembled screens on chicken coops. Although most of those details have been part of Jewish custom for centuries, the novelist focuses on them as an example of the human tendency toward architectonic separation. Bassani stresses that individuals feel apart from the socioreligious world surrounding them. Even among members of the same religious community, one that should have the strongest bonds because of millenia of persectution, individuals find themselves isolated from their coreligionists. The narrator comments that frequently the sense of community between members of the Italian temple arose from a few banal greetings exchanged in the darkness of the synagogue's entrance hall before or after the ceremonies of major holidays like Yom Kippur and Passover. Throughout the world of Bassani's novel, the dimensions that are usually lacking are closeness and openness, since even those of the same religion establish barriers of exclusiveness.

THE WALLED FORTRESS OF LANGUAGE

In more than any other work by the author, a sense of immurement dominates the human and linguistic space of the novel whose characters increasingly complain of being shut in by the city's narrow confines. The terms of spatial obstruction that occur most frequently are *mura* (outer walls), *pareti* (interior walls), *isolamento* (isolation) and *separazione*. The town's inhabitants always speak of Ferrara as a medieval fortress prison with its restricting circuit of walls and lofty parapets that peasants climb as a short cut on their way to market. Only an outsider like the Milanese industrial chemist Malnate can avoid the city's claustrophobic oppressiveness and imagine an escape beyond the municipal borders to the countryside and nearby sea. To the Ferrarese, the country is merely a distant zone where nighttime lay desolately like a "black wall (*muraglia nera*). The city's various districts and social circles resemble so many distinct areas with metaphorical walls, preventing free movement from one place to another, especially after the passage of racial laws. Ironically, those laws barred gentiles from business and legal transactions with Jews, including medical services. Gentiles also lost jobs with Hebrew employers.

Bassani constructs his novel on a language of hermetic closure whose very exactness intensifies the impression of living in an era of political and social oppression. The author continues the practice from his tales of so accurately locating events on obscure streets in Ferrara that present-day scholars must carefully examine city maps from that period to identify the sites.[5] Sometimes names of historical persons prominent in that society, such as Roberto Longhi, appear in the text as the narrator's professor of art history at the University of Bologna. Trade names from the period also occur with frequency: Celestino rides a Wolsit bicylce; young Alberto Finzi-Contini uses Maryland pipe tobacco and prefers to purchase Dawson shoes of English leather. Contemporary motion pictures provide a full range of experiences and metaphors: Celestino wonders if Micòl paces around her personal telephone like the caged tiger in the 1935 movie *Nocturno* by the Czech director Gustav Machaty. One of the Aryan guests at the tennis matches at the Finzi-Continis' home is Bruno Lattes's beloved Adriana Trentini, whose beautiful complexion is described as resembling that of the American movie actress Carole Lombard. The sight of that beauty is denied to Bruno by spring 1939 when local authorities forbid the Finzi-Continis to invite non-Jews to their social gatherings. When the narrator and Malnate see a German movie with the star Christina Söderbaum, a nasty racial incident almost brings Celestino to blows with an obnoxious spectator. Music and theater also offer ironic comparisons between the world of Ferrara and that of general culture. The grandiose Finzi-Contini mausoleum in the town's Hebrew cemetery recalls the theatrical artifice of stage productions of Verdi operas *Nabucco* (set in Babylon at the time of the Jewish captivity) and *Aïda* (set in ancient Egypt of the pharoahs). When the relationship between the narrator and Micòl becomes one of frustration and hostility, Celestino's outbursts of self-pitying and disdainful laughter remind the young woman of the snickering derision by the jester in *La Cena delle beffe* (1909, *The Banquet of Jests*) by the Italian Jewish playwright Sem Benelli. Micòl's brother, Alberto tries to impress Malnate and the narrator with a comprehensive collection of American jazz records featuring Duke Ellington, Fats Waller, Benny Goodman, and Louie Armstrong.

To a certain extent, as time passes, many of the references to trade names and contemporary movie stars lose their effectiveness and make the novel appear dated in a pejorative sense. Neither of the two American translators of the novel have tried to assist English readers with footnotes on most of those now-obscure contemporary allusions. Bassani has answered critics accusing him of paying attention to trifles by stating that he was combatting the abstractions of officially approved Fascist literature by producing narrative with a strong link to reality. His express task consisted in reconstructing an historical period down to minute details to render an exact image of a provincial Italian city at the time of racial legislation. Brand names also indicate the tastes and pretentions of the novel's condemned characters.[6]

Throughout the text, numerous phrases and entire sentences in both nonstandard Italian dialects and foreign languages break up the artfully contrived prose, recalling the novels of D'Annunzio and the belles-lettres fragments of the Rondists. Here, too, the novel's language recreates that world's tense diversity. The author renders most of the town's commentary about the behavior and superiority of the Finzi-Continis through substitutionary speech by the narrator's parents, particularly his exasperated father, who employs Emilian dialect and Jewish slang (part Hebrew, part Sephardic Spanish, part Yiddish) to express his dissatisfaction with the haughtiness of that wealthy family who seemed to welcome discriminatory laws. Cunning old Moisè Finzi-Contini, who made possible the move from ghetto to Renaissance palace, is known as *al gatt*, Emilian for the cat. Typical of Italian folk humor and custom is the practice of nicknaming someone after an outstanding trait of physical appearance or dress; consequently, townspeople used to call Moisè's son Menotti *al matt mugnàga*, the apricot madman, after the color of his bizarrely styled but expensive fur-lined overcoat. Nicknames like those often replace the individual's actual name and may continue for generations as part of local history. Non-Emilian dialect invades the conversations of the tennis players in the garden world with the presence of Alberto's former university schoolmate Malnate, who feels most at ease quoting the verses of Lombard poets like his favorite writer, the Milanese Carlo Porta (d. 1821). By using phrases in Emilian and Milanese dialects, the author enables readers to approach the mentality of his characters, from the mean, closed suspiciousness of the Ferrarese (gentiles and Jews alike) to the naïve optimism of the Lombards. Bassani aims his book at well-educated, linguistically alert readers.

Words from ancient classical languages like Latin and Hebrew add solemnity to the novel's lexicon, in contrast to Jewish slang. To the narrator, the Finzi-Continis' mansion is the *magna domus* (great house). Moisè Finzi-Contini ordered the construction of an ostentatious tomb *sibi et suis*, for himself and his own. And, of course, to be able to understand the reasons for the existence and continuance of rival sects among Ferrara's Hebrews, one has to have lived *intra muros*, within the city's walls. Tension takes place not only between different Jewish groups but also between *judim* and *goyim* (sometimes a very negative *negri goyim*—filthy outsiders). Whenever a gentile shows him- or herself to be particularly insensitive to Jewish customs, he or she proves to be *goyish*. Bassani does not insert Hebrew terms gratuitously for local color but because language determines reality for individuals as well as entire groups.

Many of the Hebrew words appear quite early in the novel, in the fourth chapter of part 1, to describe the rituals of the Italian temple at the time of high holidays: *tevà* (the synagogue's lectern); the *sefarim* (scrolls of the law); the *taled* (talit—a prayer shawl belonging to a particular family and passed from generation to generation that, at the celebration of certain services, is spread like a canopy over the congregation's children); the *berachà* (the benediction intoned by the rabbi). Hebrew words from religious services convey the image of the aloof and exotic Finzi-Contini family who fascinated the narrator as a boy in temple. Although Alberto (born 1915) was a year older than Celestino, the narrator preceded the Finzi-Contini son in the honor of entering the *mignàn* (the minyan—the designated number of male adults, thirteen years old or older, required to hold public religious services). When the Finzi-Continis later move to their own private temple, the family shows its pretentiousness by furnishing it with such items as a *parochet* (parokhet: ark curtain) of authentic Spanish Sephardic origin. One of the most significant sequences in the novel is the two seders (Passover dinner services) in which the narrator participates. Most of the Hebrew terms occur in relationship to Celestino and the Finzi-Continis, thereby suggesting that despite their common religious background, a gulf separates them, so that Celestino's yearning to become part of the *magna domus* cannot be realized.[7]

Modern languages like German, French, and English intensify the memories of the era which marked the decline and eventual destruction of the dwellers in the secluded manor house. Ominously in the novel's prologue chapter the narrator compares the cone-shaped tombs in an Etruscan necropolis which he visits in the late 1950's to the *bunkers* that German soldiers built all over Europe in a vain attempt to secure mastery over occupied nations. During the first visits of the tennis players to the Barchetto del Duca, Adriana Trentini sharply

distinguishes between young Micòl and Alberto as opposed to the "old guard" of
parents, grandmother and uncles whom she calls in allusion to the volumes of
Marcel Proust's *A la recherche du temps perdu* as the *"côté vecchi."*

With their elitist aspirations, Alberto and Micòl fabricate their own language,
Finzi-Continico, from the Venetian dialect and the Ladino spoken by their
mother, Olga Herrera, and her brothers, along with fashionable Tuscan, French,
German, and a great deal of English. An expert at foiling her verbal adversaries,
Micòl demolishes the narrator in his erotic thrusts at her with sentences in
English like, "You're fishing for compliments." Majoring in literature at the
University of Venice, the Finzi-Contini's daughter sees life recreating situations
and attitudes from classic works, and consequently, she quotes from Baudelaire,
Mallarmé, Melville, or Emily Dickinson to establish a parallel for every new
happening. Although Micòl knows all the rare trees in the garden by their
scientific names (to the point of regarding Celestino's lack of botanical knowledge with astonishment), the young woman refers to familiar fruit trees like the
plum in Emilian dialect as the tongue most appropriate for discussing hor-
ticulture with the peasants tending the park's plants. The composite Finzi-
Continian language reflects to an extreme degree the desire of well-educated
members of the Italian middle class in the period just preceding World War II to
fashion a cultured *lingua franca* in order to overcome the verbal provincialism of
the conservative standard Italian with its basis in Tuscan. Determined to
distinguish themselves from others, Micòl and her brother assert their social and
intellectual superiority through language.[8]

Tennis, with its terminology of serves and drives, becomes a metaphor for
struggle in the novel, symbolizing the disruptive forces at working within and
without the walls of the Barchetto del Duca. At the time of events in the novel,
tennis held an enormous snob appeal among the wealthy like the Finzi-Continis
and the ambitious middle class like the narrator's family. It is a letter from
Marquis Barbicinti, secretary of the Eleonora D'Este Club, to the association's
Jewish members informing them of their forced resignation that causes the
owners of the manor house to open their doors to the excluded youths. As
always, the author focuses on a linguistic detail by having his narrator comment
with irritation over Barbicinti's typical misspelling, a trait that once seemed
amusing but under the circumstances exacerbates his resentment. Toward the
close of the fall 1938 tennis tournaments, Barbicinti also permits politics to
interfere with sports by suspending a game early one evening to prevent a Jew,
Bruno Lattes, from winning the club's finals on the day preceding receipt of his
letter of expulsion. That same marquis later takes steps to prevent Aryans from
joining tennis games at the Barchetto del Duca. The narrator's disenchantment
with the garden world begins with the inadequacies of the Finzi-Continis' tennis
court: its white earthen surface, narrow out-of-bounds zone, and poor drainage;
almost a potato patch compared to the court at the Eleonora D'Este Club. By the
summer of 1939, Professor Ermanno Finzi-Contini does take steps to improve the

court's surface and extend the out-of-bounds zone with a new fence—all while willfully ignoring the global war about to engulf Italy's Jews and refusing to recognize the fatal illness afflicting his son, Alberto.

Among the garden's players of mixed doubles, each one's attitude toward the game reveals an essential element of moral character. Although Alberto sometimes appears bored while playing, he regards tennis as not only a sport but an art requiring the particular talent of individuals with a certain natural sense of class. His friend Giampiero Malnate so lacks style that he often ends up refereeing games. Because tennis is a sport that requires a certain ferocity, it is not surprising that Micòl is highly skilled at the game, working with the destructive force of an artillery shot to attain victory even when she plays *all'americana* as a single against two male partners. Determined to be free, athletic, and modern, Micòl, in tennis, shows nearly the same fierce determination that she uses to oppose the narrator when he tries to win her love. For even though Celestino knows how to play the game well, he alienates Micòl with his erotic insistence and self-pity and loses his place in the mixed doubles. The narrator never summons forth the ferocity to triumph in love or tennis.

Nonstandard Italian dialects, ancient classical languages, and modern European tongues add a linguistic perspective to Bassani's presentation of the state of inner emigration or spiritual exile of life in Ferrara that the racial laws only intensified. Those various linguistic codes, with their restrictive patterns, illustrate the complex problem of communication between Ferrarese of different social classes and even among members of the same religion but in rival sects. Those who employ a tongue different from the standard one are exiles.[9]

DWELLERS WITHIN THE ENCLOSED KINGDOM

Lordly isolation, of course, marks the Finzi-Continis' style of life within their retreat behind the Wall of the Angels in Ferrara's northern section along the majestic boulevard, Corso Ercole I D'Este, made famous by the verses of Giosuè Carducci and D'Annunzio. In creating an artificial paradise, that aristocratic family expresses its Decadentist aestheticism, which eventually has to yield to the political reality of Fascist and Nazi anti-Semitism. To the chagrin of the narrator's well-assimilated and pro-Fascist father, in 1933, the Finzi-Continis protested the eagerness of their fellow Jews to respond positively to the recent decision of the Fascist party to open membership to all interested citizens by withdrawing from the congregation of the Italian synagogue. The Finzi-Continis did not return to the Italian synagogue until Roshashanà (Jewish New Year festival) 1938, after the discriminatory laws had vindicated their distrust of the party's generosity. Hebraic tradition, especially Sephardic customs and rites, shelter the aloof family, and until racial legislation confirmed their doubts about the sincerity of Fascist officials in particular and gentiles in general, the Finzi-

Continis live as if encased in a protective wall of glass (*parete di cristallo*). Their return to the Italian synagogue also coincides with their invitation to the excluded youths to use the garden's tennis court. In the opinion of the narrator's father, it seemed that the Finzi-Continis actually welcomed governmental segregation despite the hardships it caused Hebrews less fortunate than they. In fact, with their wealth and the corruptibility of Fascist authorities, the family easily circumvented many of the government's decrees until the advent of the Nazi-dominated Italian Social Republic. Because of their satisfaction over the new climate of discrimination, the Finzi-Continis willingly surrender part of their isolated splendor to create what other Jews contemptuously referred to as a kibbutz for the new generation of social refugees.

An atmosphere of isolationism also envelopes Alberto and Micòl, who, due to the death of the Finzi-Contini's son, Guido, in 1914, from infantile paralysis, were not allowed to leave the safety of the Barchetto del Duca for fear of contamination. Later, when tutors visited the *magna domus* to give private lessons, the town's middle-class Jewish parents reacted with their usual indignation at still another example of noncollaboration by that haughty family. By sending their children to public schools, most Jews felt they were performing a patriotic duty out of gratitude to the nation that accepted them as equals with other citizens. The only time the Finzi-Contini children associated with their contemporaries was at the state-required final examinations in June. Even then, Micòl and Alberto stayed apart from other children because Perotti drove them to the examination in the family carriage while other students walked to school or rode bicycles. To the Ferrarese children at the public school, Alberto and Micòl seemed to be "among these *others*" (p. 267, italics Bassani's) who came from outside the city. The narrator remarks that brother and sister were "always courteous, even somewhat too polite: just like guests" (ibid.). With his nearly cinematic art of distantiation, Bassani presents Micòl and Alberto as if they were photographed from behind a gauze screen.

Even in their own home, the Finzi-Continis behaved toward each other with the decorum of guests. Each member of the family had his or her own suite of rooms, and the walls of their suites constituted boundaries that the others never violated. Those stuffy, centrally heated rooms recall Bachelard's description of man-made shells and corners that ensured a comforting sense of immobility. The one zone of daily familial encounter was the dining room with its art nouveau furnishings of reddish wood and huge fireplace that on wintry evenings radiated a roseate conviviality and gentle intimacy that shone across the room's wall-length window. Celestino feels sheltered in that dining room, which is ideally suited to protect the "slow-burning coal" of the hearts of the young. But to the dining room and the entire Barchetto del Duca as well as to all of Ferrara, the narrator applies an adjectival past participle that signifies both comfort and death—*sepolto* (buried) cut off from life and its vital challenges.

Celestino's first guide into the complexities of the *magna domus* is none other than its proprietor, Dr. Ermanno, who welcomes the youth almost as a disciple of the manor's mysteries. During the course of most days, Professor Ermanno would retire to his study which, in its disarray of scattered books, globe, lectern, microscope, half dozen barometers, surgeon's cot and strong box, reminded the narrator of Dr. Faustus's quarters but would actually suggest Dürer's engraving of *Melancholia* with its many instruments of frustration and futility. For Professor Ermanno's erudite activities produced almost no positive results. The one time that the door to this study opened to the adjoining billiard room took place during the brief period when Celestino was consulting the family's superb collection of nineteenth-century Italian writers to compose his dissertation, and from their respective rooms he and the professor would exchange casual comments. A few years later, during the winter of 1944, the narrator would similarly communicate with a fellow political prisoner in the next cell.

It was the style of the Finzi-Contini family to determine the perimeter of its own luxurious cells and to stay at a polite distance from each other. As creatures of habit, the Finzi-Continis have to incorporate even the minor intrusion of Celestino's research visits into the routine of the manor house, and consequently, every day at eleven in the morning, Perotti brought the guest a cup of coffee to establish still another ritual at the estate. Mental rigidity prevents the Finzi-Continis from adapting to even the idea of change, let alone the experience of novelty that might have rescued them from physical danger. Of all the older generation of the family, only Professor Ermanno, with his scholarly eccentricities, emerges from the manor's shadows; his wife, Olga, remains a lugubrious figure; her mother, Regina Herrera, appears from a distance in the garden as a spectral form, and Olga's two brothers from Venice are caricatures, speaking a combination of Spanish and Venetian.[10]

Among the Finzi-Continis, Alberto is the least capable of establishing rapport with others, despite his pathetic efforts to play the perfect host whenever he entertained in his studio. During a prolonged absence by Micòl to finish her doctoral dissertation in Venice, her brother makes possible Celestino's transition from the garden world to the *magna domus* by inviting the narrator to his rooms. The narrator, Alberto, and Malnate form a threesome from winter 1938 to 1939 in Alberto's apartment. The narrator finds the apartment strangely oppressive, with its indirect lighting and austere modern decor that clashes with the florid architectual style in the rest of the mansion. Although the rational and functional furnishings appeared to be the outward expression of a young man in complete control of his emotions, Celestino senses the inner agitation that undermines Alberto's precarious equilibrium and prevents him from ever feeling at ease with his companions and especially with women. The aesthete youth seemed to fear exposing a secret self if he became close to someone. Bassani merely hints at a possible homoeroticism in Alberto: A small male nude painting by De Pisis decorated the young man's apartment. During their university days together in Milan, Malnate and Alberto became acquainted with a vaudeville dancer named Gladys, but unlike his sexually assertive friend, Alberto refused to have an affair with her. Similarly, Alberto declines all of Malnate's suggestions that they visit a brothel, in contrast to Celestino who once during summer 1939 accompanies Malnate to a Ferrarese bordello.

Alberto belongs to that class of Bassani's enigmatic characters whose inner drama remains a mystery not through the author's failure to investigate thoroughly but because of his artistic determination to respect the puzzle that is the human heart. All of the Finzi-Continis, even the vibrant Micòl, by the very nature of their self-chosen roles as creatures in isolation persist in their bewildering remoteness. The reader glimpses the intimate secrets of characters like Alberto only after having penetrated their private space, as here in the young man's ultramodern rooms. Never once does Bassani suggest the possibility of an erotic liaison between Alberto and Malnate. Instead, the novelist concentrates on the complexities of personal attachment as the chemist gradually moves away from intimacy with the possessive brother to form a friendship with the competitive sister. Yet, despite the tension of the strained relationships in Alberto's apartment, the narrator finds a kind of narcotic to soothe the pain of his solitude.

Surrounded by mechancial objects symbolizing inertia and repression, Alberto awaits death in the *magna domus* by slowly asphyxiating malignant lymphogranuloma; in 1942, he is the last member of his family and the final male heir to die at the Barchetto del Duca and to be buried in the family's mausoleum. The young architectural student continues the nineteenth-century literary tradition of romantic illness, although it is not consumption here but a respiratory condition that required ever-increasing quantities of oxygen. This pale, progressively emaciated and prematurely aged youth recalls the tubercular heroes of romantic writers who regarded that fatal illness as the sign of a defective vitality of will. And by retreating into a world where he relies on machines like his multispeaker phonograph to sustain him in life, Alberto has already lost the will to live. Never exhibiting his sister's fierce resolve to succeed, the young man does not even bother to return to Milan to complete his university degree. The victim of a spiritual disease, Alberto Finzi-Contini merely marks time in ever-agonzing attempts to breathe until physical death liberates him from both life that has ceased to hold interest and from the fate that befalls his family in the autumn of 1943.[11]

Micòl's turreted rooms are located on the highest level of the mansion, expressing the home's vertical thrust. Being in her apartment gave the feeling of sailing in an ocean liner. Although a spiral stairway led to her rooms, the most convenient way of reaching them was by an elevator, which the narrator considered a coffinlike antedeluvian box, with its pungent odor of wine-colored velvet cushions and turpentine that recalled the estate's carriage house. The cagelike interior of the elevator seemed to be a miniature world in itself on the way to still another world in Micòl's apartment. This high tower whose uppermost chamber is reached only after great difficulty suggests fairy tales and princesses in impenetrable castles. In her blonde beauty, Micòl brings to mind the "Blessed Damozel" of Dante Gabriel Rossetti with hair "yellow like ripe corn."[12] The remoteness of the young woman's rooms symbolizes her insistence on preserving a domain that in her own words would be *verboten, privat*. When Celestino eventually ascends to those rooms, he is at the apex of his experiences in the *magna domus* but the nadir of his romantic expectations.

All around her Micòl had to give everything her peronal touch. After she discovered a refreshing beverage during a skiing trip to Austria,*Skiwasser*, the young woman changed its contents by adding grapes for an Italianate and Finzi-Continian flavor. Life for her had to possess an ambivalent bittersweet taste like that of unripened plums or certain brands of Swiss chocolates. Every personal experience for her would hold beauty and sadness at the same time, as in her relationship with Celestino. For his part, during the time the narrator succeeds in participating in the Finzi-Continis' world, he never attempts to meet Micòl outside her home, whether in Venice or the synagogue. Celestino instinctively realizes that contact with her must take place in her own territory where she retains the home court advantage over him. The young man longs to find a permanent place in the world of Micòl's rooms. His arrival in that very private domain is achieved in three stages. First, Celestino learns the details of the rooms from descriptions he persuades Micòl to give him over the telephone. Then, on the night before she leaves for Venice, the youth dreams about those rooms, but resentment for having been excluded causes him to distort the reality of the objects there. After he finally penetrates that special chamber, Celestino marvels over the apartment's two high windows, whose southern exposure overlooks the garden's desert palms (the *Washingtoniae graciles* of biblical memory), relieving the room's overcrowded atmosphere with the liberating view of treetops. In contrast to her brother's preference for a modernistic interior decor, Micol furnishes her rooms aiming at an air of cozy comfort and traditional elegance with a Persian carpet, a Récamier sofa, over stuffed armchairs, and most surprising of all to the narrator shelves full of opalines called *lattimi* because of their milky white color, from the Italian word *latte* for "milk". Micòl tells Celestino that one should respect the transiency of objects by never trying to prolong their life: "Even things die, my dear. And then, if even they must die, it's so much better to let them go. There's much more style about it, after all, don't you think so?" (p. 327). Her statement about the need for objects to pass away occurs at the strategic close of part 2, as the couple take shelter from autumn's first rain in the carriage house. In that afternoon's dusty luminescence, the old carriage seems to retain the luxurious perfection of Celestino's childhood memories of trips to the schoolhouse by Micòl and Alberto for the required annual final examination. But in pointing out the carriage's deterioration, which Perotti's painstaking care could not correct, Micòl directs the narrator's attention to another object in the carriage house: the children's old canoe in which brother and sister once dreamed of voyages on the Po, now abandoned in its full decay. For the young woman, there is more dignity in the canoe's passing than in the carriage's, with the servant's futile attempt to reverse the destructive effects of time.

Through objects, Bassani's characters come to know space and time as contingency reveals reality. Contact with the world comes in part from objects, and a character like Micòl seeks control over the world and time by both acquiring objects and disposing of them before their total decline. Victor Hugo once remarked, "We deposit ourselves in the objects that surround us!"[13] Objects here do not recall the past through the memories they hold; instead, Bassani concentrates on objects of actuality whose "pastness" eventually condemns them for the present and future. Celestino resents the collection of opalines (*lattimi*) in Micòl's apartment, and in his dream, he transforms them into pieces of cheese that he can devour, in an attempt to obliterate them as objects usurping Micòl's affections so that she cannot care for another person. He cannot understand that the mania for collecting *lattimi* is another Finzi-Contini peculiarity: including Thanatos into a pattern of apparent permanence.

On that oneiric level, the narrator imagines that the young woman's room is floating above the Venetian lagoon, with the threat of death with the rising tide. His tormented sleep also returns him to the enclosure of the carriage, where servants peer in at Celestino and his beloved. Those intermittent dreams ilustrate the novel's final centrifugal movement: The narrator must leave Micòl's room and life at the Barchetto del Duca.

As a child, Micòl had felt empathy for Celestino. They were contemporaries whose lives seemed destined to coincide no matter what obstacles Professor Ermanno and his wife placed between their children and the contaminating outside world. During temple ceremonies, Micòl always wanted to put Celestino under her father's *taled*, acknowledging the boy's spiritual affinities with the Finzi-Continis. For that reason, she had hoped to introduce the mysteries of the garden and home to him, as a schoolboy in 1929 weeping over a failing grade in mathematics. Micòl wanted to introduce Celestino to the permanence and transitoriness of things. What is intuitive to her at last becomes part of the narrator's awareness during an exile journey to France in the second half of April 1939. Recognizing that in paradoxes one can discover the true meaning of continuity and transiency, Celestino sends Micòl a postcard from Grenoble with a quotation from Stendhal's notebooks, "All lost, nothing lost."

Their closest bond is their perception of time, contrasted with the dialectical optimism of their tennis companion Giampiero Malnate. For although the young Milanese chemist regards objects as surrogates for moral ideals producing a state of reification that makes objects masters of their owners, he looks forward to a liberating future under socialism. Rejecting that naïve hope in progress, Micòl quotes Mallarmé, declaring that she worships "*le vierge, le vivace et le bel aujuord'hui*" and especiallty the past. The young woman wants to seize every today in its ever renewing and ever fresh "nowness" of infinite possibilities. Micòl glories in the instant while the narrator, in presenting the story of the *magna domus*, its inhabitants, and its brief guests strives to recapture a duration of pain and loss. In an unfinished diary from winter 1944, Bassani observes that during the German occupation of Rome, some Italians lived on past memories, others on hopes for the future, but no one lived in the present. Micòl teaches Celestino to long for the present to fade away into a past of fond memories. Like the swan in Mallarmé's poem, through memory one can defeat temporal flux. Rather than move toward the future like Malnate, the young woman hopes to defy time in the eternity of the instant. Micòl wishes to go through life looking back on its todays, the very task that the narrator achieves with his text.[14]

Rapprochement between the two young people always appears imminent, but it never occurs as life constantly comes between them. Nine years separate the June afternoon when Micòl summoned Celestino to the garden wall from the Saturday morning in October 1938 when he arrives at the manor house for the first tennis match. Neither one of them ever dares take the decisive step of forming a liaison. Micòl the child failed to follow the schoolboy into the subterranean storehouse where he left his bicycle so that he could afterward climb the wall. On that rainy afternoon in autumn 1938 that ends part 2, Celestino the university student does not seize the promise of a moment when he and Micòl find themselves alone in the intimate enclosure of the old carriage during one of their tours to the coach house. As Celestino later reproaches himself again and again, a gesture like a kiss might have realized the possibilities of that instant. But the embarrassed silence of his hesitation drove Micòl away into a corner of the carriage. Her withdrawal before Celestino's inability to make up his mind about his feeling and declare them openly is never reversed no matter how often and how insistently the narrator later attempts to recover the lost promise. Those disappointing moments in the carriage, of course, return to haunt Celestino in his dreams, where he tries to seek the sensual love his faltering forever denied him.

After the debacle in the coach house, Micòl physically vanishes for an entire season from the narrator's life as she put herself at a distance. Her telephone calls to Celestino's home serve intentionally to separate rather than unite them, so that the young woman fades away into a voice before she leaves for Venice. Micòl deliberately becomes an absence in the narrator's existence, creating a void that he has to fill with his nearly daily visits to the *magna domus* to see Professor Ermanno and join Alberto and Malnate. Not until the evening of the Passover celebration in 1939 does Celestino at last kiss Micòl on her return from Venice—too late, however, to overcome the barriers that have risen between them. By that time, Micòl has developed the philosophy of freedom and noncollaboration, which she learned from Herman Melville's scrivener Bartleby, with his firm declaration of autonomy to the employer who wanted to send him on an errand outside the office: "I prefer not to."[15] Life holds no greater means of asserting independence than by rejecting another's entreaties.

In Micòl's view love is a ferocious game of spatial maneuvering in which participants stand in front of each other *(di fronte)* in an effort to gain supremacy. She desires Celestino's position to remain that of a brother, *di fianco,* at her side; otherwise, he does not fit into her scheme of life. For Micòl love equals contention. When Celestino at last visits Micòl in her rooom during her recovery from a cold, she rebuffs his ill-timed and clumsy erotic assault. She attempts to make the narrator understand that she does not personify Eros; she merely experienced it but never with him. In warning, she quotes Baudelaire's censured poem "Delphine et Hippolyte":

> Maudit soit à jamais le rêveur inutile
> qui voulut le premier, dans sa stupidité,
> s'éprenant d'un problème insoluble et stérile,
> aux choses de l'amour mêler l'honnêtetè!
>
> (Whoever would try to be the first to confuse
> virtue with love should be forever cursed as a
> useless dreamer struggling in his stupidity
> with an insoluble and fruitless problem.)

Celestino's sentimentality conflicts with Micòl's view of love as perpetual strife from which one party emerges the victor. After having been rejected, the narrator takes a trip of voluntary exile to Grenoble, France, supposedly to smuggle funds to his younger brother who is studying there because of Italian racial laws. Yet, during the weeks in France, Micòl's reproaches echo in his ears until, early in May, he returns to Ferrara. Because of the young man's obdurate resolve to force his way into Micòl's life, their relationship deteriorates, so that he finally agrees to being banned from the manor house for three weeks and thereafter to visit only on Tuesdays and Fridays. Celestino sees himself *cacciato dal Paradiso* (expelled from Paradise), and waits to be readmitted. Although the narrator does not always comply exactly with the visitation terms of their truce, Celestino and Micòl manage to establish their friendship in a neutral zone of mutual respect where excessive coldness and familiarity are avoided. However, the narrator then finds himself maneuvered outside the space of loving intimacy.

In his despair at never being more than a guest in the garden world, the young man senses that a new triangular relationship has developed: between Micòl, Malnate, and himself. Suspecting that the Milanese chemist is his superior in playing the fierce game of love with Micòl, the narrator for the first time begins to cultivate a friendship with Malnate. He and Alberto had already revealed their tacit admiration for the self-confident communist by imitating his pipe smoking. Because the narrator believes that the hirsute, muscular chemist has succeeded in becoming part (if only secretly, *di nascosto*) of Micòl's life, he studies him as that privileged Other who possesses the object of Celestino's desire. In Malnate's company, the youth tries to take a surrogate for Micòl in the person of a prostitute at a bordello they visit together; the girl even calls him *celestino* because of the color of his eyes. On another evening, the narrator does not join Giampiero for dinner so that he may watch him at a restaurant from the vantage point of one of the Este Castle's drawbridges as if the Milanese chemist were an actor in some play. Celestino understands that with Micòl he is neither "in front" nor "to the side" but "outside."

Ironically, that outsider from Lombardy seems to have taken the longed-for post as lover meeting Micòl in her rooms. From their conversations on art and literature, the narrator gains insight into Malnate's determination to seize reality in its positive nature. The young industrial scientist rejects the still lifes of an artist like Morandi because he sees in them a fear of reality that the Bolognese painter tried to evade with monotonous arrangements of bottles or flowers. Poets of lachrymose negativity could never attract Malnate, who prefers the satiric versifiers of his native city. With his self-affirming optimism, the Lombard seemed to have penetrated the mysterious core of Micòl's life. Even though Malnate was a *goy*, who could never understand the conspiratorial winks exchanged by his Jewish friends, that supreme Aryan, in the narrator's opinion, had overcome the obstacles to Micòl's affection.[16]

With the irony underlying most of Bassani's narrative works, Celestino does at last scale the garden wall to the Barchetto del Duca, ten years and two months too late, toward the end of August 1939. In discovering that the ladder of years before is still in its place on the other side of the wall, he concludes that Micòl has left it there for Malnate. Celestino's surreptitious penetration of the garden world occurs on a brilliant moonlit night of orgiastic frenzy, when more than thirty couples are stretched out on the grassy bastions beyond the estate's walls. At all those erotic events—those actually occurring before his eyes in the nocturnal light or the imaginary liaison between Malnate and Micòl in the *Hütte*—the narrator is condemned to be the unwanted, solitary outsider. Most significantly, Celestino does not pursue his frustrating quest although nothing stands in his way, since the dog greets him on the grounds as a friend. The anguished young man does not proceed to the cottage to confirm his suspicions about Micòl and Malnate, for he finally understands that his place will forever be away from the Barchetto del Duca. It is the sound of his beloved city clock that recalls the narrator to his true home in the city with his family. That love for his native city acquires an intense irony becaue as a Jew, the youth will suffer further discrimination and persecution in the years immediately following his renunciation of the world of the manor house. Celestino's failure must be interpreted in terms of spatial displacement from the cosmos of the Finzi-Continis once he recognizes himself to be a trespasser or intruder among the permanent dwellers of the enclosed kingdom.[17]

TEMPORAL STRUCTURES

With the original dedication of this novel to Micòl, the work of art attempts to defeat the destructiveness of time. Celestino eventually learns the perfection of absence over the years expressed by Mallarmé: "Separated we are together."[18]

Time and space in Bassani's novel form part of a continuum in which the Finzi-Continis vainly struggle to resist time as flux in the protective enclosure of the garden wall. The intentional disarticulation of time so that past, present, and future shift back and forth only to be recombined produces the effect of spatialized time replacing linear succession.[19] Because the prologue already announces the deaths of the last Finzi-Continis, the narrative arrests the movement of time so that readers experience the fate of the members of that family as if predestined.[20]

This work displays a double perspective because the "binocular I" dominates the narration. The one "I" is a man in his early forties looking back on events of 1938 and 1939, while the other "I" is a stunned Jewish youth of twenty-two compelled to bicycle down the side streets of Ferrara to elude the intimidating stares of Fascist hierarchs in the town's center. To adopt the terminology of St. Augustine, one views from the present of things future on the present of things past. Frequently, when some major event occurs during that first traumatic year of Fascist racial legislation, the reader shares the perspective of the middle-aged narrator who has succeeded in surviving that catastrophic period and who alone among the novel's main characters spiritually matured from the state of rejection. Bassani's narrative art functions through the juxtaposition of two principal temporal levels.[21]

This novel's controlling temporal perspective remains that of the narrator, who in 1957 decides to salvage the fragments of the past by writing down his recollections. Having lived in Rome for years, "the recording "I" yearns to reexperience Ferrara's past. The novel in part examines making connections with the world in time and space. There once was a time in the narrator's life when he felt he was part of society, a time when life's greatest tragedy consisted in flunking a final examination in mathematics. Even living under a dictatorial regime made no difference to the child and young man. When the narrator's relationship with society at large is severed by force, the dwellers of the *magna domus* initially but temporarily offer him a relationship with life in their artificial paradise. As the middle-aged narrator recaptures the lost colors and aromas of the mansion's past, he never allows the reader to forget the present-day condition of the Barchetto del Duca stripped of its great trees, with wartime evacuees occupying the bombed-out ruin of the manor house and wrecking the last remnants of its Renaissance paintings. By telling the story of the garden world, the narrator becomes a witness to the painful truth that must be remembered.

In its outer formal structure, the novel follows a concentric pattern and even recalls a musical round, with its prologue, four parts, and epilogue, which completes the circle by recounting the destinies of the Finzi-Continis. In part 1, the narrator traces the history of the Finzi-Continis' spirit of isolation up to the fateful afternoon in June 1929. Part 2 begins in October 1938 (shortly after the enactment of racial laws) and describes the admission of outsiders to the garden, closing with the scene between Micòl and Celestino in the carriage on that symbolically rainy afternoon that ends the luminous Indian summer of 1938. With the narrator's entrance through the great gate begins the partial loss of the esteem that the previous isolationist attitude of the Finzi-Continis had inspired in the young man. Imaginary and actual walls command an admiration that perishes when gates open to reveal such imperfections as a malfunctioning doorbell or a poorly surfaced tennis court. By part 3, the ground-floor door of the manor house opens to admit the narrator to the library and Alberto's apartment, but at the close of that section, the Passover reunion between Celestino and Micòl already foreshadows their total separation. For although in part 4, the narrator visits the young woman's rooms, his belated scaling of the garden wall and his furtive exploration of the grounds convince Celestino to renounce hope of ever sharing the Finzi-Continis' world. Part 4 carries the narrative to August 1939, the very eve of the maelstrom that engulfs and destroys the Finzi-Continis' universe.

At the end of each of the four sections, Micól plays a decisively negative role: her disappearance from outside the wall when the schoolboy Celestino climbs up from the storehouse; her sudden withdrawal from the narrator in the carriage; Micól's cold submission to her friend's welcoming kiss at the Passover festival; and her definitive absence from the scene of Celestino's nocturnal wanderings through the estate. According to one critic, the novel's structure is governed in each section, respectively, by one of four fundamental elements: Love—a dream of adolescence; Death—acceptance of the death of people and things even within the garden paradise; Time—recognizing the rituals at the Barchetto del Duca as a means of transforming temporal duration into an idyllic eternity; and Truth—acknowledging the human limitations of the Finzi-Continis and abandoning any pretentions to a life among them. Thus, the garden is dominated by the forces of illness, decay, and death, which Celestino must overcome through his Dantesque descent into the underworld of the estate to gain illuminating and liberating self-knowledge.[22] In its formal and interior structures, the novel relates a quest through time and space to transcend death.

Bassani is representing here the salient features of a world just before it falls apart with a narrative technique that resembles De Pisis's in depicting a moment of brilliant vitality preceding disintegration. Consequently, the pivotal section of the novel occurs in autumn, the season of natural crisis and deepening coloration, whose evanescent vibrancy bears the promise of its own decomposition. The disillusionment caused by the racial decrees in autumn 1938 starts the slow decline of the Finzi-Continis, which ends with their deportation in September 1943. The narrator's recollections recreate all the seasons of the manor house: the vacant expansiveness of winter snow surrounding the mansion's hermetic warmth and creating in its seemingly permanent iciness an illusion of eternity; then the luxuriant resurgence of motionless and deceptively time-free greenery in May; the stifling heat of summer settling over a tennis court and intensifying the combativeness of the players. Cyclic time across the seasons becomes time as a quality of human experience rather than objective fact that can be chronicled in a linear sequence of intervals. Love permits the narrator to recreate the past of individuals whose tragedy is that they never had a future. Through the narrator's redemptive vision, the shattered world of the Finzi-Continis regains unity.

THE PLACES OF DEATH

With this work, the novelist creates a story of death recollected. The text's initial acknowledgment of the human and material destruction wrought by World War II leads it into another of the author's meditations on the places and theme of death. Bassani's fascination with tombs (the first words in part 1, chapt. 1 are *La tomba*) is partly derived from the funerary tradition inspired by the poet–novelist Ugo Foscolo (1778–1827), whose hymn "Dei sepolcri" ("On Sepulchers," 1807) declares that tombs unite the dead with the living to encourage future generatioins to aspire to greatness. But the novelist's irony undermines the lyrical intensity of a Foscolo whenever it concentrates on the theatric pretentiousness of a tomb like the Finzi-Continis' mausoleum. It is a chance visit to an Etruscan necropolis at Cerveteri in April 1957 through the section of northern Latium that is almost an unbroken cemetery that convinced Celestino to write his story. The naïve perspective of a nine-year-old girl, Giannina, who was accompanying the narrator and her parents on the weekend excursion, awakened Celestino's attention to an analogy between the Etruscan *montarozzi* (burial mounds) and the Finzi-Continis' tomb in Ferrara's Jewish cemetery at the end of Via Montebello. Giannina raises an essential question about the calming effect of time's passing on the anguish caused by death: "why do ancient tombs arouse less sadness than more recent ones?" (p. 251). After more than two millenia, it seemed as if the Etruscans had always been dead. Similarly, this novel creates an impression of timelessness because from the prologue on, readers know that the Finzi-Continis are dead.[23] At Cerveteri, the burial mounds compel Celestino to acknowledge the human need to construct a world safe from historical time: "Past the cemetery threshold . . . each of them possessed a second home . . . eternity no longer had to seem an illusion, a fable, a promise by priests. Even if the future overturned the world at its caprice, there no matter what else in that small closing sacred to the family's dead, in the heart of those tombs where they had taken care to bring along not only their dead but many of the things that made life beautiful and desirable, in that protected, privileged, well-defended corner of the world: at least there nothing would ever change . . ." (p. 252). The eternity of the tomb in the Jewish cemetery might have defeated time if historical and political circumstances had permitted burial there in the family mausoleum for the last of the Finzi-Continis.

That visit to the Etruscan necropolis reminded Celestino of the garish tomb that the patriarchal Moisè had erected for himself and his descendants in an extravagant combination of ancient Egyptian, Minoan, late imperial Roman, and Ostrogothic architectural styles to express the family's desire for isolated grandeur even in the graveyard. But over the years, with the steady advance of vegetation and subsequent neglect, the ostentatious structure had become a grotesque monument to a family's vanity. The mixture of nouveau riche display and subsequent neglectfulness indicate the moral flaws of the Finzi-Continis and prefigure their eventual decline. One could note a disturbing lack of congruence in the architectural styles of the mausoleum and the tasteful, perfect fusion of Renaissance palace with Victorian neo-Gothic mansion in the *magna domus*. The Finzi-Continis, of course, made a cult of death. One of the few projects that Professor Ermanno ever completed was a paper on the inscriptions of the tombstones in the Jewish cemetery at Venice's Lido, which, he decared to the narrator, was one of the most beautiful cemeteries in Europe and where he and Olga had become engaged. After the death of Guido Finzi-Contini in 1914 and his burial in the family mausoleum, Signora Olga continues to dress in mourning: Death and its attributes are distinguishing features of life within the Barchetto del Duca.

In his adoring imitation of the Finzi-Continis, the narrator begins to consider life with a similar funereal visiion that transformed various sites into graveyards: He sees the entrance hall of th public school where final examinations were held as cool and dark like a crypt; the Renaissance-period undeground storehouse where Celestino hid his bicycle in June 1929 resembles one of the Etruscan burial mounds on a small scale. The idea of death so obsesses the narrator that even in his dreams he visualizes the old Finzi-Contini carriage as a hearse to be escorted by the spectral couple of Perotti and his wife, Vittorina. Celestino succumbs to the funereal vision of the Finzi-Continis at the very moment when the earliest Fascist decrees on race forbade newspapers to publish obituary notices about Jews. What the narrator gains from his lordly hosts is the knowledge that individuals often matter most after they die.

For her university degree, Micòl writes a dissertation on Emily Dickinson, who, like Micòl, had cherished life most in the awareness of death's certainty. Micòl once referred to the American poet in English as "Alas poor Emily" (p. 353). A similar sense of barrenness oppressed the lives of both women, for neither married. Micòl doubted if she would ever wed. Her name, in fact, comes from the biblical Michal, David's first and sterile wife. During her absence in Venice, Micòl sends Celestino a translation of a little-discussed poem by Emily Dickinson:

> I died for beauty, but was scarce
> Adjusted in the tomb,
> When one who died for truth was lain
> In an adjoining room.

> He questioned softly why I failed?
> "For beauty," I replied.
> "And I for truth—the two are one;
> We brethren are," he said.
>
> And so, as kinsmen met a night,
> We talked between the rooms,
> Until the moss had reached our lips,
> And covered up our names.

The translation appears almost precisely at the novel's center. In his reply to Micòl, the narrator revises her work by replacing her rendering of *moss* in the last strophe as Italian *erba* (grass) with the literal *muschio*. While Micòl in her study of the American poet can be thought of as the advocate of beauty, Celestino makes himself the interpreter of a pedantic truth. A wedding of beauty and truth occurs only in death, as happens with this novel dedicated to Micòl's memory. For although the dead couple in the poem are separated in adjacent chambers, they manage to communicate until their names are obliterated on the funerary inscriptions. Death and the ending of relationships predominate in Dickinson's poems. The idea of passing from life and being obliterated at its end constitute a challenge in the American poet's work that is paralleled in the Italian novel:

> We must be less than Death
> to be lessened by it—for
> nothing is irrevocable but
> ourselves.[24]

Dickinson recognized a sameness in death and parting, loss and mourning, that made contemplating death a form of dying. The poet, as in the example cited, explored beyond the moment of passing to listen to the voice of the departed within the grave, which stands for physical weariness and spiritual wavering. Ultimately, death appeared as a negative event taking away nature's vitality and beauty. Micòl's version of the American poem is cast in the style of the post romantic Italian poet Giosuè Carducci (1835–1907), who in this novel was a living presence in the Finzi-Contini home because of his supposed letters to Ermanno's mother, Josette, after he had been a guest at the mansion. Carducci's grief before death the destroyer who robs us of loved ones merges with Dickinson's tense consciousness of the paradoxical separation and union in dying. Micòl discerns in Dickinson's poem a kinship of souls in death such as would develop between her and Celestino.

The novel's preoccupation with burial sites transcends Decadentist morbidity, since the tomb figures as the ultimate corner of rest and peace for which the characters yearn. But the pathos of Bassani's work arises from the realization that except for Alberto, the Finzi-Contini family never knew the consolation of burial in the mausoleum because of their death in concentration camps. Instead of representing continuity between generations living in the manor house and forbears in the mausoleum, that monument came to symbolize the brutal interruption of power seeking to make death an instrument of annihilation that obliterates the values that transform dying. As noted before, one of the important words here is *sepolto* (buried), for even the living are buried away: the Finzi-Continis voluntarily behind their walls, the Jews in their spiritual ghettos, and other citizens in fear of living under a totalitarian regime.

CONCLUSION: In solitudine cordis

Space is compressed time, and every spatial image that Celestino evokes renews a precious moment of the past. The pious pilgrimages that the narrator makes with Micòl to sacred places on the estate, like the embarcadero or the coach house, represent a return to stasis that halts time as a bringer of change. All the Finzi-Continis share the fatal illusion that they can sustain the static inertia behind their grand style of life against the pressures of the outside political world. But across the desolation of history, the narrator attempts to achieve a harmony of continuity by integrating the scattered elements of a vanished reality in order to transform successive time into a spatialized time that interrelates all temporal dimensions. Against this aesthetic time, however, there stands destructive time, which constantly introduces dispersal and disunity. The Finzi-Continis exemplify the refusal to accept life as successive time. Two key terms that apply to their attitude and behavior are the verb *fingere* (to pretend) and the adverbial phrase *di nascosto* (secretly): Everyone in the house pretends to ignore the seriousness of Alberto's disease and to dismiss quite lightly the impending political disaster as just another historical lesson of the impossibility of ever becoming assimilated into mainstream society. Secrecy for members of the family and their staff are equivalent to privacy. Deep in her heart, Micòl seems to be aware of their destiny but makes no effort to alter the future course of events. All that concerned Micòl was a present in which she could assert an identity undefined by her relationship with males.

Places and moments join in a lived duration where spatial intervals and temporal phases are fused in the narrator's memories as they gain structure in the novel. By moving on the lofty plane of the Finzi-Contini world, the narrator believes he is entering a terrestrial paradise. In his great novel, Proust makes an observation about the vanished opportunity to know perfection on earth that refers to Celestino's situation: "The only true paradise is always the paradise we have lost."[25] An early poem of Bassani's from the collection *Te lucis ante* (1947) identifies the wasted garden with unrealized happiness: "But here,/here, in this lost garden, here is my paradise." For a long period, Celestino resists acknowledging the false security on which the garden world is founded. The youth has to learn that the insouciance of the Finzi-Continis reflects a spirit of passivity, surrender, and unwillingness to confront reality, for death reigns in the defeated souls of the garden. But before he totally comprehends the menace lurking within the estate's walls, Celestino has to lose his paradise twice: first through rejection by Micòl and later, at the family's destruction.

After the enactment of discriminatory laws, the narrator begins to desert his own home as a place of gloom and despair. He anxiously rushes to the narrow telephone cubicle in his house to receive the calls inviting him to the *magna domus*, in whose warmth and vitality he feels truly alive. In episodes toward the end of part 3 that mark two celebrations of Passover 1939, Celestino's antagonisms toward his family and his rapture at being a guest at the Finzi-Continis' reach a climax of self-delusion that early in part 4 precipitate his exile at Micòl's command. Since Passover commemorates the exodus from Egypt, it affirms the Jewish faith in past, present, and future. When the seder ends with the words "next year in Jerusalem," Hebrews joyously declare their optimism for future liberation from the exile of diaspora. But the 1939 Passover dinner at the narrator's home recalls a funeral or Yom Kippur (the Day of Atonement) because the racial laws renew an earlier age of slavery. The narrator's home on Via Scandiana in the old part of town is so frigid that the dreary holiday meal has to be served in the breakfast room instead of the generally festive living room. Surrounded by relatives mourning recent political events, the young man rebels against the attitude of consternation on the faces of the hopeless celebrants: "I was not dead . . . I was very much alive! . . . Why didn't I run away immediately from that desperate and grotesque gathering of ghosts . . . ?" (p. 374). The novel's binocular vision transfigures this scene by the 1957 narrator's comments on how many of the relatives at that dinner were victims in Nazi crematoria.[26]

When an unexpected phone call invites Celestino to the seder at the Finzi-Continis' home, his gloom at once becomes ecstasy. He dashes into the icy night as if embarking on an adventure. The glacial season is not so much a consideration of low temperatures and incessant northern winds but the reflection of a state of mind: despondency in the household on Via Scandiana over the racial laws; defiant jubilation at the manor house. In contrast to the anguished discussions over subtle interpretations of discrimination on the basis of blood by Celestino's relatives, his hosts at the estate are playing a game of prophecy with a miraculous chalice that predicts the eventual repairs of the tennis court, Alberto's abandonment of his university studies, the coming war, and the triumph of Stalin's forces but resorts to a sibyline mysteriousness regarding possible marriage by Micòl. As for the Finzi-Continis and many of the narrator's family members, a similar fate awaited them despite their mood that night of the two seders, since they all failed to realize the enormity of the threat requiring them to flee their homes. That unwillingness to accept reality is reflected by the fact that the author does not truly bring either dinner to an end. The narrator merely imagines the first part breaking up, with guests departing but lingering to exchange worried, fearful "good" wishes by the wind-swept front door. To render that unreal close, verbs in the past conditional and past perfect tense predominate. Similarly, festivities at the mansion do not cease when the chapter concludes: "That night would never end" (p. 383). As some critics have remarked,[27] the Passover celebrations, in truth, resemble the Last Supper, where death follows. With the loss of relatives and his friends, on that night which should never have drawn to a close, the narrator foresees the end of his hope for winning Micòl's love.

Of the novel's major characters, only Celestino survives the war years. Malnate, the communist, ironically dies fighting for Italy's Anti-Bolshevik Expeditionary Force in the Soviet Union. Even by having survived, the narrator remains isolated from the others in the garden's magical circle; and his survival inspires a responsibility to search through and understand the past: a task to be continued in Bassani's following novel, *Behind the Door*. It is Celestino's father, rather than the Finzi-Continis, who gives him the insight and inspires the strength of will to abandon empty illusions and gain the maturity that does save his life. Coming home late one night during the summer of 1939, the narrator for the first time recognizes in his father's ghostly pallor all the suffering that has drained away his parent's vitality following the Fascists' betrayal of Italian Jews. The rebellious son's fierce resentment toward the father as an authority figure vanishes in the awareness that the older man has also recently endured loss and rejection. Because the father understands Celestino's torment on failing to conquer Micòl's resistance, he attempts to make his son see that ordeal as a form of death that could lead to a new life: "In life, if one wants to understand, really understand how affairs of this world stand, a person *has to* die at least once. And since that's the law, it's better to die young when one has so much time ahead to pull oneself together and start all over . . . ." (p. 441, italics Bassani's). The end of estrangement between the narrator and his father, expressed by a tender embrace between the former combatants, moves Celestino to renounce his love for Micòl and the cosmos of the Finzi-Continis. Because of his experiences within the confines of the Barchetto del Duca, the narrator spiritually died. If he had succeeded in marrying Micòl and taking a place in the *magna domus*, Celestino would have perished with the members of the family deported to Germany. Disappointment in love brings the narrator to knowledge of himself. Unlike their young guest, the Finzi-Continis lack the ability to integrate their experiences and live again. Theirs proves to be a vocation for solitude that leads to extermination. Because Celestino has briefly visited the garden of the Finzi-Continis, he learns that the sole reality is that of the heart—changing and forever changed. The place where the Finzi-Continis were to find their eternal paradise was in the heart and memory of an admiring outsider.

4

The Place of Betrayal

Toward an Inner Chronology

Toward an Inner Chronology

It would have been tempting to analyze *Dietro la porta (Behind the Door)* before studying Bassani's other two novels in first-person narration, since events in this work begin in autumn 1929 following the narrator's June meeting with Micòl Finzi-Contini outside the walls of her estate and continue through the school year to the summer vacation 1930. Since the action of *The Gold-Rimmed Eyeglasses* occurs most importantly in 1937 and that of *The Garden of the Finzi-Continis* from October 1938 to the end of August 1939, one might conform to an outward chronology by examining the narrator's adolescent development as Bassani represents it in *Behind the Door.* The author expressly indicates that the literary *persona* of this third and final novel of first-person narrative is the same individual who, in *The Garden of the Finzi-Continis,* failed his final examination in mathematics for the academic year 1928–29 and later had to pass a second test before the beginning of the fall term.[1] But in determining the structure of *The Romance of Ferrara,* Bassani decided on an arrangement according to original date of publication.

As a novel issued in 1964, *Behind the Door* presents the reflections of a Jewish narrator in his late forties looking back at the period from October 1929 to June 1930, long before the Fascist government ever contemplated an anti-Semitic policy. The author also assumes that his readers are acquainted with the preceding two novels and will evaluate this work as illuminating a dark period in the narrator's life. Instead of studying the corrosive effects of racial legislation, this novel examines the pain that people of the same age and social class cause one other without specific regard to religion or ethnic origin.[2] Consequently, it is imperative to respect Bassani's ordering of experience to appreciate the narrator's attempt to arrive at an understanding of the traumatic events of his lifetime.

Here, for the first time, the narrator ceases to be a witness or a secondary actor to become the novel's protagonist. As the work's primary figure, the adolescent hero studies himself as a victim of both his own undisclosed impulses and the treachery of his classmates in the initial year of the *liceo*, the higher division of Italy's secondary schools. The movement across Bassani's fictional writings is that of an extradiegetic narrator in the five nuclear tales of Ferrara commenting from outside the main actions toward an increasingly intradiegetic narrator in *The Gold-Rimmed Eyeglasses* and *The Garden of the Finzi-Continis* participating in major events until with *Behind the Door* the narrator becomes the protagonist. As a self-reflexive work of fiction, this novel functions like an autobiography, since it creates its own voice to comment on its inner life—not because it resembles the author's life.[3] At the beginning of the epilogue in *The Garden of the Finzi-Continis*, one can anticipate the transformation of the secondary narrator into a primary figure: "My story with Micòl Finzi-Contini ends here. And thus it is proper that this tale should also come to an end, now, since all that I could add to it would no longer regard her but, as the case would be, only myself." (p. 449). At last, the recording "I" moves to the fiction's foreground as its central character in his painful effort to question his conscience and assess his guilt in life's all-pervasive evil. Instead of relating the acts of exclusion that follow official anti-Semitism, the present novel transcends political considerations to portray a youth's awakening to a dreadful sense of isolation and his fear of never belonging to the world of his contemporaries.

Bassani has written this work on more than one level, sometimes speaking with the voice of an adolescent interacting with his contemporaries at school, sometimes as an adult with knowledge of the deaths of the parents of his peers and the chaos that the Second World War caused in the careers of former classmates. The narrator succeeds in recreating how he once viewed reality as an adolescent, so that the work reflects the presence of a bewildered, lonely boy and a middle-aged man who still bears the psychic scars of his first year of *liceo* in Ferrara. What the narrator records here is the anguished separation from a childhood sense of being able to participate in the society of his classmates. This book seems to contradict itself because on one level, it recognizes that the past always remains part of an individual's present and future, but, on another, it is an attempt to evade and conceal a past and enduring truth.

With the movement in narrative voice between the past "I" of 1929–30 and the writing "I," one notes the function of memory that permits the adult to discover meaning in events from his early adolescence that he could not interpret at the time he experienced them. As frequently in Bassani's fiction, the mind recalls the past with extreme precision, as in mentioning the exact number of doors along the gloomy corridor of the Guarini Liceo or the make of the bicycle owned by the narrator's chief academic rival, Carlo Cattolica. As a voluntary act of human reason, memory allows the narrator to bridge the years that racist laws, the war, and the regime of terror during the Fascist Social

Republic seemingly disrupted forever. But memory here is one of affliction
without hope of ever restoring individual integrity.

An oppressive feeling of pathology and spiritual darkness predominates from
this novel's opening paragraph:

> The years past . . . have not succeeded in healing a pain that has remained
> there like a secret wound, bleeding in secret. To cure it? To free myself of it? I
> do not know if it will ever be possible? (p. 453)

Frustration prevails here in the present because of an incurable wound that
secretly (note the repetition of *segreta* and *in segreto* to stress the hidden pain that
always throbs beneath the surface of everyday existence) persists from a period in
the narrator's life that he calls among the darkest (*più neri*) that he ever
experienced. The mere passage of time fails to heal the sorrow that the protagonist hopes to understand and make his readers understand. For the narrator
continues to believe that in his soul he was contaminated by a metaphorical
infectious social disease carried by his treacherous classmate and false friend,
Luciano Pulga, during the winter and spring of 1930. Not only did the puny
Pulga bear in him the plague that afflicted the narrator, but the deceitful boy
used to amuse himself with thoughts of being reincarnated as a microbe like the
syphilis bacillus or tuberculosis germ that gnawed away at its host over decades.
Syphilis and tuberculosis depend on time—they secretly fester and destroy the
stricken individual. While tuberculosis casts a romantic aura of lost vitality over
its victims, venereal disease debases with a corruption that appears moral as well
as physical. The contagious wound that the hero contracts from his devious
classmate would, in his theory, touch other members of his family, especially his
mother. Actual illness, such as the continual sore throats that bother the
protagonist and occasion a very significant absence from school, serves as an ego
defence mechanism regressing him to an oral stage away from the genital threat
posed by his faithless "friend."[4] As within a circle of despair, the novel's final
chapter begins by speaking of an ulcer that secretly, slowly, and lazily festers away
with no hope of medication. For although recalling the past does produce a
continuous self, memory offers no healing power to treat the spiritual wound.[5]
Remembering renews the affliction.

As a novel that examines the moment in life when a youth crosses the
threshold between the unawareness of childhood and the disruptive adoslecent
awakening to sexual capacities, this work can be classified as a juvenile novel,
especially since its main characters are all secondary-school students. Although
Bassani has never stated that he intended *Behind the Door* primarily for adolescent readers, it has exerted an enormous appeal on the young for portraying the
sensual and social crisis of a boy at the onset of puberty. In Italian literature, it
brings to mind Alberto Moravia's two novellas of adolescence, *Agostino* (1945)
and *La Disubbidienza* (*Disobedience*, 1948), particularly the former for the pro-

tagonist's agonizing discovery of his mother as a sexual creature. For its compression (running only ninety pages in the 1980 edition of *The Romance of Ferrara*), the work is reminiscent of Robert Musil's brief novel *Young Törless* (1906), depicting school as an arena of unrelenting cruelty and erotic experimentation of a humiliating nature.

With its first-person point of view and its distinction between the hero as a sensitive outsider and his contemporaries as self-assertive vulgarians, the Italian novel also recalls J. D. Salinger's *The Catcher in the Rye* (1951), although *Behind the Door* possesses little of the humor pervading the American tale of a young man's isolation. Writing in the early 1960s during a period of ever-increasing restlessness and discontent among young people in Western Europe, Bassani moved beyond what James in his nouvelle *The Pupil* called "the morning twilight of childhood" to represent the lonely darkness of adolescence.[6]

In its compact structure, *Behind the Door* falls into four parts. The first part covers the opening three chapters during the fall term of 1929, with the protagonist's unhappy advancement from the lower *ginnasio* division to the *liceo*, where his Section B class is merged with the haughty members of Section A. That initial part introduces the leitmotif of exile and the hero's contradictory longing to establish a rapport with his academic competitor, Carlo Cattolica. In chapter 4, the second part beings after Christmas vacation, with the arrival in class of the future traitor, Luciano Pulga, who at once arouses repugnance and pity in the narrator until Pulga succeeds in insinuating himself into the latter's home as a study companion. At the end of chapter 5, Pulga's influence over the protagonist is revealed by his host's growing dependence on the flattering attention of an admirer, who in the following two chapters gains ascendancy over his passive friend. A campaign by the gang of three—Cattolica and his liegemen Boldini and Grassi—occupies the novel's third part from chapters 8–12, with their cruel scheme to wound the hero by luring him to Cattolica's home where his illusions of friendship are shattered by Pulga's treachery. The concluding three chaptrs make up part 4 and the protagonist's flight from truth past the title's door, his retreat within his classroom, the end of the school year, and his farewell encounter with the disloyal Pulga during a beachside vacation. During those two academic semesters, the unconsciously ordered world of the hero's childhood is destroyed by treachery, savage intrigue, and the revelation of his barely repressed sexuality.[7]

Language in this novel both reflects the crudities of the main character's scholastic milieu and ironically comments on the pettiness of his classmates and the arrogance of his instructors. To recapture the explosive resentment and confusion of adolescence, Bassani abandoned the art prose of *The Garden of the Finzi-Continis* for a deliberately unpolished style corresponding to the vernacular of *liceo* students. Throughout the work, the voice of loneliness from the adult narrator predominates from a distance of more than thirty years. Fragmentation in both direct dialogue and substitutionary speech indicates the psychological tensions in the protagonist, who consistently strives to suppress before others and himself disturbing erotic drives. The author here wishes to employ language to reproduce mental process during a period of physical and emotional upheaval. In rendering the self-betraying speech of schoolboys, the text shifts from the pretentiousness of middle-class youths rigorously educated in classical and modern languages to the crude reality of describing a classmate like Pulga as a *leccaculo* (ass licker). Luciano reveals his vulgar nature by dismissing his father, a village physician of limited income, as a *testardo di un cretino* (a stubborn idiot), while referring to older women who meet young lovers in hotels of ill repute as *pollastre* (pullets).

Similes describing beings as animals in appearance and behavior become one of the motifs of the novel. On entering the classroom, Pulga first suggests to the protagonist a wading bird with thin legs, beaklike nose, and in his search for an empty desk, a pathetic need to find a nest. Depth psychologists interpret the comparison to a bird with an open beak as a projection of oral-sadistic impulses.[8] Luciano's resemblance to winged creatures becomes less horrid when he cautiously explores the hero's garden on first visiting there: groping around unknown territory like a small, lonely swamp bird. Even late in the work, when the narrator originally learns of Pulga's possible faithlessness, the former holds onto the image of a defenseless, puny child with flamingo legs desperately needing protection. There exists here an ambivalence between the bird of prey and the frightened little bird seeking refuge. But in Cattolica's cynically accurate evaluation, Pulga recalls a mongrel totally lacking in dignity as he begs for admission to others' homes. Those animal references form a network that strips most characters of their human status: the Latin professor has eyes like a green lizard; Cattolica and the hero tentatively draw close to each other in the manner of cuttlefish (perhaps an allusion to Eugenio Montale's famous poetic text, *Cuttlefish Bones* of 1925) stretching forth tentacles in an ink-colored sea; Cattolica ensnares Luciano in the betrayal scene like a cat playing with a mouse; and a nouveau riche family like the protagonist's brings to mind sharks (*pescecani*, dogfish). The world of this novel turns into a jungle with wild, devouring, or slow-witted beasts until, in the eleventh chapter, a verbal explosion takes place when Pulga affirms his fascination with the theory of metempsychosis in Plato's *Phaedo* and proceeds to characterize classmates and teachers as vipers, cobras, owls, ducks, earthworms (an instructor already called half-pint due to his short stature), pigs, hyenas, moles, camels, horses, lice, eagles, falcons, and elephants. Luciano regards his "protector" (the hero) as a large dog of good breeding though not pedigreed waiting for a little mongrel to come along and lead it through the streets. This novelistic bestiary reflects the work's concentration on experiences that debase individuals.[9]

Sports also function as a metaphor for life with its competitive striving to surpass others. Although, ideally, participating in a sport like soccer should socialize biological drives by teaching young people to cooperate in a team effort, in this novel, struggle rather than collaboration results from participating in games. Taking part in athletic events is also related to libidinal urges with an underlying genital symbolism. Thus, the protagonist's desire to play soccer is derived from a failed attempt to overcompensate sexual anxieties, particularly the castration fear of being defeated by his rivals. Demonstrating skill in athletic competitions enables the narrator to withstand the criticisms of his seemingly never satisifed father. Sports also permit the protagonist to avoid the temptation to masturbate, a habit that he had not developed at the time of the novel's events, to the derision of the experienced Pulga.[10] The ambiguity between sports and sexuality emerges in chapter 6 in what the narrator in recalling it admits might have been only a dream: an Easter vacation game on the parade ground where he fell down, slightly injuring his knee, and pretended to pass out in order to enjoy the concerned attention of his soccer teammates. But on opening his eyes, the youth saw only Pulga standing over him. The language of the Italian original betrays an obsessive gentital preoccupation: *dritto* (erect), *enorme* (enormous), *gigantesco* (gigantic), either describing Luciano looming over him or imagining his phallus. For elsewhere in the novel, some of the same adjectives unequivocally refer to Pulga's exposed penis. In addition to their subliminatory role, sports also symbolize the fight to emerge as the champion performer, paralleling contention in the classroom for academic prominence. Excelling in games brings power, status, and admiration among peers. It is, in fact, both sexual and social insecurity that propels the hero to join in the battle of games.

Whether the narrator looks back to the playing field, school, or his classmates' homes, it is an overwhelming need to communicate to others the life-long pain experienced during that first *liceo* year that summons forth his multileveled linguistic resources. In order to study that attempt at communication this chapter, as already demonstrated, sometimes employs psychoanalytic theory to probe beneath the surface of statements. Examining scenes of exile, relationships of dominance and subservience, and symbolic structure of motives and episodes also involves comparing variations between the original version of 1964 and the revision in *The Romance of Ferrara* that reveal patterns of repression. All the linguistic resources in this text are attempts to translate and understand the depths of *human* suffering.

THE DIVIDING LINE OF EXILE

Perhaps more than in any other fictional work by Bassani, the first-person narrator moves along the darkest corridors of past memories in *Behind the Door*. Images of interiority and prison closure entrap the protagonist without avenues of escape. In contrast to *The Catcher in the Rye*, the hero in the Italian novel never enjoys a temporary flight from reality as does Holden Caulfield in his odyssey through New York City. While in Bassani's tales and other novels descriptions of landscape and seasonal changes offer a brief outlet from op-pressive situations, here nature descriptions are almost completely absent from the work's static, tense scenes. Setting emphasizes isolation, whether sought as voluntary exile or imposed as a form of exclusion. Repeatedly, the narrator speaks of invisible lines of demarcation or imaginary (but all too real) barriers that separate students in his new class from each other, even when, as in his case with Cattolica, two pupils share the same desk.

The novel moves through gloomy tunnels and hallways in the protagonist's mind where he can see no way out of his degrading reliance on the compan-ionship of the debased and debasing Luciano Pulga. Those dark, endless pas-sageways through the psyche symbolize the subterranean depths of the unconscious with hidden threats of sexual aggression. In his determined effort to hide the truth from himself and others, the hero never succeeds in making his way through those narrow tunnels of the soul.

Recognition of oneself as an alien and the need to mark clearly the confines of one's personal exile are the major themes of this novel. Because of his earlier failure in mathematics, the protagonist began the school year in 1929 feeling cut off from other students, including those from his original section. The youth took as his motto a line from a canzone by Dante: "The exile which is given to me, I hold as an honor unto myself." Just as the Florentine poet had risen above the bitterness of an unjust banishment, the schoolboy cherishes his exile as a challenge to resist the pettiness and cruelty of his contemporaries. Like Dante, this *liceo* student seeks a retreat of noble solitude away from a world that ridicules tender sentiments and repays kindness with treachery. Here, as elsewhere in Bassani's writings, two verbs that rarely occur are *avvicinarsi* and *venire vicino* (to draw near, to come near), since rapprochement between individuals almost always leads to compromise and disappointment. There can be no private sectors for friendship to develop—merely continual alienation.

Until his entrance at the Guarini Liceo, the protagonist seems to have adjusted quite well to school. But starting the upper division coincides with the beginning of puberty, and the hero displaces sexual anxieties with intellectual and social fears. School always forces students to sublimate their libidinal drives, and that demand for sublimation is achieved by strict teachers acting as parent surrogates, especially at the time of this novel's action, when public education in Fascist Italy rigorously followed the guidelines of reforms by the philosopher Giovanni Gentile, minister of education from 1922 to 1924. The authoritarian attitude of teachers transformed them in the eyes of students into castrating figures of vengeance as they ruled the classrooms by intimidation and arousing guilt in their pupils. In the protagonist's reaction to school, one can observe a paradigm of his relationship to society at large: anguished withdrawal for feeling different from an uncomprehending world.

That new academic environment so acutely stirs the hero's discontent that on the book's first page the impersonal verb *piacere* occurs three times in parallel negative phrases to underscore the vehemence of his emotions: "Non mi piaceva l'aula . . . " ("I did not like the classroom . . . "); "Non mi piacevano i nuovi insegnanti . . . " ("I did not like the new teachers . . . "); "Non mi piacevano i nuovi compagni . . . " ("I did not like the new classmates . . . ," p. 453). Such resistance to change, accompanied by self-admitted absurd attachment to his original section of classmates, discloses a deep-seated unhappiness that involves far more than the school setting. At times, the main character tries to relieve his anxiety by playing trite adolescent word games involving observations about his schoolmates, remarking that the surnames of most of the female students ended in *-ini*, such as Bergamini, Bolognini, Santini, in a comical evocation of families of grocers, tradesmen, and cattle dealers. But such infantile pastimes failed to lessen his depression.

At school, the place that a student either chose to occupy in a classroom or was made to occupy not only communicated relative rank and peer esteem but determined an individual's attitude toward the academic setting. Position expressed status. The classroom was a battleground for the favored seats nearest the teacher's desk, while boys with prior failures in major subjects and all girls sat in the back of the room close to the window. Those students who usually ended up in the back of the classroom were accustomed to viewing school as a prison. Formal arrangement, then, followed a prisonlike system of punishments and rewards according to space. Angry and ashamed over his earlier failure in mathematics, the protagonist seeks exile in the back row. But escape proves impossible when the professor of classical languages compels him to share a desk in the front with Cattolica, the student with the highest grades in the combined sections. From that involuntary cooccupation would come no comradeship but the entrapment that wounded the hero for his entire life.

Because two students had to share a desk, the selection of a desk companion could increase prestige or cause ridicule. As a newcomer from out of town, Luciano Pulga did not fit into either the old A or B sections, and he encountered such a frigid reception that he had to take the solitary seat in the back that the narrator had initially attempted to occupy. Caught between the rival factions, Pulga would never have belonged anywhere if the protagonist had not made him a protégé. Throughout the novel, the miniature society of schoolboys extends the maliciousness of the classroom to the outer world by sharing space or denying admission into their cliques. On street corners, closely knit groups gathered, companions clinging tenaciously to each other to prevent newcomers from usurping their posts. The most eagerly sought after place for students to band together was at each other's homes, meeting in late afternoon to review assignments. As Bassani emphasizes, those homes sometimes became places of conspiracy and betrayal. Until fall 1929, the hero had always studied at the home of Otello Forti, his deskmate since elementary school. But after failing a make-up examination, Otello suddenly summoned up the courage of the defeated and decided on self-imposed exile at a boarding school in Padua. For the whole autumn term the main character must study in solitude. A Christmas vacation reunion at Otello's home on Via Montebello on the elegant northern side of town leaves the protagonist even more desolate than before, since his former friend, by then growing remote, keeps him at a formal distance, seated in an armchair in a room that he once considered almost his own. That loss of friendship causes the hero to feel like a widower (*vedovo*) and leaves him open to exploitation by an ingratiating traitor hoping to find admission to a comfortable home.

Pride in one's home characterizes that band of schoolboys, all of whom come from middle-class professional backgrounds. Unlike the situation in Moravia's *Agostino,* this novel does not involve the confrontation between a boy of well-to-do bourgeois circumstances and contemporaries from the lowest economic class. Although Pulga stands somewhat apart from the others, since his father does not enjoy the income of a private medical practice and the family has to settle in a modest apartment in an unfashionable district, the boy still shares the outlook and expectations of his middle-class peers. The enormity of Luciano's betrayal of the protagonist is evident when considering Pulga's delight at being invited to study at his friend's large, pleasant home, whose size amazes the guest with its fifty rooms on several floors divided into apartments paying rent to the hero's father, while an entire floor of twenty rooms is reserved for the protagonist's family. But the difference in the two families' economic means (the hero's father held a medical degree but never practiced the profession as a point of honor) along with similarity in aspirations also accounts for the fierce resentment that consumes Luciano. For Pulga's charge against the central character is his intolerable vanity over his home and its possessions, which he shared condescendingly with Pulga as if granting a special privilege that required undying gratitude. Luciano correctly understands that his friend's material possessions demand admiration.

Perhaps the chief reason for the wall between the protagonist and his competitor, Carlo Cattolica, is each one's insistence on the superiority of his home and belongings. The two boys hold too much in common simply to yield a point to the other. Cattolica acts as if only his world exists and to enter it is a unique pleasure, so that he never deigns to visit the homes of other classmates. In the spacious bedroom-study of his modern-styled townhouse, Cattolica rules like a medieval lord with his vassals Boldini and Grassi treating other guests, such as Pulga and the protagonist, to their scorn. Impelled by a desire to demonstrate his superiority, Cattolica invites the hero to his luxurious home with the aim of stripping him of the illusion of friendship with Pulga. In their vicious assault, Cattolica and his fellow conspirators closet the protagonist in the parents' bedroom, which adjoins the study area, so that he may listen to his new-found friend mock him and his family. That dimly lit bedroom, which becomes the tomb of the narrator's dream of having a companion, takes on a sepulchral irreality in his eyes—reminding him of an underground crypt with the twin beds as massive gravestones in an association of Thanatos and Eros. The space of disenchantment and betrayal seems immense like the ocean, sweeping the hero along on waves of despair to drown him. After Cattolica's accusation of Pulga's faithlessness is confirmed, the protagonist does not emerge from behind the door to confront the traitor and satisfy the sadistic conspirators by turning the study into a boxing ring. For here, the only door that has opened—to the home of a desk mate—led to unrelenting aggression against the hero.

In the dark bedroom of Cattolica's parents, the hero discovers a mirror of his martyrdom: a holy picture of an androgynous Christ (illuminated by a very low-wattage bulb) with blond hair and blue eyes. In the image of Jesus' large red heart, the Jewish youth discovers a projection of his own suffering spirit. But, of course, the Hebrew outsider realizes that he can never fully conform to that Nordic portrayal of the supreme victim of treachery. Once before in the novel, the hero identified with Christ—just after Epiphany, in early January 1930, at the opening of the winter semester when, one morning, he visited the Church of Jesus for the first time. The baroque theatricality of the Chiesa di Gesù immediately impressed the non-Christian observer with its attempt to arouse lachrymose sentiments by exhibiting life-sized painted wooden statues of the Pietà with attendant holy figures in petrified gestures and attitudes. Both the protagonist and Christ were betrayed by a Judas and suffered from the plots of hostile conspirators. But, as frequently in Bassani's works, a heavy irony pervades the two episodes of identification between the hero and Christ. A morbid, pathological quality characterizes the religious outsider's fascination with grotesque and even banal images of Christianity. Also in the church episode, the protagonist encounters Cattolica at prayer and joins him in their first extended conversation. Christ and Cattolica represent that otherness to which the Hebrew youth is condemned to remain alien.[11]

When action does arise away from the enclosed oppressiveness of school, home, or church, it is usually outside on the battleground of athletic events. Although Cattolica always remains in the narrator's recollections as the first time he saw him running in the school courtyard like a champion racer, the haughty youth never voluntarily participates in sports because he feels superior to such childish activities. With his puny physique, Pulga succeeds in being exempted from physical education classes, and of the novel's central triad of characters, only the protagonist wants to be on the playing field trying to be one with his teammates. But after his springtime bout of tonsilitis, the convalescent hero becomes a wretched spectator feeling sorry for himself. In that abject state of self-pity, the main character easily falls prey to Cattolica's deceitful display of sympathetic interest. Thus, even the sidelines of athletic events become a site for entrapment and treachery.

As usual in Bassani's literary world, window vistas and interior gardens provide temporary relief from imprisoning restrictions. Even Guzzo, the tyrannical instructor of Greek and Latin, liked to pause a few minutes before class to look out the window. On a warm spring night, after a telephone conversation with Cattolica, who accuses the protagonist of being naïve about Pulga, the narrator opens his bedroom window:

> It was a lovely starry night, moonless but very bright. Down in the garden the shapes of the trees stood out distinctly: first the magnolia, a bit farther on the fir, and down there (in the corner where the three arches of the portico entrance ended) the linden. Among the flower beds, the milky white of the gravel, and in the midst of the open court (even brighter) that was situated before the dark hollow of the portico a black dot, unmoving: perhaps a stone, or maybe Philomena, the century-old family tortoise . . . . (Pp. 507–8)

The pet does not respond to the boy's call. A perfect symmetry occurs between the trees and the archway of the portico entrance to encapsule this enclosed, human-made inner world. But it is a rather sterile inscape shining with gravel and not wide open like a large park or the woods; in truth, an unresponsive space. The garden that holds the happiest memories for the hero is the one at Otello Forti's home, since it was a place of experience shared in friendship: a model Mediterranean house garden with a handsome central lawn used for croquet games, a rustic hut, and even a small wooded hillock to breed rabbits. Aside from that garden recollection in bluish, chiaroscuro light emblematic of childhood playtime, the protagonist gains another outlook on a lost world when he visits Cattolica's house to prepare for the arrival of Luciano Pulga. Turning away from Carlo and his two henchmen, the Hebrew youth peers out the study window to behold a panorama that stretches into the valley of the flooding Po:

> Having disappeared a few seconds before behind the sugar refinery opposite the railway station, the sun was no longer bothersome, and the vista of the area was all vegetable and flower gardens that extended from the Cattolica house to the city walls and then beyond the unbounded plain. The view at once made me want to be over there together with those little boys atop the walls running after a ball . . . . (P. 514)

The adolescent's thoughts move spatially and temporally: back to the time when he was a little child chasing balls and unaware of plots and betrayals. Or else he longs to be on a train with open windows, setting out from town or perhaps on a trolley that follows the river's right bank. All the images are ones of escape in time or space, but the protagonist at that moment has no where to go except behind the dreaded door from which he will emerge "alone, forever" (p. 514). This window vista outward to a boundless expanse stands in ironical juxtaposition to the central character's hemmed-in isolation. Neither interior nor exterior views ultimately offer evasion from loneliness.[12]

Feeling a metaphorical door slammed in his face for life after the revelation of betrayal, the hero never fully leaves his protective hiding place, not even in the confessions of this text. After stealing out of Cattolica's house without assaulting Pulga, this victim of treachery later completes his total exile with a dignity and courage worthy of Dante by requesting to move from his seat beside Carlo to exchange a post in the back row with Luciano—thus appropriately placing tormentor and betrayer side by side. Forming a party unto himself like the medieval Florentine poet, the narrator never gives his false companion the satisfaction of explaining why he broke off with him.

In the novel's final chapter, there occurs the work's only scene of uninterrupted natural view, at the beach resort where the hero and Pulga say goodby to each other forever, since Luciano's father is establishing a private practice in Bologna. The Adriatic stretches out to meet the sky in a mother-of-pearl mergence that recalls a canvas by De Pisis. The boys become part of that seascape by rowing into the water, with the protagonist later swimming while Luciano crouches in fear in their boat. Ordinarily, on an unconscious level, swimming represents Eros, but here the sexually expert youth can not swim, unlike his chaste companion exhibiting the Hawaian crawl stroke. Ironically, though, the hero holds a limited advantage over the traitor, for by withholding the truth from him, the hero is denying it to himself. Living in a world without enclaves of sincerity or purity,[13] the main character looks to the sea here as he had to window and garden vistas for renewal of values of personal worth and integrity. But the space in which the protagonist forever dwells is an inner state of personal exile.

THE MONSTRUOUS ENCOUNTER WITH EVIL

Bassani constructs the novel around the triangular relationship between the hero, Cattolica, and Pulga. All attempts by the central character to reach the other two classmates end in disaster. Cattolica is the supreme godlike figure, who ends the school year with highest honors while the hero takes second place. When the protagonist tries to bring Carlo down to his alien level by commenting that Cattolica might be of Jewish origin since his surname was the name of a town and many Italian Hebrews were named after towns, the rival reacts with outrage to confirm his family's status as old Christians. Indeed, Carlo's last name has the ring of age-old Catholicism. Cattolica's physical image in the narrator's mind remains that of a face in profile, like a portrait on a coin to impart a stamp of singular importance. On a nonverbal level, Cattolica always sends his competitor, from the beginning of their forced relationship as deskmates, numerous cues to contradict the charade of mutual courtesy and respect they acted out in class: a frigid turning of Carlo's face to signify rejection, the refusal to lean over and "collaborate" on a difficult Latin assignment, a manner of holding his neck and back perfectly rigid to stay apart. The hero reveals his subjection to the rival by imitating some of those physical traits. Unlike any of his classmates, Cattolica has a regular girlfriend to whom he is engaged—a sign of his maturity and commitment compared to the others. Carlo delights in playing puppetmaster to those who submit to his dominance, like Grassi and Boldini. His plan to debase his chief rival by luring Pulga to the study indicates, however, a basic insecurity that seeks a victim to reaffirm supremacy. Whenever someone or something interests him, Cattolica has the habit of bending his head forward like an animal evaluating possible prey. Because Carlo's family moves to Turin in 1933 just after his successful graduation from *liceo*, the narrator never learns what becomes of him. Cattolica remains attached to the events of that traumatic year in the hero's life as one of its two enormous disappointments. The victorious rival has an emasculating effect on his defeated competitor. Every art of dissimulation seems to be in Carlo's grasp as he draws the protagonist into his trap by feigned displays of sympathy and repeated telephone calls of concern at his being duped by Luciano. The traits of will power, tenacity, discipline, and mental concentration that bring Cattolica success in his studies figure in his assault on his competitor. It is that very confidence in exercising his powers and judgment that causes the hero to admire Carlo. The central character's weakness and passivity become evident in comparison to Cattolica's decisiveness. Because of Carlo Cattolica's apparent near perfection, the hero will always adore and hate him.[14]

Although Pulga's originally seems to be a slave, the devious boy soon proves who the actual master is in regard to his Jewish benefactor. The weakest in physical stature among the novel's central triad of characters, Luciano displays equivocal traits: a bluish stare from his eyes as cold as an Alpine glacier; droplets of perspiration over his upper lip indicating tension at not being accepted by the class; blond hair offensively redolent with brilliantine, recalling adult males on the prowl for women. With Pulga, the narrator devotes more attention to details of person and clothing than with any other character in the attempt to develop a word painting of evil incarnate. Above all, Luciano wishes to invade the privacy of others. As a voyeur, he used to peer through a keyhole at erotic liaisons in the low-class Ferrarese hotel where he and his family stayed before finding an apartment. The hero's casual question whether or not the Pulga apartment has central heating occasions the breakdown in formality that at first kept their study sessions at a safe distance. Luciano's crime against his generous friend constitutes a rape of the soul. By compelling the protagonist to join him in mutual phallic exhibitions Pulga asserts his physical superiority as a male and ridicules his host for having always refrained from indulging his libidinal urges. But Luciano's greatest act of cruelty consists in denouncing the moral character of the hero's mother before Cattolica and his two friends, portraying her in lascivious terms that forever destroy that protagonist's pure and virtuous image of her. The boy poisons his friend's entire future existence. From an admiring underling with ingratiatingly courteous manners that charmed the hero's mother, Pulga reverses roles to triumph as a superior, if nonhuman creature.[15]

If envy corrupts Pulga, then feelings of inferiority condition the hero's relationship with Luciano and Carlo. Although the protagonist senses that intimacy with Pulga involves some vague menace, his ambivalent emotions of repulsion and attraction leave him powerless to resist Pulga's manipulative strategies. Even when that relationship brings no warmth but only a degrading realization that familiarity deprives him of the respect assured by social distance, the protagonist at least has the illusion that in the eyes of other classmates there is one person who values his friendship. Entrapment by Cattolica, of course, robs the hero of any illusions and forces him into an all-encompassing isolation.

Between the protagonist and Pulga there develops a sadomasochistic relationship with definite homoerotic overtones. Nothing ever occurs, since both boys retreat at tense moments, as when Luciano hurries home one evening during a storm rather than stay for dinner and spend the night sleeping in his friend's bedroom. Because of the hero's extreme agitation at the time of mutual exhibitionism, Pulga later denounces him in the betrayal scene as a latent homosexual, labeling him *finocchio*—the equivalent of queer or fairy. Even though some homosexual play fits into adolescent sensual experimentation and comparing individual physiological development is considered normal behavior by psychologists,[16] the protagonist's sudden pallor and loss of composure alert Luciano to a possible erotic attraction. In the ninth chapter, following the call from Cattolica first accusing Pulga of treachery, the hero lies naked in bed imagining a violent confrontation at school with Luciano where he thrashes Luciano like a gangster being punished in the movies by a ferocious James Cagney. Significantly, the 1980 version of the novel for *The Romance of Ferrara* does not include the movie simile, nor does it feature the following passage blending violence with sexuality:

> I saw myself striking him without pity; and meanwhile my penis had stiffened, as when, a child, I would spy unseen through the half-opened kitchen door at the cook (she was named Ines, a big, complacent peasant women with a maternal manner) as she disemboweled a chicken.

What the hero experienced as a child in the kitchen was the connection between cruelty and sexuality. Thoughts of brutality arouse an erection, for both striking Pulga and witnessing the disemboweling symbolize genital excitation. Since the penis often functions as the executive organ of the ego, the stiffening of the member represents the violent assertion of the self. The passage cited here (which appeared in the original 1964 version) does suggest transferred voyeurism and Oedipal desire through a strengthened genital position.[17] While Pulga initiates the hero to evil, an act of vengeance against the traitor would function as the protagonist's initiation into manhood. The central character, however, always remains a passive creature accustomed to sitting and watching.

Pulga's savagery consists in striking the Jewish youth in the most vulnerable part of his psychic being: his bond with his mother. Luciano and the narrator both perceive that the signora is overjoyed to use the guest as a means of keeping her son at home in the afternoons and evenings. The woman rewards the visitor with an abundant five o'clock snack with delicious pastries, for one of the first weapons of maternal control is the gratification of oral desire. On the day when final grades were posted, the hero returns home and tries to evade his mother's inquiries about his marks by going to his room. With her repeated calls from her seat in the garden she appears, like a princess, to be courting her son, a prince, on his balcony. The family structure reveals a somewhat prematurely aged husband (sign of declining potency) yielding with some protests to a sweetly insistent wife.

The hero's vulnerability in regard to his mother is derived from his not having yet established an identity independent from his parents; he simply does not know who he is at that age. Luciano's description of the signora as a ravishing woman intent on seducing youths like him injures the protagonist in his self-image, pushing him toward a chaos of thoughts and feelings. During all their study sessions, the mother's presence, aside from serving refreshments, is expressed by the creaking parquet floor in the adjacent room. When Pulga crudely speaks of the woman's sagging breasts, he causes the narrator to become confused between the forbiddn genital mother and the tenderly loving breast mother of earliest experience. Luciano demolishes his friend's prepubescent devotion to the mother by making her the object of his vulgar wit. In this novel, the central character has no one to love other than his mother, but after Pulga's attack on her, that love can never be the same. The toxin of Luciano's treachery forever destroys the precarious paradise of the asexual love between mother and son.

The Guilt beyond the Door

Throughout Bassani's three novels in the first person, a sense of guilt torments the central Jewish youth; Dr. Fadigati's ghost, too, haunts all those works. Whether in a veiled allusion to the physician by the young man's father in *The Garden of the Finzi-Continis* or a house call to treat the adolescent for an infected throat in *Behind the Door,* the figure of the doomed invert hovers obsessively and stirs the narrator with a feeling of guilt by association. Pulga's accusation of latent homosexuality merely affirms the protagonist's underlying conviction that he is different from others and must isolate himself from them. Entrapment and betrayal in *Behind the Door* confirm the awareness of being unlike others and anticipate in a nonpolitical spirit the exclusion that comes eight years later with racial laws. For by being a Hebrew, though during a period of fairly widespread religious tolerance, the hero was truly different from his classmates, even by dint of the circumcision that marked his person for life. Guilt in this work incapacitates and isolates the victimized protagonist forever struggling to accept himself.

In early editions, this novel bore as motto a couplet from Baudelaire's poem "Un voyage à Cythère" ("A Voyage to Cythera"):

> Ah! Seigneur! donnez-moi la force et le courage
> De contempler mon coeur et mon corps sans dégoût!
> (Ah! Lord! Give me the strength and the courage
> To contemplate my heart and my body without disgust!)

Strength of will and courage are the very qualities the hero fails to display when he witnesses Pulga's disloyalty. The psychic conflict present in the protagonist from the novel's start (long before any acts of hostility toward him) never does achieve a cathartic resolution, as evidenced by the pathological disturbance oppressing the narrator in middle age. There is no growth by the adolescent hero toward adulthood. Friedrich Nietzsche in *The Birth of Tragedy* has defined a condition like the protagonist's as decadent, when spiritual illness does not pass through conflict and bewilderment to a state of creative renascence.

Despite the text's apparent candor, pathological evasion persists, since the main character hides *(nascondere)* an essential truth from himself. In the concluding paragraph of the 1964 version, the narrator confesses to paralysis of soul:

> something then had to tell me that if he, Luciano Pulga, was certainly capable of looking at it in the face, the whole truth, I was not. Slow in understanding, unable to carry out a single gesture or pronounce a single word, riveted to my cowardice and my resentment, I remained the little impotent *killer* as always. And the door behind which I was once more hiding myself (from him, Luciano, and together from my mother), neither now nor ever would I be able to find in myself the strength and the courage to throw it open. (Italics my own)

The last line echoes without hope the verse from Baudelaire. That self-accusatory designation as a killer or assassin *(sicario)* does not appear in *The Romance of Ferrara* version, where, instead, the narrator stresses that he is bound to a destiny of separation. It is to himself and not the traitor that the hero attributes the label of murderer. Pulga forces the protagonist to look behind the everyday mask he wore before the world in order to see with disgust the sexual creature of repressed desires. The narrator even has to concede to the faithless companion a degree of admiration for being able to behold the truth behind their troubled relationship. But for the hero, the dreadful door not only represents eternal separation but unwanted and rejected knowledge because the door will remain shut throughout time.[18]

Behind the door the narrator learned that sharing experience leaves one vulnerable to the maliciousness of others, making exile not the choice of a noble soul but the flight necessary to escape a mocking injustice. Compelled to recognize evil, the protagonist cannot bring himself to accept it, and he chooses to withdraw from situations of moral and social compromise. While the narrator of the book has not opened the door which conceals the evil intrinsic to life, the narrator, through his writing of the book, has done so. If the narrator telling the retrospective story of this novel is taken into account, the subject of this text would seem to be not the concealing or repression of evil but its disclosure and consequent catharsis for both writer and reader, if not for the work's principal character. According to Bassani's (perhaps decadent) artistic ideology, art has the power to conquer a certain sort of evil through the revelation and dispassionate consideration of that evil. Despite what he says, the narrator of this book is *not* a "sicario"; we know this to be so because his suffering has been mediated to us through the superior position of the elegiacizing narrator.

Behind the Door illustrates how painful the formation of one's identity can be with the pressures of adolescent sexuality, parental control, scholastic authority, and peer persuasion. Here, the ultimate enigma is the hero, whether as victim or killer. With the loss of possibility for a creative life and the exhaustion of resources for spiritual discovery and self-recovery, there occurs a return to third-person narration in the author's final novel, which examines the descent into self-destruction.

5

The Fatal Circle

In *The Heron* of 1968, Bassani creates a victim hero of Faulknerian dimensions totally isolated from a once-sustaining world and eventually devoted to the idea and act of death. For the protagonist Edgardo Limentani recalls in his self-annihilating attitude some of the tormented heroes in Faulkner's novels, like Quentin Compson in *The Sound and the Fury*, with his similar languishing of the will and passive surrender to the reverses of fortune. As in Quentin's section of the American novel, this Italian narrative recaptures a moment of suspension before the chief character's suicide, with the difference that Bassani represents each instant in the process of Limentani's decision rather than showing self-destruction to be the result of a life-long dedication to the negative values of death as with Faulkner's character. Through this work, the Ferrarese novelist attempts to remove his hero from treacherous time to a life beyond decay.[1]

A Decadentist sense of lateness predominates in the Italian novel, set like a classical drama on the last day of Edgardo's life on a Sunday in the end of December 1947. Both the season and the year bear a bleak significance: the private desperation of the Christmas holidays preceding the New Year and just following the darkness of the winter solstice; the postwar anarchy prevailing in Italy and its threat of a communist-led revolution that would sweep away agrarian magnates like Limentani. As always, Bassani constructs his narrative with an ironical version. The Jewish hero has to live surrounded with Christmas decorations because in 1938 he married his gentile mistress to avoid government confiscation of his town and country properties. Instead of sharing the joy of the season with his wife and their infant, Catholic-baptized daughter, Edgardo experiences only the spiritual emptiness that makes Christmas an ideal time for suicide. For the protagonist here has come to view himself as a temporally

displaced person, not just as a Hebrew who succeeded in surviving the war years
through his marriage and flight to Switzerland during the period of the Italian
Social Republic but even more as a gentleman farmer representing an obsolete
class.

Bassani structures this narrative of the hero's final day of life as a fatal circle
that begins and ends at his townhouse on Via Mentana, in the fashionable
northern section of Ferrara, with central events occurring in the marshlands of
the Po valley where Limentani returns on a bird-hunting holiday after an
absence of fifteen years. But instead of being a tale of return and restoration at
the sources of life, the novel follows a circuit of frustration and revulsion in
irreversible emotional decline from psychic numbness to intensified sensitivity at
the brink of death. The text's four parts function as acts in a play, symmetrically
divided into six chapters each, presenting different levels of the hero's consciousness as he moves to his deadly decision. Chapters 1–3 of the first part all
take place in the townhouse, from Edgardo's difficult predawn awakening to his
delayed departure for the hunting trip. In the following three chapters, the
protagonist pauses in the country town of Codigoro, site of the gigantic Reclamation Bureau pumps that drain the Po valley and make its cultivation possible.
In Codigoro, Limentani attempts in vain to telephone his one-time inseparable
hunting companion: his cousin Ulderico, from whom he became estranged
during the era of racial legislation and moral compromise. That abortive phone
call marks a failure to reestablish a vital link with the past and concludes part 1.

The actual hunting scenes occupy part 2 in an atmosphere of paralysis of will
where the alienated hero declines even to shoot at the game fowl and hands his
best shotgun over to his guide as a gesture of surrender to the new ascendant class
of communist workers and peasants. Toward the novel's very center, from the
fourth through the sixth chapters, occur the book's emblematic events: the
appearance on scene of the red heron from which comes the work's title; its
flight against the wind; the bird's return over the marshes, where it is shot by the
guide; and its prolonged death agony that compels Limentani to acknowledge
the ridiculousness and futility of his own existence. The reader never beholds the
bird's exact moment of dying, in anticipation of Edgardo's suicide that occurs off
stage after the novel's conclusion just as in classical tragedy.

While the protagonist's first stopover in Codigoro represents his effort at
communication with the past, in part 3 Limentani's return trip through that
dreary provincial hamlet confirms his resolve to detach himself from others and
life itself in order to preclude any possible future for him. The circle turns in on
itself in the concluding section where the central character returns to his
townhouse to prepare for his death and bid his elderly mother farewell, for at the
start of that last part, he gained a glimpse of absolute peace and perfection safe
from life's reverses in the display window of a taxidermist's shop in Codigoro.
From its structure, the novel emerges as a study in enlightenment through

negation that severs its hero from a past of self-serving compromises and a future of meaningless social and family relationships.[2]

Through the technique of interior monologue, readers share the protagonist's growing awareness of his existence of "being-a-corpse among people."[3] As Bassani reveals more and more of Limentani's past and its impact on that holiday season hunting trip in 1947, the importance of every fragment increases with the hero's movement toward self-destruction. It is through Edgardo's tormented angle of vision that readers regard the course of events on that Sunday and all the preceding forty-five years of his life. Although the novelist has stated that he was seeking to achieve the objectivity of narrative distance, by recreating the forcefulness of the protagonist's psychological nature, he involves his readers directly in Limentani's subject being.[4] Interior monologue discloses how the main character comes to recognize and then evade the demands of reality. Structurally, there is an aesthetically unresolved tension between the author's intention to represent and decode his hero's movement to suicide from exterior gestures and attitudes and the in-depth exploration of inner life.

To depict the troubled flow of memory and immediate perceptions in Edgardo's mind, Bassani frequently employs complex syntax where the logic of main clauses seeks an elusive meaning of events and places followed by subordinate clauses expressing disappointment. The writer avoids brief declarative sentences to accomplish tonal variety, employing a tortured rhythm of haunted thoughts and mental images of a lost pre-1938 paradise when all the personal relationships in Limentani's life were in their proper place. Frequently, the sentences move toward an emphatic, emblematic final word like *invidia* (envy) or *solo* (alone) to point out the protagonist's attitude or situation. Transitions in time return to a past before discriminatory laws and move forward with the past conditional tense to a barren future that Edgardo imagines in his absence following the suicide. Since the novel's main events take place in the recent past of the immediate post-World War II period, the text's rapid-fire verbs in the past absolute possess the vividness of present actions. In passages like the description of the heron's death, verbs in the imperfect agonizingly prolong the scenes. The novel aims at reaching a dream time beyond the chronology of minutes and hours where Limentani will seek salvation in self-inflicted death. Through this third-person narrative, Bassani attempts to portray his protagonist's painful recognition of a life that has led to loss, fall, and failure.

More than in his other novels and major tales, the writer here employs extended dialogue in Emilian dialect. Edgardo often remarks how well certain characters like his hunting guide Gavino or the ex-Fascist proprietor of a Codigoro hotel, Gino Bellagamba, speaks standard Italian, but these figures come to life most effectively in the native dialect of their region. The movement between standard tongue and provincial speech is a form of code switching by characters caught between two cultures: the traditional life of their home territory and the educational linguistic norms imposed by national laws. Local dialect provides a stable link with the past, as in an episode of part 1 when Edgardo gains a sense of reassurement visiting the carriage apartment of his porters, the Manzolis, who have continued to respect him as their sole master. While Romeo Manzoli can resort to a rather slowly paced standard Italian for a ceremonious moment, the servant at once returns to the familiar refuge of dialect. It is only through the use of dialect that Limentani at all succeeds in establishing a bond with others, though significantly it is mostly with characters who represent the past for him.

Through exterior structuring, interior monologue, syntax, tense, and regional dialect, the author creates a novel with a total vision of despair that paradoxically becomes an affirmation of faith in nonlife. The text finds order and coherence in its portrait of an anti-hero who confronts and embraces his nothingness.

The Alien to Life

Edgardo Limentani survived Fascist racial legislation and subsequent Nazi domination, but he can not overcome his existential situation. Even more than Geo Josz, this novel's central character fails to adjust to the social circumstances following the war when he denies the instinct of self-preservation that sustained him during the time of persecution. His abnormal mourning prevents him from being able to feel secure in his inner or outer life.[5] Edgardo never frees himself from the grief of the life that was taken away from him. Bassani describes his last novelistic protagonist in very Pirandellian terms as an *escluso*, an excluded one who is no longer within life, a character who, as in the title of a tale by Pirandello, bears "Death upon him." Edgardo, for the author, is an "object in a world of objects,"[6] which are listed in the novel in typical detail by brand names. Those objects are lost to him because of the race laws and the communist-inspired peasant rebellion ensuing after the war. For instance, since April 1947, this great landowner could not even visit his farms because of the hostility of sharecroppers demanding a new contract for harvest distribution favorable to their interests. And not once during the circular course of his fatal journey does Edgardo dare approach his fiefdom, La Montina, which in legal terms no longer belongs to him but instead to that Catholic peasant woman who formerly was suitable merely to be his mistress. Survival for the hero requires a psychic closing-off as a defense mechanism, which by the end of 1947, no longer continues to protect him.

Without a foothold on life, this estranged gentleman landlord is seeking something that will give coherence, pattern, and meaning to his life. Although others address Limentani as *avvocato* (attorney) in recognition of his membership in the professional class of Ferrara that before the war included many prominent Hebrews, this anti-hero never made the practice of law a major pursuit of his life, with the result that after the war, he felt no compelling need to resume a career. His hunting trip is a vain attempt to discover a distant place of peace and security. Edgardo feels so alienated that he pronounces his own surname with a sense of repulsion and embarrassment. During his trip outside Ferrara, the one person with whom Limentani can establish a bond of common identity and destiny is that former Fascist militiaman Bellagamba, since the two of them are relics of the past in the proletariat world of postwar Italy, and it is to that hotel proprietor that the huntsman donates the day's catch of forty birds as if in tribute to the era they shared with each other. Being Jewish and an agrarian magnate make life intolerable for Bassani's anti-hero, who assumes all his resentment toward those responsible and directs it against himself.

Fundamentally, Limentani has broken away from members of his family, whether from the period before his marriage (his mother and cousin Ulderico) or his wife and daughter. Even though he has continued to live in the same house with his mother, Erminia, his wife, Nives Pimpinati, and little Rory, Edgardo has retreated to the same bedroom and bed where he was born and spent most of his time at home before marrying as if returning to the safety of the womb. He displays the spirit of detachment from others that the psychiatrist Alfred Adler has attributed to the suicidal type who can no longer function in the company of other people.[7]

The protagonist has, in fact, never recovered from the radical disruption in social relationships brought by the anti-Semitic laws. The lack of fellowship follows the shock caused by discrimination, with resulting accumulated self-contempt and the inclination to life in imagination. While the tendency to isolation characterizes many figures in Bassani's literary world, with Limentani that exclusiveness leads to the most complete form of withdrawal—suicide. The enforced segregation of the race laws and the post-war turmoil among peasants who no longer bow to town-dwelling lords have irreparably injured Edgardo's self-esteem, which depends on the value that other people attach to him.

His elderly mother, the original representative of the outer world for most children, inspires a feeling of scorn in him for her infantile inability to recognize how time has changed their lives. With Nives, he has experienced alienation in its legalistic meaning: the transferral of his property, which the woman considers her own and administers with the assistance of an accountant whom Limentani suspects to be her lover. The wife's hooked nose reminds Edgardo of a bird of prey, a horrid devouring creature of oral-sadistic impulses. Toward his cousin, the anti-hero projects envy for the other's ability to play a chamaleon: marrying a gentile and converting to Catholicism well before any discriminatory legislation was passed, even accepting a Fascist party card, always managing to manipulate people and circumstances despite bureaucratic regulations in order not just to survive but to prevail. For Edgardo, his cousin signifies two moments of life: a past of fellowship shared on hunting trips, a future full of the hope promised by a large family with several children. For Ulderico possesses the qualities lacking in the protagonist: vitality, flexibility, virile force. Never once does the self-assertive cousin appear in the text, not even as a disembodied voice on the telephone. Ulderico figures as possibilities that Limentani can never realize. Instead, the hero severs himself from the entire network of family relationships where he does not effectively function as a vital participant.

Edgardo's conflict with life as process manifests itself in his difficulty to relate to his body and its needs. Food does not bring him the satisfaction of experiencing the world as a generous, maternal force. Whether eating sandwiches purchased at a country grocery store, consuming an abundant meal at Bellagamba's hotel, or contemplating evening dinner at home, he fails to overcome a distaste for what could sustain and nourish his physical existence. He barely eats, giving his sandwiches to the hunting guide and later declining to join in what would have been his last dinner at home. Not fully exhibiting the nausea before life of Jean Paul Sartre's Roquentin in *La Nausée*, Limentani instead never succeeds in satiating his at times intense hunger and thirst, since life forever disappoints and frustrates him. Edgardo fails to cope with his animal, physical self. Bassani does not hesitate to detail bodily processes, like urination and especially defecation, that have often been taboo subjects for Italian writers because his hero's sometimes embarrassing inability to regulate elimination indicates an underlying problem in controlling his life. For an individual experiencing those difficulties, suicide is a means of evasion, as the author Antonin Artaud once remarked: "[Through suicide] I free myself from the conditioned reflexes of my organs, which are so badly adjusted to my inner self. . . ."[8] The body is a prison from which death offers liberation. In no sense is Limentani an anal-retentive personality, since he forever struggles to rid himself of the filthy burden that is physical life. But the protagonist cannot overcome a form of constipation that is as much psychic as physiological. Self-hatred and anxiety frequently attack certain parts of the body in order to transfer distress from the mind to various offending organs. Regularity and ease of elimination express the integrative capacities of the personality, which, in Limentani, break down in rebellious disorder.[9]

Edgardo's desire to renounce his body's tormenting functions has already brought him to a state of near sexual impotence. In his conjugal relationship, he readily yields his place as Nives's lover to the accountant Prearo, tacitly in the present and almost enthusiastically in his imagination of the future after his death. Ulderico appears in his thoughts as an erotic alter ego, virilely triumphant with his many children; and Limentani fantasizes about betraying his cousin through an adulterous affair with his wife, Cesarina. Edgardo even suspects that the hunting guide is Ulderico's illegitimate son. In the text's phallic symbolism, the hero never shoots the birds with his superannuated Krupp rifle, while Gavino uses Limentani's brand-new Browning for his successful shooting.

The protagonist looks at his penis with an ironic sense of detachment as an instrument more for urination than erotic self-assertion. His castration complex carries over to a dream during a nap at the Bellagamba hotel. In this dream, he sees himself with a prostitute, who was actually one of the patrons at the afternoon dinner; he cannot respond to the woman because he has lost his penis. Edgardo's vitality has shriveled to nothing, just like the phallus in his oppressive dream. Freud, in his early treatise, *The Interpretation of Dreams*, noted obsessive patterns of wish fulfillment in dreams, and he later wrote of repetitious compulsions where psychically troubled individuals suffer again and again overwhelming libidinal frustrations,[10] because the unconscious endeavors to regain control over life forces by acting out the self-defeating erotic conflict. In both dreams and waking existence, Limentani shows a painful vulnerability to sensations of libidinal life, but the directing power of his will grows so feeble that he cannot take part in activities like hunting or even fantasize a positive reaction to a prostitute's advances. Impotence here extends beyond the sexual realm to signify a defenseless condition that ends in withdrawal from life.

Limentani retreats from Eros by idealizing his lack of virility in order to become receptive to the promise of death-in-life that leads to his suicide. His self-image is that of a victim as he identifies with journalistic accounts of postwar Jewish atrocities in communist Poland. Stories of domestic discord, like the mistreatment of Manzoli's daughter Irma by her husband, William, appeal to Edgardo's sense of victimization. With his morbid self-absorption, he succumbs to steadily growing passivity. Sometimes, in situations similar to the protagonist's, belief in a transcending spiritual ideal relieves feelings of isolation and persecution. But religion holds no solutions for Edgardo, whose daily exposure to Christianity in the image of a Catholic saint in his wife's bedroom leaves him indifferent except to underscore his otherness as a Jew. During his nocturnal wandering through the desert of Codigoro, Limentani pauses in a church where no particular service is being celebrated. The building's nearly empty interior recalls the vacuousness of a movie house between showings without any sense of quiet, peace, and spiritual restoration. That lack of consolation in a religious setting is derived from the hero's barrenness of heart, for Limentani knows neither the solace of uplifting faith nor the satisfactions of a purely sensual existence. A darkened crucifix nailed in the Codigoro church intimidates him rather than presenting still another image of victimization. Reading a pamphlet of Catholic propaganda in the church fails to convince the hero of the Christian view of an anthropomorphic world where God cares for human beings before attending to "lesser" creatures. Edgardo does not feel superior to other creatures of animal life, like the red heron killed during hunting that day. All creatures, human and animal, become life's victims. Eventually, the central character resorts to his Hebrew identity as a means of finding community, not in religious belief shared with others of the same faith but as the final retreat to be enjoyed in Ferrara's Jewish cemetery.

One critic has recently referred to the anti-Semitic laws of 1938 as a "time bomb" whose delayed explosion decimated individuals like Limentani and

Josz.[11] Certainly, those laws negated previous social acceptance, created a present nightmare, and for Limentani, prevented a secure future. Edgardo feels the past as a deadening pressure on his present postwar existence that denies him any hope of rebuilding his life. As always in Bassani's narrative works, life is not a simple chronological sequence, for Limentani dwells in interrupted time. The last day of the protagonist's life appears as an attempted return to the past of fifteen years before but without any opportunity for relief from his burden of regret and loss. Bassani juxtaposes the pre-1938 world with that of 1947 to point out the pathos of a time without redeeming faith in life.

SYMBOLS OF FATALITY

Throughout this final novel, the author develops symbolic patterns to express the fatality dominating the protagonist's circular journey. At the beginning and end of the novel, there are references to alarm clocks in the bedrooms of Limentani's townhouse: symbols of time drawing to a close. Space, too, becomes a major part of the work's symbolic network: As in *The Gold-Rimmed Eyeglasses*, a deceptive sense of openness characterizes the narrative's literary space, which moves beyond Ferrara's walls to the expansiveness of the Valle Nuova (the New Valley), with the suggestion of hope for a renewed life that recalls Dante's *Vita Nova*. In that unbroken landscape, Edgardo seeks to breathe freely as he passes through marshlands that paradoxically appear stagnant but are filled with water flowing in from the sea. A surface impression of stasis gives way to nature's dynamic force. Over the fifteen years of the hero's absence from this area, drainage efforts of the Reclamation Bureau have changed the topography, thereby throwing the huntsman off his bearings. The only direction Limentani finds is back to town and death. During his sojourn in the valley, however, Edgardo's spirit finds consolation in the aesthetic beauty of the intense blue of the area's water basins: a color reminiscent of canvases by De Pisis diaphanously bathed in a twilight of redemptive peace and death shining across Italy's marshlands. In his movement away from the city, the anti-hero is searching for a source of salvation for his futile existence. Wanting desperately to find a place to which he can belong, Edgardo briefly rejoices as he drives by the medieval Benedictine Abbey of Pomposa whose reassuringly unaltered appearance reminds him of a past era when social relationships were clearly defined and respectfully observed. But the wind-tossed marshlands are also a scene of slaughter, a place of purposeless transience whose sole pattern is one of life-in-death and death-in-life as wild birds struggle to escape relentless predators. One critic has noted that rivers and the wind symbolize the otherness of nature,[12] sought after by characters fleeing a closed human world. That quest for nature's otherness will lead to an acknowledgment of the nothingness in death.

Just as the flow of the Po di Volano becomes part of Edgardo's consciousness, the town of Codigoro is tied to his memories and failed expectations. Not just his failures but those of the Fascists are recalled there by the old party headquarters and the pompous monuments to war dead. Recent postwar attempts to erase reminders of the past by altering street names are already beginning to deteriorate under the force of rain and snow that have obliterated entire letters on street signs. Especially during the hero's return trip through the provincial city, his estrangement renders him a spectator to dramas without design or significance. Wandering the streets, he witnesses scenes of debauchery as if they were an absurd puppet show. When life becomes a distant theatrical performance viewed in numbness, an acceptance of death follows as a necessary release. Every sense of joy, life, and freedom vanishes amidst squalid, crowded cafés and irreparably neglected mansions in the grand Venetian style. As with the street names, efforts at covering up decay prove vain in an atmosphere of desolation that effaces earlier Fascist rhetoric and present-day Marxist pretentions to Liberation-era glory. No matter what governing party reigns in the town, Codigoro is a metaphor for spiritual emptiness and deadening entrapment.

Throughout his trip across the valley and in and out of Codigoro, Limentani travels in his old car, an Aprilia, which partially symbolizes stability in time.[13] That one-time petty Fascist officer Bellagamba would like to purchase the automobile, not only to appropriate that tie to a shared past but to convert it into a truck to be used for the daily acquisition of foodstuffs for his hotel. Thus, the past would be adjusted to the new present as elegance yields to utility. Cars are cultural artifacts that people use to shield themselves from the outer world through which they pass in an illusion of decreased motion.[14] At certain moments, the hero sees his car as a familiar, trusted confidant; at other instants, it is no more than a heap of rusted scrap metal that he should discard at a profit. In the crystaline atmosphere of an evening in Codigoro, the parked Aprilia takes on a spectral appearance as it joins the faded provincial world around the town's center square. That melancholy blue car represents Edgardo's past lordly life that cannot move into the postwar period with him.

Telephones function in this novel not as instruments of communication but as symbols of alienation. At their Ferrarese home, Edgardo's peasant wife refuses to use the house telephone to give orders to the Manzolis; instead, she betrays her rustic background by shouting to the servants from the upper windows facing the building's central courtyard. In Codigoro, the phone's ring has a strident metallic sound in contrast to the sophisticated muffled tone in Ferrara. The narrow, vertical closet of the wood and glass phone both at a Codigoro café where Limentani tries to call Ulderico suggests a coffin. Edgardo's first attempted call marks one of the most pathetic moments in the book as he listens enviously to the sounds of his cousin's children playing ball in their living room. Except for an unsuccessful exchange with a maid at the beginning of the call, Limentani does not speak with an adult because Ulderico is away from home and his wife is in the bath. For a few moments, the alienated huntsman sustains a conversation with Ulderico's six-year-old son Andrea, but for most of the time on the phone, Edgardo becomes a spy overhearing the playful noises in the Cavaglieri household. The entire final chapter of part 3 is occupied with Edgardo's phone conversation with Ulderico's wife, Cesarina, a former trouser maker, from a background obviously inferior to that of the family into which she married, but who at once assumes the familiar pronoun in speaking to Limentani. During the course of that conversation, the novelist moves beyond actual dialogue to the thoughts of the caller who endeavors in vain to imagine himself in the role of a pleasantly misanthropic uncle visiting the Cavaglieris but ultimately becomes a traitor by destroying the domestic tranquility of his intended hosts. Both calls to Ulderico's home are futile since Edgardo never visits the Cavaglieri apartment, whose boisterous activities arouse such intense envy in him when compared to the tense atmosphere in the Limentani townhouse. Although telephones make it possible for people to extend themselves to others, Bassani represents this invention as a source of loneliness, disappointment, and frustration.

An enormous psychic distance prevents Limentani from making vital contact with another individual. The author's symbol of separation is a well or pit (*pozzo*) of desperation; occasionally, he varies the image with the word *baratro* (abyss). In the first sentence, the novel describes the "bottomless pit of unconsciousness" from which the awakening hero must climb. One critic has called the well "the parent image" for all the other closure images in the text.[15]

Literal and figurative wells abound in the book: There is a well in the midst of the courtyard at the Ferrarese townhouse. Going down the stairs of that home is similar for Edgardo to lowering himself into a well, while the stairway at Bellagamba's hotel suggests a dark abyss. The entrance portico of the house on Via Mentana is as cold as a well in a cellar. After passing the Abbey of Pomposa on his way to the hunting party, the hero considers returning directly to Ferrara, but to do so would mean hurling himself again down that "dark well of slothful sadness" (p. 588) from which he was struggling from the day's start to escape.[16] Death can release one from the uncertainty of life. By plunging himself into the abyss, Edgardo would attain an inhuman state of perfection.

Juxtaposed to the symbol of the darkly threatening pit is the den, lair, or hiding place where the protagonist can find refuge. The idea of hiding, indicated by variations of the verb *nascondere*, is essential to understanding Bassani's literary world where everyone (not just Jews after fall 1938) feels insecure, either somewhat ill at ease in another's company, or fears imminent loss of life. Limentani's hunting trip is a vain attempt to discover a place of peace and safety. Each pause in his journey represents a stage in the hero's efforts to estabish attachment to, and familiarity with, the land: the warmth and aroma of a fireplace in a roadside grocery, the roar of the large drainage pumps at Codigoro, the sight of barges moored at a riverside port. Limentani desperately wants to discover a place to which he can belong, but spiritual displacement has haunted him ever since passage of the racial laws. He feels torn between a need for flight and a longing to bury himself. During the war, he did, of course, take refuge in Switzerland, and since spring 1947, he has had to be a fugitive from the sharecropprs at La Montina. A commonplace irony in narrative literature involves the hunter becoming the hunted. The alienated Jew is indeed a hunted victim seeking to hide from persecution. Considering himself displaced even in his own home, Edgardo views the strong, white light coming from the kitchen window of the Manzolis' apartment as the promise of a temporary refuge. Although on his first trip through Codigoro, the Bellagamba hotel, with its odor of fried fish, seemed like the cavern of a wild animal, on his return home, Limentani seeks a sense of calm, safety, and stability of mood in the establishment's dining room. But in the midst of the hotel's apparently self-assured neocapitalistic dining patrons, Limentani once again feels himself to be the anachronistic outsider. Because the womb is the original hiding place, this novel closes with Edgardo's final ritualistic visit to his mother's bedroom. Beyond that return to the source of life lies the supreme hiding place of burial in Ferrara's Hebrew cemetery. Herein arises the paradox of Limentani's character: Throughout the novel (and ever since autumn 1938), the protagonist runs away from the darkness and cold of the abyss only to plunge into the security of the grave.

One of the ties to life that the hero must renounce is money, the symbol of frequently disappointing exchange in the book. Edgardo married beneath his class merely to hold onto the estate that provided all his income—only to be displaced by his socially ambitious wife and their accountant who want to change the kind of crops being raised on the farm. The sharecroppers violently insist on a new contract in order to win what they believe to be a fair portion of La Montina's profits. Because Limentani arrives hours late for his hunting appointment with the guide Gavino, he fears the young man may accuse him of trying to avoid paying the fee previously arranged by Ulderico. When Edgardo asks Bellagamba to give him the bill for his dinner and the use of a sleeping room, the hotel proprietor refuses payment, exclaiming that the gift of the day's game more than suffices for the expenses incurred by his guest. The tranquility that Limentani enjoys with the Manzolis ends abruptly in domestic disputes about their shiftless son-in-law William, who, with his communist leanings, refuses to work and exploits the elderly couple's love for their daughter Irma. Reliance on money as a form of communication betrays a radical alienation in spirit in people who no longer rely on their animal instincts but employ a totally artificial medium of exchange. Edgardo's destiny is to draw close to the instinctual life of hunted animals—away from the contrived world of monetary transactions.

The hemmed-in, wounded, red heron clutching to life reminds Limentani of himself as a member of a disappearing social class. The death scenes of this emblematic bird possess the vividness and ferocity of a De Pisis animal painting. Through the hauntingly persistent image of the bird's fight to stay alive, the protagonist realizes the uselessness of struggling to survive. That awkward, ill-proportioned creature had the chance to escape destruction but instead flew back to the lagoons where the hunting was taking place. Compared to other game fowl, the heron has little value as a foodstuff because of its fishlike taste; it would serve as only a stuffed trophy. Edgardo the agrarian magnate has lost his historical raison d'être in Ferrarese and Emilian society. For the gentleman hunter to fire at the bird requires a cruel courage that he finally summons only to end his own existence. That bird's death compels Limentani to see that he, too, has lost vitality. This shooting scene is the last major twilight incident in Bassani's most significant narrative work. During a subsequent conversation between Edgardo and Bellagamba in Codigoro about the day's hunting, a flashback occurs in Limentani's mind to the crepuscular moment following the bird's death: as in motion pictures, a close-up technique focuses on the heron as a lifeless victim of brutality. As a Decadentist, the author concentrates on instants of anguished realization when his protagonists acknowledge their fall.

For the novel's supreme symbol of separation, the author employs glass in various forms: glass walls, mirrors, house windows, and display windows. Like other leading characters in Bassani's works, Edgardo feels that a sheet of glass divides him from other people (even his wife and family) and objects. In contrast to other walls, glass is transparent, permitting individuals on either side to see each other but never to touch. Consequently, a glass partition proves more frustrating than opaque barriers because contemplation never results in contact. Absurdity has settled around Limentani like a thin sheet of glass to separate him from the bewildering convergence of sheer being in all its physical flux.

In this self-reflexive novel, mirrors objectify the protagonist's identity in the image of himself that he regards in near admiration because his aristocratic features resemble King Umberto. For Edgardo is concerned about his physical appearance, or to be precise, about an idealized image of himself. In preparation for his last visit with his mother and his ensuing suicide, he bathes, shaves, and combs his hair to preserve his perfect image to the end. This concern with grooming is common to some suicidal individuals, whose narcissism is not love of the actual self but of an idealized image.[17] Verbs of vision, usually in the reflexive form, like *osserversi* (to observe oneself), *guardarsi* (to look at oneself), and *intravedersi* (to gain a glimpse of oneself), abound in Edgardo's preoccupation with his physical being in all its manifestations. In the optics of the novel, the protagonist attempts to hold onto a cherished mirror image of himself that becomes as elusive as his identity.

Windows in this work paradoxically reinforce the sense of alienating otherness while providing an image of liberating identification, as in two sequences during Limentani's final stroll through Codigoro in the early evening. Outside a building that he takes for a wine shop, he looks through a window at a group of men playing cards—a scene that makes him feel like a useless alien without any precise function standing before a picture in a frame. A critic has compared this episode to the immobility of a painting by Cézanne.[18] Edgardo recognizes that he can never fit into that unapproachable scene and thus finds another hiding place closed to him as he stands outside (not behind) the window. But a display window at last frees Limentani from his state of dividedness after he wanders over to the establishment of a taxidermist. Viewing the display of stuffed animals, Edgardo begins to yearn for their eternal life free from mortal decay. While the cardplayers seemed to be frozen like figures in a painting, the artificially preserved animals possess a marvelous lifelike quality in their cheerfully bright arrangement. For the display animals dwell in a condition of "silence, absolute stillness, peace" (p. 650) where death infuses them with vitality and perfection. Window and mirror symbols merge as Limentani moves away from the almost theatrical scene to study a detail of the spectacle and then suddenly catches a glimpse of himself on the glass surface. For once, Limentani is neither *behind* nor *outside* but *on* the window and to a certain degree, *within*, as he imagines that he, too, can participate in the perfectly preserved life of the dead animals. Herein occurs what critics have called Edgardo's "conversion to death."[19] Suicide offers him a form of salvation. Like the heron, he transcends his death agony, longing only for the artificial paradise of escape from mutability. Standing on the brink of self-dissolution, Edgardo Limentani finds an enduring sense of harmony in death, which will release him from the strain of an ever-changing reality.

Bassani creates a network of symbols that express his hero's alienation and intense desire for peace. As the work's carefully controlled symbols unfold, its protagonist at first tries to flee but eventually descends into a grim well of self-destruction.

A DEATH-AFFIRMING NOVEL

Limentani's choice of salvation through death reflects his anomic situation of having experienced the forced dispersal of his accustomed way of life without any hope for renewal. In truth, by the close of 1947, there were signs for optimism that the postwar crisis of communist aggression in Italy would give away to normalcy. Like Geo Josz, the anti-hero of *L'Airone*, could never succeed in reintegrating himself into a community that had once rejected him. Edgardo's death as an affective human being with social affiliations took place in 1938 when he became the victim of his past without any possibility for deliverance except through suicide.[20] At the collapse of his privileged world, the will to live diminished so that only escape from the confines of his bodily prison promises spiritual restoration.

This novel examines the disintegration of the central character who destroys himself because his identity has been shattered. The book moves from the desolation following the trauma of discrimination to the discovery of consolation in self-inflicted death. Like the character in a Pirandello novella who commits suicide to cheat involuntary death by tuberculosis, Limentani moves toward a conversion that is purely self-negating. But his is a hollow triumph instead of a resurrection of spirit attained through an act of free will. In contemplating the display in the taxidermist's shop, the anti-hero seems to achieve an insight that allows him to view life in all its grotesque dimensions from the perspective of death. Suicide often bears the illusion of rebirth of the self beyond contingency. But the reality of the act is inverted murder in vindictive anger toward the family and community who have deserted the victim. Rather than a novel of victorious martyrdom, this work becomes a study of a retreat into nihilism.

Is there any hope of restoration in Bassani's final novel? The author, of course, also began his career as a novelist in *The Gold-Rimmed Eyeglasses* with a story of suicide. As the original epigraph for *The Heron*, the writer selected some lines by Arthur Rimbaud that point the way to transcendence: "It is found again!/ What? Eternity." As in Rimbaud's *A Season in Hell*, where the sea fuses with the sun in a reconciliation of opposites, life and death in Bassani's works may enter into a liberation of an eternity beyond disruptive time. Edgardo Limentani attempts to recover eternity in the vision of a perfect life safeguarded from decay. Willed death is his effort to experience the absolute, through the eternal.

In this last novel, the author moves toward completing his literary world of Ferrara. The ironic situation of salvation through suicide marks the achievement of a creative quest to overcome the destructive fragmentation of human experience. With a final volume of tales and essays, Bassani presents his farewell to narrative writing.

Conclusion:
The Leave-Taking

Closing the Circle

A Decadentist fragmentism characterizes the tales, personal sketches, anecdotes, and essays that comprise *The Odor of Hay* (1972), the last volume in *The
Romance of Ferrara*. The overall impression that one gains from the final section
is that the writer, creatively exhausted, has substituted a highly polished art
prose for insight into time and the suffering it brings his characters. Bassani's
attempt to effect organic unity never succeeds in this collage text. A sense of
surrender pervades the brief pieces in this collection where the author gathers
his final reflections on his native city and its inhabitants. A plurality of voices
arises throughout the text's various levels: the comments of a detached first-
person observer; fairy tales with a legendary tone or a surrealistic timelessness
that recalls the late novelle of Pirandello; third-person tales that complete the
history of individual characters from the original *Storie ferraresi*; and vignettes of
eccentric figures from the Emilian capital.

Although the time period for tales in this volume ranges from the anarchic
days following World War I and the march on Rome to the comfortable mate-
rialism of the recent Italian economic miracle, there is a dominant temporal
shifting from the ebullience of late 1945 back to the final oppressive phase of the
Fascist alliance with nazism. Throughout the pieces in the text, one notes a
stylistic involution in the author's return to aesthetic and thematic preoccupa-
tions of the *Storie ferraresi* that culminate a year later in the publication of the
revised five nuclear stories of *Within the Walls*. Here, Bassani permits his authorial voice to intrude and override his fictional world because he assumes the
role of witness to the society at the center of his compositional work. Behind the
historical episodes that the writer renders in a fictional guise emerges his own
authorial personality.

An elegiac vein permeates this assemblage as Bassani makes his last effort to
identify in prose narrative what his favorite American writer Hawthorne calls

"the deep warm secret" that "gives substance to a world of shadow." Bassani structures this volume in seven sections that conclude with reflections on his beginnings as a narrative writer in the *Storie ferraresi*. In the opening "Two Fairy Tales," he focuses on the optimism of the immediate postwar period that creates a genuine community in Ferrara ("Necesity is the Veil of God") and then turns back to present "a dream within a dream" ("At the Time of the Resistance") about a mysterious traveler passing through town with a mission to distribute underground leaflets. A three-part section ("More News about Bruno Lattes") functions like a flashback to show Bruno as a child and a youth bewildered by the initial consequences of the racial laws. An autobiographic sketch, "Ravenna," not only marks the physical limits of Bassani's literary world but also establishes the mood for this collection as one of a "secret sadness, totally steeped in farewell" (p. 698), since the writer is preparing here his leave-taking from narrative composition. In the two tales of "Les Neiges d'antan," the author returns to familiar situations in the difficult relationships between gentiles and Hebrews ("Rawhide") and the enigma of an individual ("Pelandra") to adjust to a secure if somewhat monotonous existence. Autobiographic sketches become allegoric investigations about accepting life in a metropolis like Rome ("Apologue") after knowing the humanely slow pace of provincial towns, while in the tale "A Mouse in the Cheese," Bassani recalls the all-consuming appetite for life that sustained him during his late-war participation in the work of the Action Party in Naples. A writer's responsibility for transforming historical reality into fictive fantasy occupies the essay "Tennis Shoes." With the article "Down There, at the End of the Corridor," he presents the journal for the tales in the *Storie ferraresi*, discussing their interior structures in geometric terms. The original epigraph for the volume *The Odor of Hay* comes from Simone Weil: "One can offer only one's self. If not, everything that one calls an offering is nothing but a label placed on an a revenge of the self." Through this last volume of reflections, the author acknowledges the gift of himself that his narrative productions represent. In this concluding chapter, I shall examine only those tales that complete Bassani's portrait of the romance of Ferrara in that past era from which the writer could never separate himself.

"Necessity is the Veil of God"

Some critics interpret the fairy tale "Necessity is the Viel of God" ("La Necessita è il velo di Dio") as a literary antidote to the despair of *The Heron*.[1] For the first time in Bassani's writings, and placed as the initial piece of his last narrative work, the traditional segregation of women from men in the Ferrarese temple vanishes at a celebration ceremony where survivors of the Holocaust rejoice together at the end of 1945 over their deliverance from destruction. While the first edition of *The Odor of Hay* indicates that the reunion is taking place in the German synagogue, in the 1980 edition, the century-old division of Hebrews into different *schuls* ends with a meeting for all in the Italian synagogue. But the scene of universal harmony occurs in a piece that the writer calls a *fiaba* (fable, fairy tale, moral tale) and not a *storia* of historical inspiration. While the novel *The Heron* explores death as liberation, this fairy tale optimistically stresses how "life . . . eternally ends and begins again" (p. 672) in a story about God's thinly veiled plan to save His chosen people. Starting in the fabled time of fairy tales with the words "Many and many years ago . . . " (p. 669), the story relates the sweet deception that led to the romance and marriage between the Ferrarese maiden lady Egle Levi-Minzi and the Ukrainian emigrant Yuri Rotstein during the period of the greatest accommodation of Italy's Hebrews to Fascism in the mid-1930s.

Bassani merges history with legend to describe Egle as a damsel awaiting her golden knight in recollection of the violently erotic heroes of the early Fascist squads until Yuri arrived in Ferrara as a sojourner with his parents, staying at the Hebrew communal asylum. The Rotsteins would all suffer for deviating from their fate as wandering Jews, for the brief period of rest they asked of their Ferrarese coreligionists, before moving on to Palestine or America, became a protracted visit that ended only with their deportation in fall 1943 to Nazi extermination camps. By lingering too long in their haven, the Rotsteins had their names recorded on that infamous plaque on Via Mazzini along with 180 other Ferrarese victims of racial persecution.

Bassani chose the mystic number three for the visitors from Odessa who capture the admiration of the uneasily satisfied Emilian Jews through their quiet sense of dignity. Out of the marriage between the demanding Egle and the naïve Eastern refugee comes hope for future renewal in a handsome son also named Yuri. In a fairy tale, time can circle around in a spirit of renascent promise. The barriers that distinguish Bassani's literary realm disappear, but only in an atmosphere of loving enchantment that dissipates the menacing shadows of Nazi lager concentration camps.

"MORE NEWS ABOUT BRUNO LATTES"

Clelia Trotti's clandestine companion Bruno Lattes reappears in three episodes that begin with the volume's title tale, "The Odor of Hay," which Bassani reworked from the opening frame story "The Enclosing Wall ("Il Muro di cinta") from the enlarged 1960 edition of the *Storie ferraresi*. That earlier prologue tale presents the enclosure that shuts off people from one another. The dividing wall ("il muro di divisione," p. 8, Einaudi edition: Turin, 1960) surrounds Ferrara's Hebrew cemetery, where a solitary and silent sentry stands guard as if to protect the dead from the living. There, in the first version, which describes a funeral in the Camaioli family as viewed by the youth Girolamo, a refrain arises that only the dead are well off, since they no longer have to face the surprising challenges of life. No possibility exists for the living and the dead to communicate; instead, a feeling bordering on resentment prevails among the Camaioli survivors who all fear that they will fall victim to cancer. The atmosphere in the 1960 tale is a pathological one about the conviction among many Jews that they are a race tainted with disease. Girolamo regrets the atavistic inheritance that causes him to resemble his Semitic relatives while he envies his Catholic friends for their good health. One member of the Camaioli clan, Uncle Giacomo, has attempted to elude their accursed fate by converting to Catholicism and having his children baptized in that faith; but his relations doubt that Christianity will absolve the apostate from their pathogenic history. While the burial ceremony is taking place, the mourners think of earlier deaths and funerals in that same cemetery; yet there emerges no sense of consolation or comforting continuity, only a depressing awareness of the suffering that awaits every individual until the moment of final destruction. In that early version, Bassani demonstrates that even within the close kinship structure of Hebrew families individuals remain isolated from each other behind an invisible wall from birth to the grave.

A liberating impression of expansiveness emanates from the Hebrew cemetery in the reworking as "The Odor of Hay," with its vast meadows full of riotously growing grass where the vital force triumphs over death. While the 1960 version presents an unrelievably lugubrious atmosphere of mourning in which survivors recognize no reassuring bond with the deceased but actually envy their dead relative for putting agony behind him, the reworking transforms the dreary setting into an environment of cheerful magnificent trees that outlasted the devastation of the Second World War. Bassani constructs the reworking according to a complex temporal plan that resembles music.

The primary time period is 1932, when the protagonist Bruno Lattes is a seventeen-year-old adolescent attending the funeral of his uncle Celio. But the temporal reference in the tale's initial section is the early 1970s, which celebrates the lush exuberance of the cemetery grounds. The ceremony in 1932 causes Bruno to remember his first visit to the Jewish graveyard, in 1924 as a child of nine for the burial of his grandfather Benedetto. At that previous interment, swarms of mosquitoes circled around the little boy reminding him of another August evening sometime during the First World War when, as an infant at Benedetto's home, he had looked out the kitchen window at military pursuit planes crossing the sky in squadrons. Four time periods—1971, 1932, 1924, 1917, or 1918—are juxtaposed to one another to create a positive feeling of continuity over the years and generations. Whereas Girolamo in "The Enclosing Wall" has to acknowledge his genetic lineage, Bruno totally rejects his Jewish identity in both his physical appearance and moral character. Since Lattes's mother is a gentile, by Hebrew matriarchal tradition, the youth can rightfully disavow any Jewish identification. Both Girolamo and Bruno display an ardent adolescent longing for companionship with the lonely sentry who stands as an emblematic figure of independent otherness. The beguiling sounds of life intrude into the story's revision with the nearby music from an accordion and the voice of a woman singing of love. In the second version, the graveyard turns into a child's playground where hopefulness prevails amid the funerary monuments. This revision demonstrates Bassani's acceptance of a cemetery setting not just as an environment of death and resentment but as an almost idyllic locale where fieldworkers mow the grass that provides the pungent hay symbolizing life's rebirth.[2]

From the peaceful retreat of the Hebrew cemetery, the narrative passes to two unrelieved episodes of oppressive separation in "The Rifle Girl" ("La Ragazza dei fucili") and "A Race to Abbazia" ("Una corsa ad Abbazia"), which study the deterioration of intimate ties between Hebrews and gentile fellow citizens after the promulgation of racial laws. Until passage of that legislation, Bruno shared with other Italian Jews the certain belief of their full and equal membership in the Fascist-ruled society. With his half-Aryan family background, he took as his tennis partner and lover the blonde, blue-eyed Adriana Trentini, who, under normal circumstances, would have become his fiancée and wife. But by the onset of the first chilling fogs of autumn 1938, even before the wide-sweeping consequences of the government decrees were evident, Adriana announced her retreat from adult responsibility by ending her relationship with the moody Hebrew youth so that at the age of seventeen, she could again be a child free to enjoy life without fear of any political repercussions. The shock of discrimination drove Bruno into an instant maturity that, however, left him a pariah wandering back streets in a desire for protective invisibility. In his despair he frequented an area near the city's bastions where there had been an amusement park the previous summer, for there, the young man had first glimpsed the uncrossable gulf that separated people from each other's company. He had made the acquaintance of a girl operating a shooting gallery, and her attractiveness had fired a passion that he felt she might reciprocate. But one night, with only a wink toward her gypsy caravan, the rifle girl let Bruno understand that she already had a lover. Bassani employs the sign language of nonverbal communication to represent the awakening in Lattes of a feeling of suffering, humiliation, and isolation that the subsequent edicts of segregation merely reinforce.

A fundamental dualism lies at the core of the romance of Ferrara. Although Hebrew characters like Bruno lived in the illusion of belonging to a collective "we" that included all Italians, even before the time of official discrimination, many Jews were aware of their essential dissimilarity from gentiles that created a situation of "us" versus "them". Before government statutes forbade intermarriage as miscegenation, Aryans were attainable objects of desire to be possessed through civilly recognized matrimony.

This tale completes a symbolic circle with the story of Lida Mantovani at the start of Bassani's fiction. Like Jewish authors in other countries, such as Philip Roth in the United States, a persistent theme with Bassani is the relationship between a Hebrew male and a "Schiksa" (gentile woman). While economic status and urban background make the Jew David the superior to the impoverished Lida Mantovani of peasant origin, in the play of master and slave Bruno in the aftermath of racial laws finds himself abandoned by his former gentile lover.

Authorized exclusion established a rift between Hebrews and gentiles that could be overcome only by the police accusation of "pietism" (sympathy for Jews) for the Aryan and forced residence for the Jew in some remote corner of Italy. Since Bassani explores an underlying sense of separateness in all people, which transcends officially sanctioned intolerance, in these final notices about Bruno Lattes, the author uses the very grammar of pronouns to show how the "we" of "us persecuted Hebrews" becomes in the young protagonist a fully isolated "I" unable to communicate with his parents, coreligionists, and university peers.[3]

Frontiers of space and time carry the world of Ferrara to its outermost limits in "A Race to Abbazia," where Bruno makes a last desperate effort at intimate contact with Adriana. Knowing the impossibility of meeting in town or at vacation resorts like Rimini and Riccione, frequented by large numbers of the Ferrarese middle class, Lattes rejoices after learning that the Trentini family has gone in late summer 1939 to the distant Istrian seashore city Abbazia. There, just beyond Trieste and close to the border of Yugoslavia, far away from the spying eyes of their townspeople, Bruno dreams of resuming for a final instant their passionate relationship. But this story involves barriers—courteous remoteness and family conspiracy—as Adriana, her mother, her slightly younger sister Rosanna, and their little brother Cesarino, politely treat Lattes as an acquaintance to be held at a respectful distance. Not once does the anxious youth succeed in being alone with Adriana, whose attractiveness recalls that of a vamp in American movies of the 1930s. As elsewhere in Bassani's writings, swimming is a metaphor for failed human relations; here, Adriana is an excellent swimmer who outdistances her former lover, left behind in the shallow water near the beach. Once again, nonverbal language marks a line of exclusion when the Trentinis signal each other with meaningful private glances to bar all access to Bruno. A sense of finality, not just in the contact between an optimistically secure Ferrarese bourgeois family and a Hebrew outcast but for all human associations represented by the seashore vacationers, haunts this episode because the dates of Bruno's visit to Abbazia are 30 and 31 August 1939, exactly the eve of the outbreak of the war, which everyone in the tale wishes to declare an impossibility.

Lattes realizes that time has run out for him when during an evening stroll he meets Cesarino out for a bicycle ride. Hanging from the handlebars of the bicycle is a red banner that Bruno unrolls to reveal a swastika. Cesarino dismisses the significance of the banner as nothing but a decoration. Herein lies the great mistake of Italy's professional middle class toward Fascism and its pact with Nazi persecution: People saw only the ornamental spectacle of strength, splendor, and international prestige without recognizing the underlying evil. Throughout all three episodes, the author presents a paradox in settings: Grave-yards provide pleasant retreats for a life-renewing experience, while an amuse-ment park brings sad memories of separation, and a beach resort seems to be located on the abyss of war. Hope for the future completely recedes, for as readers of the *Storie ferraresi* already know, Bruno's parents face extermination although he will seek survival through exile.

"Les Neiges d'antan"

François Villon's *Ballade des dames du temps jadis* provided Bassani with the title for a two-part section dealing with disenchantment and flight. The refrain in the French poem about the gently melting "snows of yesteryear" creates a feeling of tranquility rather than horror before irreparable loss. Like Thomas Wolfe, the Italian author asserts in the first tale, "Rawhide" ("Cuio grasso"), that one can not spiritually return home after years of separation. The original version of this story was entitled "In esilio" ("In exile") and stood as the epilogue of the 1960 edition of *Storie ferraresi*. First time and then geographical distance prevented the first-person narrator of the original version from becoming the friend of the handsome and aristocratic Marco Giori. Because the narrator was a Ferrarese high school student six years younger than Giori at the time of their first encounter, the two could not strike up a close acquaintanceship. There is an air of ambiguity in the 1960 edition, deliberately making it difficult to discern whether the admiring narrator or the inaccessible Giori is the one in exile. Both versions present the image of a prison in the village townhouse where Marco's mother is held prisoner by her jealous husband, Signor Amleto. A prisoner like his mother, Marco, with the looks of a movie star and the manners of an English gentleman, never even completes his university education: For although the peasant can leave the farm, the farm never leaves the peasant and eventually compels his return to the land. The hold that future ownership of a thousand-acre estate exerts on Marco causes him to abandon dreams of a charmed existence in cosmopolitan centers like Paris, London, and New York. One of the forces that always separates Giori and the narrator is the contrast between rustic and urban cultures that runs throughout Bassani's writings, preventing an ex-change of basic values between the Emilian peasant and the Ferrarese city dweller. In the revised tale, the narrator does not regard himself to be in exile in Rome, where he affirms he has "put down roots" to start his own family and establish a literary career. Marco, instead, as the narrator observes one autumn evening on a rare journey from Rome to Ferrara with a stop in the hamlet of Ambrogio, has succumbed to the lethargy of provincial life in the farmlands. The monotonous passàge of years has transformed Marco into a slovenly dressed peasant with a neck like his father's, which seems made of rawhide or literally "greasy leather." In the narrator's view, Marco's atavistic regression represents the betrayal of their youthful expectations. Between the two individuals, the opposite origins of time and place have led to an impassable gulf. A chance encounter in the present annihilates past illusions of a possible moment for the two to experience togetherness.

One of the themes recurring in Bassani's writings is the disillusioning pain of growing up. Although the most important occasion for the loss of childlike dreams is the enactment of race laws in 1938, when characters like Bruno and the first-person narrator are in their early twenties, the moment for maturing does take place as in "Rawhide" much later in life. In the first-person works, there occur instants when the past and present selves of the narrator face each other in the tormenting awareness of loss. Individuals like Marco Giori are projections of the narrator's very being, his most cherished aspirations to realize a new life free of Ferrara's petty limitations. With "Pelandra," the second tale of "Les Neiges d'antan," the narrator focuses on one of Marco's companions among the decadent young *sfatti* or café idlers in downtown Ferrara during the 1930s. For Pelandra one day astonishes his fellow citizens by emulating Geo Josz's flight into the void.

Frequently, Bassani characterizes an individual, a setting, or a situation with some material object that has the force to evoke an entire series of associations. Here, in the mystery story of the one-time Bohemian, Mario Spisani (known as Pelandra), it is through the tinted eyeglasses of the Ferrarese still photographer, Uller Tumaìni, that the first-person narrator depicts the circumstances of the *sfatto's* disappearance. Uller himself is a mysterious figure to the narrator, who does not even know if the photographer is married or where he lives. Tumaìni also seems to stand outside of time, for this sage character whom others call in dialect *al duteret* (the little doctor) for his keen insight into human motivations barely ages with the passing of years but remains the changeless image of factual reliability. The setting for Uller's documentarylike disclosures about the golden decade of the café idlers preceding Italy's entry into World War II is in the almost total darkness of the photographer's studio at nightfall, since this character who sheds light on recent and remote events peers through shaded lenses into a world of obscure emotions.

Throughout the literary world of Ferrara, there have been references to *sfatti* lolling at the tables outside the Caffè della Borsa. Gamblers, users of cocaine, habitués of bordellos, those degenerate youths from the final stable years of the Fascist epoch represent the petty meanness of provincial society, for with their ironic sneers, they form a chorus of snickering persecutors whose presence in the heart of town drives such excluded characters as Bruno Lattes and the narrator of *The Gold-Rimmed Eyeglasses* to secondary streets. In this tale, the author focuses on that vicious crowd because of his artistic need to complete the photographic album of Ferrara, presenting persecutors and their victims. The story also continues the writer's linguistic experiments in *The Heron*, since it contains whole lines of dialogue in Emilian dialect with an uncharacteristic crudeness of tone that recaptures the intrinsic vulgarity of those debauched pretenders to cosmopolitan sophistication. Among the foreign words in the text is *killer*, from the gangsters of Prohibition-era Chicago, known to Italians through American movies. The destructive idlers include among their leaders that very same Eraldo Deliliers who wrecked Dr. Fadigati's life. A sketch like this one exposes the cruelty existing at the core of the city.

Pelandra, in Uller's discreet judgment, never figured among the luminaries of the café crowd despite his eager participation in their depravity. A certain lack of conviction about the ultimate smartness of their decadent behavior denied Spisani a prominent rank among his companions. That absence of unashamed arrogance on Pelandra's part might account for his sudden conversion in mid-1938 to a model citizen with his engagement to a young woman of exemplary lower middle-class status. Individuals exhibiting this tendency for a dramatic shift from one extreme of behavior to another possess a schizophrenic nature that makes their whole existence unreal. Yet for ten years, Pelandra persisted in his role as a proper member of society: rising to the post of manager of the local branch of a Venetian insurance company, becoming a dutiful husband and loving father of four children. Tumaìni's account of Spisani's ideal married life gives a glimpse into the existence of a whole segment of Italian society who were hardly touched by the Second World War except for having to take summer vacations on family farms instead of at the seashore. To the amazement of all townspeople, on a pleasant autumn afternoon in 1948, Mario Spisani disappeared from Ferrara without leaving a trace. Here, unlike the case of Geo Josz that same year, was a gentile who had never suffered discrimination vanishing under the most mystifying circumstances: running out of the house without a top coat on the instant whim of buying cigarettes when he did not even smoke. In two weeks, Pelandra and his family would have moved into their first real home of their own. Could his sudden decision have arisen from an inability to assume responsibility? As viewed through the sensitive eyes of an observant photographer, Bassani presents the last enigma of his native city.

Throughout the fragmentary tales and sketches in *The Odor of Hay*, the writer has attempted to free himself from the burden of time. Occasionally, memory is a destructive force for the characters, a refuge where they lose themselves in illusions. For the first-person narrator, however, memory is a reliable companion that permits him to relate the past with photographic fidelity. After the anguish of separation follows the serenity of renewal through the artistic act of writing.

THE EXILE INTO ETERNITY

As the epigraph for the 1974 edition of *The Romance of Ferrara*, the author quotes Dante's *Purgatory*, 21, 136: "Treating shades as something solid." In

Bassani's stories and novels, the shades of those already dead Ferrarese characters come alive in the solidity of their shattering experiences. Aided by the distance of time since the end of the war and the relative remoteness of living in his nation's capital, Bassani through writing has succeeded in accomplishing a spiritual pilgrimage to his homeland. Ambivalent feelings of love and resentment over past exclusion have permitted him to preserve those fleeting moments of the past in the unceasing duration of his great romance. Each instant of that twilight world enters into a continuous present that transforms remembrance into actual experience. That physical place which was Ferrara from the advent of Fascism to the close of the Liberation era in 1948 contributes its spatial dimension to the force of memory across the pages of the text. The city's Jewish and Christian cemeteries, its walls and their grassy bastions, the enchanting gardens in the town's northern district, the ambitiously soaring towers of the Estense Castle, the sidewalk cafés—all serve the author in reconstructing his characters' histories. Memory in Bassani's narrative not only possesses evocative powers but also a selective quality, since the text evaluates the motives of individuals caught up in historical and political events compelling them to make decisions or surrender passively to waiting. The devastating oblivion caused by war and persecution recedes before an artistic transformation of memory that elevates everyday happenings to eternal images of human experience.

Over twenty years ago, Bassani's chief Marxist critic attempted to demonstrate a fundamental contradiction in his narrative: the conflict between historical and psychological fiction.[4] While historical fiction moves toward outward fact in linear narrative progression, psychological fiction turns to the enclosed world of inner experience in an often time-circling narrative structure. The Marxist critic questioned whether or not it was possible for a fictional author to merge the facts of historical reality with memories of enigmatic individuals lost in their private dramas. Are there two fictive planes unsuccessfully superimposed on each other and do they preclude an artistic organic unity? By his own acknowlegment, Bassani is a Crocean historicist with a vision of the continuity of events through time to the present. His characters, whether viewed from the distance of third-person narration or speaking with the vividness of the first-person voice, are actors and victims in history where public events overwhelm private stories. The objective facts of the Fascist era allow the author to arrive at a subjective interpretation of the Ferrarese society that collaborated with a totalitarian regime.

Bassani's fiction in *The Romance of Ferrara* follows a clearly discernible circular progression from the third-person narratives in the five nuclear Ferrarese tales through three novels of increasing first-person subjectivity back to the third-person voice in *The Heron*, with a final exploration of stylistic techniques in *The Odor of Hay*. With tales like "Lida Mantovani" and "The Walk before Supper," the author investigates the walls of incomprehension between gentiles and Hebrews, rustic and urban cultures that prevent authentic communication even in the presence of the strongest attachment. In "A Plaque on Via Mazzini," one witnesses the failure to reconstruct a sense of community in the doomed efforts of a solitary survivor of the Holocaust trying to force his fellow citizens to face their complicity in evil. Exclusion from society for political or racial reasons occupies "The Last Years of Clelia Trotti," with its oppressive images of enclosing personal prisons. An individual's public refusal even to recognize the occurrence of an atrocity beneath his very gaze during the Italian Social Republic illustrates in "A Night in '43" how the collapse of domestic illusions overshadows the historical and juridical importance of outside events. The parallel destinies of a homosexual and a Jewish youth at the onset of racial segregation underscore the stylistic ambiguities of the author's initial attempt at a lengthy first-person narrative in The Gold Rimmed Eyeglasses, where the highly judgmental Ferrarese community becomes a collective protagonist that casts out all undesirable elements. In The Garden of the Finzi-Continis, Bassani studies the tragic delusions of a wealthy family so accustomed to privilege that its members persist in trusting in the safety of their personal paradise, which ultimately becomes only a precious memory preserved by the first-person narrator, who could not win permanent entrance to the elegant private world. Through the confessions of Behind the Door, a sexually bewildered schoolboy relates in his own voice his first experience with treachery and admits to cowardice. With The Heron, the author returns to third-person narration to represent a protagonist reduced to being a voyeur in a life that the official discrimination of the war years prevents him from resuming with the fullness of his emotional being until he elects a peculiar form of liberation through suicide.[5] In the experimental sketches in The Odor of Hay, Bassani contrasts fairy tales of hard-won community, realistic stories about separation, and anecdotes about a puzzling flight into oblivion. Between historical objectivity and subjective exploration, the works forming The Romance of Ferrara become a coherent study of a writer's quest to combat destructive time.

What is the meaning of Ferrara presented by Bassani in his narrative writings? In the essay "Down There, at the End of the Corridor," which concludes The Odor of Hay, the author refers to his city as "Ferrara, the little, segregated universe invented by me . . ." (p. 734). Unlike Faulkner, who created the town of Jefferson and Yoknapatawpha County by "sublimating the actual into the apocryphal" from the model of Oxford, Mississippi, and Lafayette County,[6] Bassani situates his fiction in an actual city and province, carefully naming its streets and describing its geographical components with the accuracy of a scientist. Both the city's physical frame and the quality of its communal life are evident in the author's choice of such modifiers as small (piccolo) and segregated (segregato) to note the significance of exclusiveness within that immured literary universe of Bassani's Ferrara. In contrast to Faulkner, Bassani does not have to arrest the motion of life to hold the dramas of his characters within time, since he resurrects a world that has already become part of history's relentless destructiveness. All of Bassani's tales and novels are a loving gesture to restore the lost universe of Ferrara and to release its prisoner victims from exile in order to dwell in the eternity of art.

Notes

INTRODUCTION

1. Cf. Jacob Neusner, *Stranger at Home* (Chicago: University of Chicago Press, 1981), passim, for the situation of American Jews caught between the recent past of the Holocaust, the promises of Zionism, and the responsibilities of citizenship in the United States.

2. See Charles S. Aiken, "Faulkner's Yoknapatawpha County: Geographical Fact into Fiction," *The Geographical Review* 67, no. 1 (Jan. 1977): 9. Bassani, of course, works from an actual city and province.

3. Jacob Burckhardt, *The Civilization of the Renaissance in Italy,* I, trans. B. Nelson and C. Trinkhaus (New York: Harper and Row, 1958), 66–69.

4. Werner Gundersheimer, *Ferrara: The Style of a Renaissance Despotism* (Princeton: Princeton University Press, 1973), passim, analyzes the economic policies of the Estense rulers.

5. Cecil Roth, *The History of the Jews of Italy* (Philadelphia: Jewish Publication Society of America, 1946), 226, 333, 368, and passim, studies the attitude of the Estensi toward Jews. Also cf. Gundersheimer, 202, 205–7, on the enlightened views of the Este family about Hebrew immigration.

6. Ibid., 421–41.

7. Paul Corner, *Fascism in Ferrara, 1915–1925* (Oxford: Oxford University Press, 1975), 108–28, contrasts the decline of the Socialist position in Ferrara and the ascension of the Fascists through their adroit agrarian policies.

8. Ibid., 170–75, portrays Balbo's character and organizational abilities as chief of the terror squads. Renzo De Felice, *Storia degli ebrei italiani sotto il fascismo* (Turin: Einaudi, 1961), 229–38, notes that despite many later frustrating experiences with non-European Jews in Libya, Balbo never abandoned his friendship for the well-assimilated Jews from Italy.

9. Roth, *History,* 520–21, speaks of the general sympathy for Zionism among Italian Jews who had no desire to leave their country. De Felice, *Storia,* 29, provides figures on immigration.

10. Ibid., 115–22, offers details about the comprehensive laws.

11. Mair Michaelis, *Mussolini and the Jews* (London: Institute of Jewish Affairs, 1978), 112 and passim, points to the change in the Fascist attitude toward Italian Jews.

12. De Felice, *Storia,* 245–46, provides background information about the spontaneous demonstrations in Ferrara of anti-Semitic feelings. Some of the negative sentiments toward Jews resulted from antagonism by political rivals of Balbo's in resentment for his widely acknowledged pro-Hebrew sympathies.

13. Michaelis, *Mussolini,* 152–53, examines the race manifesto. M. Van Creveld, "Beyond the Finzi-Contini Garden: Mussolini's 'Fascist Racism'," *Encounter* 42 (Feb. 1974):42–47, judges the race manifesto as a desperate act by the Fascists to disprove German charges about the tainted blood of the peoples in the Italian peninsula.

14. De Felice, *Storia,* 347–50, publishes the articles of the racial legislation.

15. Neither Marshal De Bono nor Luigi Federzoni held particularly pro-Jewish views, but both felt the racial legislation was political folly.

16. Richard Collier, *Duce!* (New York: Viking, 1971), 147–48, describes Balbo's defiance of the anti-Jewish statutes.

17. S. Weil, *The Need for Roots,* trans. Arthur Wills (Boston: Beacon Press, 1952), 114.

18. Michaelis, *Mussolini,* 389–92, outlines the stages of the Holocaust in Italy, which claimed 7,682 victims among the nation's Hebrews.

19. The 1964 essay is entitled "Ancora su Soldati" (a review of Mario Soldati's novel *Le Due Città*) and has been reissued in the volume *Le Parole preparate e altri scritti di letteratura* (Turin: Einaudi, 1966), 193–94.

20. Giuseppe Raimondi, *Filippo De Pisis* (Florence: Vallecchi, 1952), 11, speaks glowingly of the year 1916.

21. See *Le Parole preparate*, 158, and Bassani's parallel between Morandi and the narrative writer Carlo Cassola for their common aversion to rhetoric.

22. For current information on Morandi, see the essays collected in *Giorgio Morandi*, ed. James T. Demetrion (Des Moines, Iowa: Des Moines Art Center, 1982).

23. Along with Raimondi's book on the painter, readers may wish to consult Sergio Solmi, *Filippo De Pisis* (Milan: Hoepli, 1946).

24. For studies of the Twilight School, see Luciano Anceschi, *Le Poetiche del novecento in Italia* (Turin: Paravia, 1972), 125–33, and Edoardo Sanguineti, *Tra liberty e crepuscolarismo* (Milan: Mursia, 1965), passim.

25. Giuseppe Cassieri presents an abridged edition of the *La Ronda* review in *La Ronda* (Turin: E. R. I. 1969), with Cardarelli's prologue on 3–6.

26. Cf. Anceschi, *Poetiche*, 191, on the reliance of the Rondists on the models of Leopardi and Manzoni.

27. Riccardo Scrivano, *Riviste, scrittori, e critica del novecento* (Florence: Sansoni, 1965), 11–61, 203–15, passes a negative judgment on the Rondists (especially Cardarelli) for their polemics on De Sanctis, Pascoli, and the Futurists. Lanfranco Caretti, *Dante, Manzoni, e altri saggi* (Milan: Ricciardi, 1964), 125–38, argues that the referendum on Pascoli was never an open debate, since Cardarelli sought only to disprove Pascoli's modernism and label the poet's adherents as backward and provincial.

28. L. Fava Guzzetta, "*La Ronda* cinquant'anni dopo: ideologia e letteratura," *Lettere italiane* 23, no. 1 (Jan.–Mar. 1971): 111–28, especially, 112, speaks of the enlightened conservatism of the Rondists.

29. C. Di Biase, *La "Ronda" e l'impegno* (Naples: Liguori, 1971), 76, comments on stylistic formalism in the journal.

30. In an interview with Stelio Cro in the *Canadian Journal of Italian Studies* 1, no. 1 (Fall 1977): 38, Bassani acknowledges his debt to Longhi in proving the reality of the historical spirit to him.

31. Readers should consult the richly illustrated *Officina ferrarese* (Rome: Le Edizioni d'Italia, 1934). Emilio Cecchi, *Letteratura italiana del novecento*, II (Milan: Mondadori, 1972), 1249–56, examines and praises Longhi as a prose stylist.

32. See the interview with Cro, *Canadian Journal* 1: 43–44.

33. H. Wildon Carr, *"Time" and "History" in Contemporary Philosophy; with Special Reference to Bergson and Croce* (London: Proceedings of the British Academy, 1918), passim, discusses Croce's idea of history as contemporaneous.

34. For Pratolini's views on history, see Frank Rosengarten, *Vasco Pratolini: The Development of a Social Novelist* (Carbondale: S. Illinois University Press, 1965), 51, 92, 127. Also cf. Nicola Tanda, *Realtà e memoria nella narrativa contemporanea* (Rome: Bulzoni, 1970), 74–75.

35. Mario Saccenti, *Riccardo Bacchelli* (Milan: Mursia, 1973), traces Bacchelli's artistic development and his historicism. Giulio Marzot, "Riccardo Bacchelli," *I Contemporanei*, 2 (Milan: Marzorati, 1963), 959–95, relates theory and practice in Bacchelli's writings.

36. The Marxist critic Gian Carlo Ferretti, in *Letteratura e ideologia* (1964: rpt. Rome: Riuniti, 1974), 24–65, argues that Bassani fails to penetrate the historical significance of an event to its depth and loses himself in individual enigmas.

37. Some of the writers who had acknowledged their rebellious inspiration from Croce are Francesco Compagna, Gino Montesanto, and Mario Pomilio; see their statements in *La Generazione degli anni difficili*, ed. E. Albertoni et al., (Bari: Laterza, 1962), 96, 189, 210.

38. Silvio Guarnieri, "La Letteratura del fascismo," *Cinquant'anni di narrativa in Italia* (Florence: Parenti, 1955), 177–87, affirms the mediocrity of Fascist literature.

39. Herbert W. Schneider, *Making the Fascist State* (Oxford: Oxford University Press, 1928), 233–34, 360–63, studies the role of Futurists in the early stages of Fascism.

40. Geno Pampaloni, "La Nuova letteratura," *Storia della letteratura italiana*, 9, ed. E. Cecchi and N. Sapegno (Milan: Garzanti, 1969), 832–34, analyzes Longanesi's paradoxical contributions.

41. H. Schneider, *Fascist State*, 238–39, 353–56, examines Malaparte's early, positive experiences with his fellow Fascists.

Chapter 1. The Community of the Excluded

1. Variations in different editions of the tales are examined by Ignazio Baldelli, "La Riscrittura 'totale' di un'opera: da Le Storie ferraresi a 'Dentro le mura' di Bassani," *Lettere italiane* 26, no. 2 (April–June 1974):180–97; and Hermann Haller, "Da Le Storie ferraresi al Romanzo di Ferrara: Varianti nell'opera di Bassani," *Canadian Journal of Italian Studies* 1, no. 1 (Fall 1977): 74–96.

2. Paul Tabori, *The Anatomy of Exile, A Semantic and Historical Study* (London: Harrap, 1972), 32, speaks of "inner exile" as the condition of being an outcast in one's own country. For some years, the Italo-Canadian critic Giusi Oddo De Stefanis and I have been engaged in a polite debate over whether or not Bassani's vision of life is one of perpetual isolation; in her text *Bassani entro il cerchio delle sue mura* (Ravenna: Longo, 1981), 180, n. 36, the critic affirms that all of Bassani's works move toward a conversion from the isolation of a Ferrarese Jew to a citizen of the world. I sustain that the "citizen of the world" will come to recognize his/her state of living "in exile."

3. See *Le Parole preparate*, 164.

4. Cf. Bergson, "Laughter," in *Comedy*, ed. Wylie Sypher (Garden City, N.Y.: Doubleday, 1956), 178–79.

5. As a guide for my exploration of Bassani's literary universe, I am following many of the investigative trails of J. Hillis Miller, *Charles Dickens: The World of His Novels* (Cambridge: Harvard University Press, 1958), lx, and xv.

6. *Il Romanzo di Ferrara* (Milan: Mondadori, 1980), 732. All subsequent page references will be to that edition unless otherwise noted; translations are my own.

7. Cited by Georges Poulet, *The Interior Distance*, trans. Elliot Coleman (Baltimore: Johns Hopkins University Press, 1959), 79.

8. Cited by Georges Poulet, *Studies in Human Time*, trans. Elliot Coleman (Baltimore: Johns Hopkins University Press, 1956), 80.

9. For an explanation of the term narrated monologue, see Dorrit Cohn, 'Narrated Monologue: Definition of a Fictional Style," *Comparative Literature* 18, no. 2 (1966):97–112. Bassani's view of dialect as a linguistic ghetto is expressed in an interview with Giorgio Varanini, *Bassani* (Florence: Castoro, 1970), 4.

10. Cf. Bassani, *Il Punto* (8 October 1960).

11. I am very deeply indebted here and elsewhere throughout my book to Professor Charles Klopp, as in his lecture "Memory and Exclusion in Bassani's 'Lida Mantovani,'" American Association for Italian Studies' Annual Conference, Bloomington, Indiana, April 1984, Professor Klopp has generously shared his very original insights and research material about Bassani with me, and my colleague's views pervade this text.

12. Detailed examination of the different versions are in Baldelli, "Riscrittura," 186–97, and Haller, "Opera di Bassani," passim.

13. Klopp "Memory and Exclusion," suggests the circular and spiraling structures. Stelio Cro, "Tempo e parola nelle Storie ferraresi di Giorgio Bassani," *Canadian Journal of Italian Studies* 1 no. 1 (Fall 1977):50, speaks of a circle of life and death in the tale.

14. Mario Boselli, "Ambiguità di Bassani," *Nuova corrente* 27 (July–Sept. 1962):14, comments on the shifts in tenses.

15. Poulet, *Human Time*, 337, in discussing Thoreau asserts that seasons are not in time but in eternity.

16. The season in the 1940 version is summer.

17. See Baldelli, "Riscrittura," 186–91, for variations in the passages about wintertime along the frozen Po.

18. Anna Dolfi, "Bassani e il diaframma speculare della distanza," *La Rassegna della letteratura*

italiana 53–54 (Jan.–June 1977):355–56, points out the doorbell and different rings of the two male callers.

19. Victor Brombert, *The Novels of Flaubert: A Study of Themes and Techniques* (Princeton: Princeton University Press, 1966), 57–61, contrasts the two opposing symbolizations of windows. Dolfi, "Bassani," 353–58, studies windows and adverbs of place, such as *dentro* (within) and *fuori* (outside).

20. In an insightful essay, Marianne Shapiro, "The *Storie ferraresi* of Giorgio Bassani," *Italica* 49, no. 1 (Spring 1972):35, speaks of such an association between Lida and Oreste because of their participation in the same class. I would speak of general domestic compatibility.

21. Ferretti, *Letteratura*, 32–33.

22. Cf. Miller, *Dickens*, 243–44.

23. Variants are noted in Haller, "Opera di Bassani," 74, 88–89.

24. In earlier versions, the mother's name is Letizia and the sister's is Cesira and Luisa. Haller, "Opera di Bassani," 83–84, quotes Bassani on the choice of the Latinized and rather allegorical name of Ausilia. Note the change from Letizia (happiness) to Dolores (sorrows, pain).

25. See Gaston Bachelard, *The Poetics of Space*, trans. Maria Jolas (New York: Orion, 1964), 72, passim.

26. Translation from *Il Romanzo di Ferrara*, 1980 edition, 54–55.

27. Edward T. Hall, *The Hidden Dimension* (Garden City, N.Y.: Doubleday, 1966), 10–14, analyzes spacing mechanism and contact versus non contact species establishing invisible bubbles around themselves.

28. Joseph Warren Beach, *The Twentieth Century Novel: Studies in Technique* (New York: Century, 1932), 345–47, analyzes indirect point of view in Conrad's narrative works.

29. Jeffrey Mehlman, *A Structural Study of Autobiography* (Ithaca, N.Y.: Cornell University Press, 1974), 79, calls the Medusa the symbol of an obsessive past that an author would eliminate through writing.

30. Cited by Poulet, *Interior Distance*, 127.

31. See De Stefanis, *Bassani*, 52, for the Shakespearean comparison.

32. Percy Lubbock, *The Craft of Fiction* (London: J. Cape, 1921), passim, contrasts drama and picture in James's narrative works.

33. De Stefanis, *Bassani*, 58, n. 8, comments that by the second printing of *Within the Walls*, the interjection of *io* is eliminated.

34. Cro, "Tempo e parola," 60–61, analyzes the use of free indirect style to express Geo's malaise over his inability to reintegrate himself into Ferrara and the fear of his fellow citizens before the estranged refugee.

35. Cf. Ferretti, *Letteratura*, 35, on Bassani's Decadentism in not reconciling history with poetic intuition.

36. Miller, *Dickens*, 256–66, discusses how a character can define his life in negative attributes and achieve an inhuman fixity.

37. David Rousset, *The Other Kingdom*, translated by Ramon Guthrie (New York: Reynal and Hitchcock, 1947), as cited by Lynn M. Gunzberg, "Down among the Dead Men: Levi and Dante in Hell," *Modern Language Notes*, 16, no. 1 (Winter 1986): 10. Gunzberg proceeds, 10–28, to relate Primo Levi's concentration camp memoirs to Dante's *Inferno*.

38. In an interview with Stelio Cro, the author has acknowledged his debt to Joyce, see the *Canadian Journal of Italian Studies* 1, no. 1 (Fall 1977):43–44.

39. I take my interpretative scheme from Bernard Benstok, "The Dead," James Joyce's 'Dubliners': *Critical Essays*, ed. Clive Hart (New York: Viking, 1969), 153–69. Benstok, 153–54, distinguishes three levels of dead in Joyce's story: the deceased, the moribund, and the living dead.

40. Ibid., 163, calls snow the most persuasive symbol of death in Joyce's tale.

41. J. Hillis Miller, *Dickens*, 53, points out the dark corridors in *Oliver Twist*. H. Stuart Hughes, *Prisoners of Hope: the Silver Age of the Italian Jews 1924–1974* (Cambridge: Harvard University Press, 1983), 132, remarks that Bruno deserts Clelia in an asexual sense with his flight to America.

42. De Stefanis, *Bassani*, 35, in comparing Proust and Bassani stresses that for the Italian writer, memory arises out of place.

43. Cro, "Tempo e parola," 73, points to the spectral, lunar atmosphere in the story. Hughes, *Prisoners*, 176, n. 7, observes that the actual Fascist rally at Verona and the massacre in Ferrara took place in November, but Bassani altered history for the dramatic effect of introducing the glistening snow.

44. Shapiro, "Giorgio Bassani" 30, comments on the lack of anonymity in Ferrara, since the town was an extended family with no intimate secrets.

45. H. Haller, "Opera di Bassani," 89, mentions the dropping of the taboo.

46. Susan Sontag, *Illness as a Metaphor* (New York: Farrar, Strauss, and Giroux, 1977), 59–60, studies the use of syphilis as a metaphor for corruption.

47. Cf. Arthur Babcock, "*La Symphonie pastorale* as Self-Conscious Fiction," *French Forum* 3 (1978):67–71.

48. Ferretti, *Letteratura*, 17–37.

49. Enzo Siciliano, *Autobiografia letteraria* (Milan: Garzanti, 1970), 117–19, refers to the idea of the wound in Henry James's fiction and its influence on Bassani.

CHAPTER 2. THE TIME OF PERSECUTION

1. H. James, *The Art of the Novel: Critical Prefaces by Henry James* (New York: Scribner's 1934), 231.

2. In a lecture given at Johns Hopkins University in fall of 1982, Jacques Derrida stressed the distinction between the author and the narrator as a literary axiom; see The *Johns Hopkins Magazine* (Dec. 1982):33.

3. De Stefanis, *Bassani*, 100–103, approaches the problem of autobiography in Bassani's fiction by referring to the theories of John Freccero on Dante's conversion. There is, of course, a difference between Dante the poet and Dante the fictitious pilgrim.

4. On 26 January 1978, Bassani delivered a lecture about the motion picture version of his novel as "Il Giardino tradito" ("The Garden Betrayed") at the Italian Institute of Culture in New York City; see the interview in the *Newsletter of the Instituto Italiano di Cultura*, no. 57 (July 1978):7–9.

5. Bruce Kawin, *The Mind of the Novel: Reflexive Fiction and the Ineffable* (Princeton: Princeton University Press, 1982), passim, contrasts primary and secondary first-person narrators. Kawin, 53, turns to Carlos Casteneda's *The Teachings of Don Juan* for the idea of the *escogido*.

6. Cf. Siciliano, *Autobiografia*, 114.

7. In a lecture for the American Association of Italian Studies on 13 April 1984, G. De Stefanis in "Gli Occhiali d'oro: i diversi piani prospecttici della narrazione" at Indiana University (Bloomington, Ind.) describes the plurality of narrative levels and the oppositions of pronoun subjects.

8. Jeffrey Meyers, *Painting and the Novel* (Manchester, Eng.: Manchester University Press, 1975), 2, passim, discusses H. James's development of the role of art to illuminate character facets.

9. Jeffrey Meyers, *Homosexuality and Literature 1890–1930* (Montreal: McGill University Press, 1977), 1–19, analyzes metaphor and allusion in literature dealing with homosexuality.

10. De Stefanis, *Bassani*, 81, 83, comments on Fadigati's masochism.

11. See Gaston Bachelard, *Imagination and Reverie*, trans. Colette Gaudin (Indianapolis: Bobbs-Merrill, 1971), xxxii, 54–59, 78–79.

12. Miller, *Dickens*, 2, 162, points out the separating force of fog.

13. Poulet, *Human Time*, 213, quotes Constant about individuals living in a swift present and becoming estranged from their homeland.

14. Siciliano, *Autobiografia*, 121–22, studies how this passage marks the narrator's rediscovery of the ties to his city's past. Charles Klopp, "Memory and Exclusion," notes that Bassani's characters sometimes recover from the shock of rejection by renewed contact with the constituent physical parts of the city: its mortar, bricks, and stones.

15. Jean Rousset, *Forme et signification: Essais sur les structures littéraires de Corneille à Claudel* (Paris: Corti, 1967), 123–31, talks of perspective from a height, in literature, as the "vue plongeante," as here on Ferrara's bastions. Yi-Fu Tuan, *Topophilia* (Englewood Cliffs, N.J.: Prentice Hall, 1974), 51, explores evanescence in the description of place by literary authors.

16. I would like to acknowledge here the insights of a former student of mine, Ronald Kotcho, in viewing this work as a study in human time with a protagonist steeped irreversibly in a fatal spirit of Decadentism.

17. Pirandello set many of his novelle in the separate compartments of passenger trains with their lonely passengers, and Elio Vittorini's novel *In Sicily (Conversazione in Sicilia*, 1941) presented a train ride as a journey into the unconscious.

CHAPTER 3. TRANSFORMATION IN THE GARDEN OF LOVE AND DEATH

1. Cf. Bachelard, *Poetics*, 72, passim.

2. From *Rudyard Kipling's Verse, Definitive Edition* (Garden City, N.Y.: Doubleday, 1949), 736.

3. As we shall discuss below, De Stefanis, *Bassani*, 118, indicates "illness, decay and death" dwelling in the garden.

4. Ibid., 129–30, refers to this episode by the wall in 1929 as being "oracular," in the terms of the critic René Girard, since the moment anticipates the final outcome of an entire relationship. Marilyn Schneider, "Mythical Dimensions of Micòl Finzi-Contini," *Italica* 51, no. 1 (Spring 1974):54–55, draws Dantesque parallels.

5. Adriano Bon, *Come leggere 'Il Giardino dei Finzi-Contini' di Giorgio Bassani* (Milan: Mursia, 1979), 59, inaccurately doubts the existence of Via Vignatagliata; but on 58–70, this critic pursues a very original and thorough study of the text's language.

6. In that interview at the Italian Institute of Culture (*Newsletter*, 8), the author emphasized that he wanted to create literature with a very strong link to reality with concrete details.

7. For information on Hebrew religious terms and ritual, consult Lewis N. Dembitz, *Jewish Services in Synagogue and Home* (New York: Arno Press, 1975), and Isaac Klein, *A Guide to Jewish Religious Practice* (New York: Jewish Theological Seminary of America, 1979).

8. The private Finzi-Continian tongue comes under scrutiny by Ilvano Caliaro, "Dal *Giardino* di Giorgio Bassani: il 'finzicontinico' di Micòl, tra dignità e stile," *Forum italicum* 15, no. 1 (Spring 1981):52–57,. where Micòl's linguistic solitude is illustrated. David Romano, "Notas sobre el judeoespañol en una obra de Bassani," *Sefarad* 30 (1970):198–200, contrasts the varying orthographic transcription of Sephardic terms in the novel according to standard Italian spelling or original Sephardic usage and occasional current Castilian practice.

9. During the academic year 1980–1981, the State University of New York at Binghamton sponsored a lecture series on "The Exile in Literature," where Rigo Mignani delivered the talk "José María Arguedas and the Novel of Exile," speaking of a language of exile for characters who employ a tongue differing from the standard.

10. H. S. Hughes, *Prisoners of Hope*, 136–40, regards Professor Ermanno as the "greatest of Bassani's Jewish characters" (p. 136) with his vague plan for the spiritual renewal of Italy's Jews in which Celestino would play a glorious role. Ermanno's superiority arises from his never having succumbed to the illusions of assimilation. To a certain extent Professor Ermanno recalls the stereotype of the frigid Jewish superintellectual as caricatured by anti-Semitic authors like Louis-Ferdinand Céline: cf. the comments on Céline by Julia Kristeva, *Powers of Horror*, translated by Leon Roudiez (New York: Columbia University Press, 1982), 184.

11. Edward Hall, *The Hidden Dimension* 101–104, analyzes semi-fixed feature space where the arrangement of furniture can be sociofugal or sociopetal. Sontag, *Illness*, 29, 31, 46, 62, presents the romantic view of tuberculosis as a disease of the will, as vitality misspent. Alberto's latent homosexuality would relate to his respiratory disease as a repression of vital energies; Sontag, 21, quotes a character in Thomas Mann's *The Magic Mountain* as stating: "Symptoms of disease are nothing but a disguised manifestation of the power of love; and all disease is only love transformed."

12. Cf. De Stefanis, *Bassani*, 97.

13. Cited by Poulet, *Interior Distance*, 166–67. Yi-Fu Tuan, *Space and Place* (Minneapolis: University of Minnesota Press, 1977), 144, discusses objects that fill a home and impart to it a sense of intimate experience and independent presence.

14. Schneider,"Mythical Dimensions," 45–46, explains Micòl's idea of time by living a "succession of presents."

15. In her conversations about Melville's story, Micòl casts Spencer Tracy in an imaginary movie version. Such a perspective illustrates the cinematic mentality of Bassani's characters.

16. Once again, following Girard's theory of triangular desire, De Stefanis, *Bassani*, 170–71, elaborately diagrams the shifting relationships among Alberto, Malnate, Micòl, and the narrator.

17. In De Sica's movie, the protagonist Giorgio plays voyeur, spying on the lovers through a window of the *Hütte*, from which Micòl sees him and turns subject into object by defiantly gazing back at him. The film has misled some critics into incorrectly interpreting the episode that the author deliberately leaves a mystery, since the narrator once again remains on the brink of realization.

18. Cited by Poulet, *Interior Distance*, 250.

19. De Stefanis, *Bassani*, 141, takes the term spatialized time from Sharon Spencer, *Space, Time, and Structure in the Modern Novel* (New York: New York University Press, 1977), 156.

20. Schneider, "Mythical Dimensions," 60, describes Bassani's manipulation of temporal levels.

21. Bruce Kawin, *The Mind of the Novel: Reflexive Fiction and the Ineffable*, (Princeton: Princeton University Press, 1982), 27–28, speaks of a third "I", the timeless self transcending the phenomenal world. There is a younger "I" in the novel: the schoolboy of June 1929 weeping over his failure in mathematics.

22. For that structural interpretation, see De Stefanis, *Bassani*, 107–118.

23. Schneider, "Mythical Dimensions," 60, notes that only the narrator progresses in time, since the other major characters are already dead.

24. Cited by Robert Weisbuch, *Emily Dickinson's Poetry* (Chicago: University of Chicago Press, 1972, 78.

25. Translated by C. K. Scott-Moncrief, *Remembrance of Things Past*, and cited by Poulet, *Human Time*, 312.

26. Stelio Cro, "Art and Death in Bassani's Poetry," *Canadian Journal of Italian Studies*1,no. 2 (Winter 1978), 155–56, studies the poem "Cena di Pasqua", in which a cold wind symbolizes Fascist persecution and on a temporal level anticipates another.

27. Both Cro, "Art and Death," 155–56, and Schneider, "Mythical Dimensions," 50–51, remark that, respectively, the festive dinners in the poem and the novel never arrive at a communion because each celebrant remains alone, enclosed in grief, nostalgia, or self-deluding hopes.

CHAPTER 4. THE PLACE OF BETRAYAL

1. There are questions about the narrator's age. His treacherous clasmate Pulga states that he is sixteen, but the *narrator* had to have been born in 1916 and could only be thirteen at the time the novel begins.

2. On the title page of a copy of this novel's English translation, a library clerk attached this summary note: "A disturbing portrait of two adolescent boys *(one Italian, one Jewish)*, and the profound psychological effect one has upon the other." The italics are my own, pointing out the exclusion that occurs, on an unconscious and unintentional level, for the Jewish adolescent is just as much an Italian as the gentile.

3. Kawin, *The Mind of the Novel*, 284, theorizes on the work as its autobiography. Giorgio Pullini, *Volti e risvolti del romanzo italiano contemporaneo* (Varese: Mursia, 1971), 99–101, contrasts this novel's apparent attempt at impersonal narration of an emblematic experience with the author's acknowledged desire to relate the story of a personal moral experience. Gérard Genette, *Figures III* (Paris: Seuil, 1972), 183–267, develops the roles of extradiegetic and intradiegetic narrators.

4. Melanie Klein, *Contributions to Psychoanalysis 1921–1945* (London: Hogarth Press, 1968), 364, calls the oral stage a defense against anxieties coming from the genital position.

5. Sontag, *Illness*, 14, considers tuberculosis a disease of time but cancer a disease of space.

6. Geraldine McBroom, "Young Adult Realistic Fiction 1967–1977," Diss., Ohio State University, 1979, 5, describes the characteristics of the juvenile novel. Hughes, *Prisoners of Hope*, 142, also

notes a similarity to the sadistic activities of students in Musil's novel. Jørn Moestrup, "*Dietro la porta di Giorgio Bassani* (1964) "*Italianistica scandinava*, ed. T. Nurmela (Turku, Finland: University of Turku Press, 1977), 282–83, relates this novel to the radical political youth movements in the 1960s and their judgment of preceding generations.

7. I have taken as a conceptual model of structural analysis the following essay: Brian Way, "A Tight Three-Movement Structure," *Studies in J. D. Salinger*, ed. M. Laser (New York: Odyssey Press, 1963), 190–201, and especially 192.

8. Klein, *Contributions*, 366.

9. De Stefanis, *Bassani*, 205–6, calls the animal references one of the novel's main leitmotives, noting that under Pulga's evil gaze, the entire human world becomes transformed into beasts.

10. See Klein, *Contributions*, 17, 119, 127–28, on the unconscious impulses behind participation in sports.

11. De Stefanis, *Bassani*, 200–203, examines the identification with Christ.

12. Moestrup, "*Dietro la porta*", 281–82, focuses on the hero's solitude by the window of Cattolica's study. De Stefanis, *Bassani*, 192, 211, discusses how the views are separate from the character.

13. H. Bungert, "Salinger's *The Catcher in the Rye*," *Studies in J. D. Salinger*, ed. M. Laser (New York: Odyssey Press, 1963) 183, observes how the American protagonist Holden Caulfield does discover such enclaves.

14. De Stefanis, *Bassani*, 194–97, employs Girardian analysis to trace triangles of worship and hatred in the novel. She asserts, 197, that Cattolica and the protagonist are symbols of two opposing worlds.

15. Luciano's father, Dr. Osvaldo Pulga, is a pathological figure in miniature. His green eyes bulge like those inflicted with Basedow's disease, perhaps a subtle literary allusion to an illness prominent in Italo Svevo's novel *La Coscienza di Zeno* (*The Confessions of Zeno*, 1923). Like his son, Osvaldo denounces his associates and hopes for their downfall.

16. Cf. Karl C. Garrison, *Psychology of Adolescence* (Englewood Cliffs, N. J.: Prentice-Hall, 1965), 72.

17. Consult Klein, *Contributions* 81, 262, 367.

18. De Stefanis, *Bassani*, 212, interprets the door as a symbol of separation. Siciliano, *Autobiografia*, 130–33, analyzes the work as a study in remorse and considers the term *sicario* as a self-indictment for refusing to understand the ambivalence of the liaison with Pulga. Brian Maloney, "Tematica e tecnica nei romanzi di Giorgio Bassani," *Convivium*, no. 5 (1966):484–95, and especially 490–92, concentrates on the epigraph from Baudelaire and its significance in the context of the entire work.

Chapter 5. The Fatal Circle

1. Moestrup, "*Dietro la porta*", 285, stresses the importance of the student revolts in Europe in 1968 and their reflection in *The Heron*. For a discussion of Faulkner's victim heroes, see Michael Milgate's analysis of the twilight mood of *The Sound and the Fury* in *Faulkner: A Collection of Critical Essays*, ed. Robert Penn Warren (Englewood Cliffs, N.J.: Prentice-Hall, 1966), 94–108.

285,

2. De Stefanis, *Bassani*, 234, examines the work's structure and its presentation of negative time.

3. Cited by A. Alvarez, *The Savage God: A Study in Suicide* (New York: Random House, 1970), 102.

4. Cf. Bassani's interview on why he wrote the novel, in "Perchè ho scritto *l'Airone*," *La Fiera letteraria*, no. 46 (14 Nov. 1968): 10–12.

5. For a psychoanalytical interpretation of extreme mourning see Klein, *Contributions*, 311–38.

6. As quoted from Bassani in La *Fiera letteraria*, 10.

7. Adler's views are summarized by Jack P. Gibb, *Suicide* (New York: Harper and Row, 1968), 126–27; and Adler's essay "Suicide" appears on 146–50.

8. Quoted by Alvarez, *The Savage God*, 131.

9. Gibb, *Suicide*, 161–62, speaks of the transferal of anxiety to organs that the neurotic patient may have removed by surgical operation.

10. Marilyn Schneider, "A Conversion to Death: Giorgio Bassani's *L'Airone,*" *Canadian Journal of Italian Studies* 1, no. 2 (Winter 1978): 123, researches the novel's phallic symbolism. Alvarez, *The Savage God*, 113, cites Freud's work on dreams and libidinal frustrations.

11. Hughes, *Prisoners*, 147.

12. Miller, *Dickens*, 312.

13. Marco Forti, "Bassani, Cattaneo," *Il Bimestre* 1, no. 1 (1969): 31–35, and particularly 31, notes the symbolism of the car.

14. Hall, *The Hidden Dimension*, 136, 165, describes cars as expressions of a culture—cocoons of metal and glass to protect their occupants.

15. M. Schneider, "Conversion," 123.

16. The well or pit is an image of entrapment that becomes internalized, particularly by people with suicidal tendencies. A patient who was admitted to a mental hospital after a suicide attempt once resorted to the image of a pit to explain how she used the self-destructive act as a means to preserve her identity: "I dreamed continually of going down in bottomless pits. I feared becoming inhuman, an outcast in the world. Death was known. It happened to everyone. To die would mean to be like other people." Gibb, *Suicide*, 159, cites this statement as evidence of the neurotic value of suicide.

17. Ibid., 163.

18. De Stefanis, *Bassani*, 235.

19. As argued by M. Schneider, "Conversion," 121–34, and previously by Geno Pampaloni in a review of the novel for the *Corriere della sera*, 20 Oct. 1968. Both the American and the Italian critics accept the idea of salvation through suicide without recognizing its total negativity.

20. Mehlman, *Autobiography*, 73, observes that in autobiography, the reverse situation may occur when an author makes a victim of his own past by writing the text, which is an attempt at deliverance, in order to begin anew.

CONCLUSION: THE LEAVE-TAKING

1. Cf. Hughes, *Prisoners*, 156–57.

2. I. Baldelli, "Riscrittura," 183–86, and De Stefanis, *Bassani*, 243–50, compare variations of the two versions of the tale. Baldelli remarks that "The Enclosing Wall" possesses a mythic vagueness, while "The Odor of Hay" plunges readers into the present of the early 1970s and then returns to the past. De Stefanis comments that the Hebrew cemetery is a symbol of Jewish alienation in the first version and a monument to life in the revision.

3. For insights about the shifting uses of personal pronouns, I again refer to the lecture by De Stefanis on "*Gli Occhiali d'oro: i diversi piani prospettici della narrazione*" of April 1984.

4. Ferretti, *Letteratura*, 38–39, particularly, and 65; the Marxist critic accurately predicts the monotonous repetition of a limited artistic repertoire of characters and places as demonstrated in the volume *The Odor of Hay*. Ferretti's observations, which go back to 1964, cannot be considered outdated, and critics like De Stefanis do well to respond to his comments.

5. Diego Bastianutti, "Giorgio Bassani: The Record of a Confession," *Queen's Quarterly* 88, no. 4 (Winter 1981): 737–47 and especially 743, refers to Edgardo's "voyeurism." Bastianutti's essay repeats the very language of some American critics without due citation.

6. Aiken, "Faulkner's Yoknapatawpha County," *Geographical Review*, 13, analyzes the transformation of objective into subjective literary locale by Faulkner.

Select Bibliography

ITALIAN EDITIONS OF BASSANI'S WORKS

Una città di pianura (under the pseudonym of Giacomo Marchi). Milan: Arte Grafica Lucini, 1940.

Storie di poveri amanti e altri versi. Rome: Astrolabio, 1945.

Cinque storie ferraresi. Turin: Einaudi, 1956.

Gli Occhiali d'oro. Turin: Einaudi, 1958.

Le Storie ferraresi. Turin: Einaudi, 1960.

Il Giardino dei Finzi-Contini. Turin: Einaudi, 1962.

Dietro la porta. Turin: Einaudi, 1964.

Le Parole preparate e altri scritti di letteratura. Turin: Einaudi, 1966.

L'Airone. Milan: Mondadori, 1968.

L'odore del fieno. Milan: Mondadori, 1972.

Il Romanzo di Ferrara. Milan: Mondadori, 1974, 1980.

ENGLISH TRANSLATIONS OF BASSANI'S NARRATIVE WORKS

Behind the Door. Translated by William Weaver. New York: Harcourt, Brace, and Jovanovich, 1972.

Five Stories of Ferrara. Translated by William Weaver. New York: Harcourt, Brace, and Jovanovich, 1971.

The Garden of the Finzi-Continis. Translated by Isabel Quigley. New York: Atheneum, 1965.

———. Translated by William Weaver. New York: Harcourt, Brace, and Jovanovich, 1977.

The Heron. Translated by William Weaver. New York: Harcourt, Brace, and World, 1970.

The Smell of Hay (Includes *The Gold-Rimmed Eyeglasses*). Translated by William Weaver. New York: Harcourt, Brace, and Jovanovich, 1972.

GENERAL STUDIES

Aiken, Charles S. "Faulkner's Yoknapatawpha County: Geographical Fact into Fiction." *The Geographical Review* 67, no. 1 (Jan. 1977): 1–21.

Albertoni, E. et al. *La Generazione degli anni difficili.* Bari: Laterza, 1962.

Alvarez, A. *The Savage God: A Study in Suicide.* New York: Random House, 1970.

Anceschi, Luciano. *Le Poetiche del novecento in Italia.* Turin: Paravia, 1972.

Bachelard, Gaston. *The Poetics of Space.* Translated by Maria Jolas. New York: Orion, 1964.

Baldelli, Ignazio. "La Riscrittura 'totale' di un'opera: da *Le Storie Ferraresi* a 'Dentro le mura' di Bassani." *Lettere italiane* 26, no. 2 (Apr.–June 1974):)180–97.

Bastianutti, Diego. "Giorgio Bassani: The Record of a Confession." *Queen's Quarterly* 88, no. 4 (Winter 1981): 737–47.

Beach, Joseph Warren. *The Twentieth Century Novel: Studies in Technique.* New York: Century, 1932.

Benstok, Bernard, "The Dead," *James Joyce's 'Dubliners': Critical Essays.* Edited by Clive Hart. New York: Viking, 1969.

Bertacchini, Renato. *Figure e problemi di narrativa contemporanea.* Rocca San Casciano: Cappelli, 1960.

Bon, Adriano. *Come leggere 'Il Giardino dei Finzi-Contini' di Giorgio Bassani.* Milan: Mursia, 1979.

Boselli, Mario. "Ambiguità di Bassani." *Nuova corrente* 27 (July–Sept. 1962): 7–27.

Brombert, Victor. *The Novels of Flaubert: A Study of Themes and Techniques.* Princeton: Princeton University Press, 1966.

Caliaro, Ilvano. "Dal *giardino* di Giorgio Bassani: il 'finzicontinico' di Micòl, tra dignità e stile." *Forum italicum* 15, no. 1 (Spring 1981): 52–57.

Caretti, Lanfranco. *Dante, Manzoni, e altri saggi.* Milan: Ricciardi, 1964.

Carr, H. Wildon. *"Time" and "History" in Contemporary Philosophy; with Special Reference to Bergson and Croce.* London: Proceedings of the British Academy, 1918.

Cecchi, Emilio. *Letteratura italiana del novecento.* Milan: Mondadori, 1972.

Cohn, Dorrit. "Narrated Monologue: Definition of a Fictional Style." *Comparative Literature* 18, no. 2 (1966): 97–112.

Corner, Paul. *Fascism in Ferrara, 1915–1925.* Oxford: Oxford University Press, 1975.

Cro, Stelio. "Tempo e parola nelle *Stori ferraresi* di Giorgio Bassani." *Canadian Journal of Italian Studies* 1, no. 1 (Fall 1977): 46–73.

———. "Art and Death in Bassani's Poetry." *Canadian Journal of Italian Studies* 1, no. 2 (Winter 1978): 153–60.

De Felice, Renzo. *Storia degli ebrei italiani sotto il fascismo.* Turin: Einaudi, 1961.

De Stefanis, Giusi Oddo. *Bassani entro il cerchio delle sue mura.* Ravenna: Longo, 1981.

Di Biase, C. *La 'Ronda' e l'impegno.* Naples: Liguori, 1971.

Dolfi, Anna. "Bassani e il diaframma speculare della distanza." *Nuovi argomenti* 53–54 (June 1977): 350–76.

Fava Guzzetta, L. "La *Ronda* cinquant'anni dopo: ideologia e letteratura." *Lettere italiane* 23, no. 1 (Jan.–Mar. 1971): 111–28.

Ferretti, Gian Carlo. *Letteratura e ideologia.* 1964: rpt. Rome: Riuniti, 1974.

Forti, Marco. "Bassani, Cattaneo." *Il Bimestre* 1, no. 1 (1969): 31–35.

Genette, Gérard. *Figures III.* Paris: Seuil, 1972.

Gibb, Jack P. *Suicide.* New York: Harper and Row, 1968.

Girard, René. *Mensonge romantique et vérité romanesque.* Paris: Grasset, 1961.

Grillandi, Massimo. *Invito alla lettura di Bassani.* Milan: Mursia, 1972.

Guarnieri, Silvio. *Cinquant'anni di narrativa in Italia.* Florence: Parenti, 1955.

Gundersheimer, Werner. *Ferrara: The Style of a Renaissance Despotism.* Princeton: Princeton University Press, 1973.

Gunzberg, Lynn M. "Down among the Dead Men: Levi and Dante in Hell." *Modern Language Studies* 16, no. 1 (Winter 1986): 10–28.

Hall, Edward T. *The Silent Language.* Garden City, N.Y.: Doubleday, 1959.

———. *The Hidden Dimension.* Garden City, N.Y.: Doubleday, 1966.

———. *Beyond Culture.* Garden City, N.Y.: Anchor Press/Doubleday, 1977.

Haller, Hermann. "Da *Le Storie ferraresi* al *Romanzo di Ferrara:* Varianti nell'opera di Bassani." *Canadian Journal of Italian Studies* 1, no. 1 (Fall 1977): 74–96.

Hughes, H. Stuart. *Prisoners of Hope: the Silver Age of the Italian Jews 1924–1974.* Cambridge: Harvard University Press, 1983.

James, Henry. *The Art of the Novel: Critical Prefaces by Henry James.* New York, Scribners, 1934.

Kawin, Bruce. *The Mind of the Novel: Reflexive Fiction and the Ineffable.* Princeton: Princeton University Press, 1982.

Klein, Melanie. *Contributions to Psychoanalysis 1921–1945.* London: Hogarth Press, 1968.

Klopp, Charles, Review of *Bassani entro il cerechio delle sue mura.* G. De Stefanis. *Italian Culture* 3 (1981): 143–46.

Kristeva, Julia. *Powers of Horror, An Essay on Abjection.* Translated by Leon Roudiez. New York: Columbia University Press, 1982.

Longhi, Roberto. *Officina ferrarese.* Rome: Le Edizioni d'Italia, 1934.

Lubbock, Percy. *The Craft of Fiction.* London: J. Cape, 1921.

McBroom, Geraldine. "Young Adult Realistic Fiction 1967–1977." Ph.D. Diss., Ohio State University, 1979. Columbus, 1979.

Maloney, Brian. "Tematica e tecnica nei romanzi di Giorgio Bassani." *Convivium* no. 5 (1966):484–95.

Mehlman, Jeffrey. *A Structural Study of Autobiography.* Ithaca, N.Y.: Cornell University Press, 1974.

Meyers, Jeffrey. *Painting and the Novel.* Manchester, Eng.: Manchester University Press, 1975.

———. *Homosexuality and Literature 1890–1930.* Montreal: McGill University Press, 1977.

Michaelis, Mair. *Mussolini and the Jews.* London: Institute of Jewish Affairs, 1978.

Miller, J. Hillis. *Charles Dickens: The World of His Novels.* Cambridge: Harvard University Press, 1958.

Moestrup, Jørn. "Lettura del *Giardino dei Finzi-Contini.*" In *Studia romana in honorem Petri Krarup Septuagenarii,* ed. K. Ascani et al. Odense, Denmark: Odense University, 1976.

———. "*Dietro la Porta* di Giorgio Bassani." In *Italianistica scandinava,* ed. T. Nurmela. Turku, Finland: University of Turku Press, 1977.

———. "Giorgio Bassani: dal racconto al romanzo." *Veltro* 25, nos. 1–3 (1981):231–38.

Pampaloni, Geno. "La Nuova letteratura." In *Storia della letteratura italiana,* ed. E. Cecchi and N. Sapegno, 832–34. Milan: Garzanti, 1969.

———. Review of *L'Airone. Corriere della Sera* (20 Oct. 1968).

Piclardi, Rosetta. "Forms and Figures in the Novels of Natalia Ginzburg." *World Literature Today* (Autumn 1979):585–89.

Poulet, Georges. *Studies in Human Time.* Translated by Elliot Coleman. Baltimore: Johns Hopkins University Press, 1956.

———. *The Interior Distance,* Translated by Elliot Coleman. Baltimore: Johns Hopkins University Press, 1959.

Pullini, Giorgio. *Volti e risvolti del romanzo italiano contemporaneo.* Varese: Mursia, 1971.

Radcliff-Umstead, Douglas. "Farsi vedere dagli altri: Bassani e Cassola." *Nuova antologia* (Nov. 1973):376–84.

———. "Transformation in Bassani's *Garden of the Finzi-Continis.*" *Modern Fiction Studies* 21, no. 4 (Winter 1975–76):521–33.

———. "Bassani: esilio nell'eternità." *Le Ragioni critiche* 7 (June 1977):113–37.

———. "Bassani: The Community of the Excluded." *Perspectives in Twentieth-Century Literature* 3, no. 2 (Nov. 1977):21–29.

———. "The Closed World of Giorgio Bassani." *Italian Culture* 3 (1981):101–130.

———. Review of *Bassani entro il cerchio delle sue mura.* By Giusi Oddo De Stefanis. *Canadian Journal of Italian Studies* 5, no. 3 (Spring 1982):269–70.

Raimondi, Giuseppe. *Filippo De Pisis.* Florence: Vallecchi, 1952.

Romano, David. "Notas sobre el judeoespañol en una obra de Bassani." *Sefarad* 30 (1970):198–200.

Ronda, La. Edited by Giuseppe Cassiere. Turin: E.R.I., 1969.

Rosengarten, Frank. *Vasco Pratolini: The Development of a Social Novelist.* Carbondale: So. Illinois University Press, 1965.

Roth, Cecil. *The History of the Jews of Italy.* Philadelphia: Jewish Publication Society of America, 1946.

Rousset, David. *The Other Kingdom.* Translated by Ramon Guthrie. New York: Reynal and Hitchcock, 1947.

Rousset, Jean. *Forme et signification: essais sur les structures littéraires de Corneille à Claudel.* Paris: Corti, 1967.

Saccenti, Mario. *Riccardo Bacchelli.* Milan: Mursia, 1973.

Sanguineti, Edoardo. *Tra liberty e crepuscolarismo.* Milan: Mursia, 1965.

Schneider, Herbert W. *Making the Fascist State.* Oxford: Oxford University Press, 1928.

Schneider, Marilyn. "Mythical Dimensions of Micòl Finzi-Contini." *Italica* 51, no. 1 (Spring 1974):43–67.

———. "A Conversation to Death: Giorgio Bassani's *L'Airone.*" *Canadian Journal of Italian Studies* 1, no. 2 (Winter 1978):121–34.

Scrivano, Roberto. *Riviste, scrittori, e critica del novecento.* Florence: Sansoni, 1965.

Shapiro, Marianne. "The *Storie ferraresi* of Giorgio Bassani." *Italica* 49, no. 1 (Spring 1972):30–48.

———. "Bassani's Ironic Mode." *Canadian Journal of Italian Studies* 1, no. 2 (Winter 1978):146–52.

Siciliano, Enzo. *Autobiografia letteraria.* Milan: Garzanti, 1970.

Solmi, Sergio, *Filippo De Pisis.* Milan: Hoepli, 1946.

Sontag, Susan. *Illness as as Metaphor.* New York: Farrar, Strauss, and Giroux, 1977.

Tabori, Paul. *The Anatomy of Exile, A Semantic and Historical Study.* London: Harrap, 1972.

Tanda, Nicola. *Realtà e memoria nella narrativa contemporanea.* Rome: Bulzoni, 1970.

Tuan, Yi-Fu, *Topophilia.* Englewood Cliffs, N.J.: Prentice-Hall, 1974.

———. *Space and Place.* Minneapolis: University of Minnesota Press, 1977.

Van Creveld, M. "Beyond the Finzi-Contini Garden: Mussolini's 'Fascist Racism.'" *Encounter* 42 (Feb. 1974):42–47.

Varanini, Giorgio. *Bassani.* Florence: Castoro, 1970.

Index

Dostoievski, Fyodor, 28, 32
Dürer, Albrecht, 101

Ellington, Duke, 96
Este, 14–15, 38, 52, 87, 107, 156

Fascism, 13, 18–23, 24, 29, 31; Fascist
literature, 33–35, 41, 47, 48, 81, 122
Faulkner, William, 13, 133, 157
Federzoni, Luigi, 22
Ferrara, 13–23, 38, 40, 50, 52, 56–57, 71–
72, 157
Forster, E. M., 80
Forzano, Giovacchino, 34
Foscolo, Ugo, 110
Franco, Francisco, 19
Futurism, 27–28, 34

Gentile, Giovanni, 122
Gide, André, 80
Ginzburg, Natalia, 62
Giolitti, Giovanni, 29
Gogol, Nikolai, 28
Goodman, Benny, 96
Govoni, Corrado, 26
Gozzano, Guido, 26

Hall, Edward T., 36
Hawthorne, Nathaniel, 29, 80, 83, 147
Historicism, 30–32
Hitler, Adolf, 20, 21, 61, 86, 92
Hugo, Victor, 65, 104

James, Henry, 29, 54, 59, 70, 75, 76, 119
Jews: in Ferrara, 15–18; Fascist racial policy
toward, 18–23, 41, 94, 97
Joubert, Joseph, 39
Joyce, James, 62, 64, 65–66, 67–68, 75

Kipling, Rudyard, 28, 91
Klein, Melanie, 36

La Fayette, Mme de, 46
Lawrence, D. H., 80
Leopardi, Giacomo, 27
Levi, Primo, 61
Longanesi, Leo, 34
Longhi, Roberto, 29–30, 95

Machaty, Gustav, 95
Malaparte, Curzio, 34–35

Mallarmé, Stéphane, 98, 104–5, 107
Manzoni, Alessandro, 27, 31, 40
Melozzo da Forlì, 79
Melville, Herman, 29, 71, 98, 105
Metaphysical School, 24
Morandi, Giorgio, 24, 28, 30, 34, 107
Moravia, Alberto, 48, 76–77, 118–19, 124
Musil, Robert, 119
Mussolini, Benito, 19, 20, 21, 23, 33–35,
61, 64, 72, 88

Nazis, 19, 20, 21, 23, 52, 61, 64, 152–53
Nietzsche, Friedrich, 131

Ojetti, Ugo, 33

Painting: and De Pisis, 24–26, 28; and
Ferrarese School, 30; Futurism, 27–28;
and Metaphysical School, 24; and Mor-
andi, 24, 28, 30, 34, 107
Pareto, Vilfredo, 29
Pascal, Blaise, 39–40
Pascoli, Giovanni, 27
Pavolini, Corrado, 33
Pirandello, Luigi, 34, 38, 42, 136, 145,
147
Poe, Edgar Allan, 71, 82
Possenti, Eligio, 33
Poulet, Georges, 36
Pratolini, Vasco, 31, 32, 35
Proust, Marcel, 52, 77, 80, 83, 88, 98, 113

Racine, Jean, 78
Raimondi, Giuseppe, 23, 28
Ravenna, Renzo, 18, 22
Rimbaud, Arthur, 28, 55, 146
Ronda, La, 26–29, 30, 32, 34, 35, 37, 74,
96
Rossetti, Dante Gabriel, 103
Rousset, David, 61

Salinger, J. D., 119, 121
Sartre, Jean Paul, 138
Shanks, Edward, 28
Söderbaum, Christina, 95
Soffici, Ardengo, 23, 34
Sophocles, 78–79
Sorel, Georges, 28
Stendhal, 105
Stevenson, Robert Louis, 28
Strapaese, 24, 25, 34

174 Index